IRAN’S NUCLEAR PROGRAM AND I

IRAN'S NUCLEAR PROGRAM AND INTERNATIONAL LAW

From Confrontation to Accord

Daniel H. Joyner

OXFORD
UNIVERSITY PRESS

OXFORD
UNIVERSITY PRESS

Oxford University Press is a department of the University of Oxford. It furthers the University's objective of excellence in research, scholarship, and education by publishing worldwide. Oxford is a registered trademark of Oxford University Press in the UK and certain other countries.

Published in the United States of America by Oxford University Press
198 Madison Avenue, New York, NY 10016, United States of America.

First Edition published in 2016

Library of Congress Cataloging-in-Publication Data

Names: Joyner, Daniel, author.
Title: Iran's nuclear program and international law : from confrontation to accord / Daniel H. Joyner.
Description: First edition. | New York : Oxford University Press, 2016. | Includes bibliographical references and index.
Identifiers: LCCN 2016011939 | ISBN 9780199377893 ((hardback) : alk. paper) | ISBN 9780190635718 ((pbk.) : alk. paper)
Subjects: LCSH: Nuclear nonproliferation—Iran.
Classification: LCC KZ5770 .J698 2016 | DDC 341.7/340955—dc23 LC record available at http://lccn.loc.gov/2016011939

To Aharon Barak. A hero of the law.

INTRODUCTION

In this book, I want to provide an international legal analysis of the most important legal questions that have been raised since 2002 regarding Iran's nuclear program, and to set those legal questions in their historical and diplomatic context. My purpose is to clarify how the relevant sources of international law—including primarily the 1968 Nuclear Nonproliferation Treaty and International Atomic Energy Agency (IAEA) treaty law—should be properly applied in the context of the Iran case. My hope is thereby to provide an instructional case study of the application of these sources of international law, the lessons from which can be applied to inform both the ongoing legal and diplomatic dynamics surrounding the Iran nuclear dispute itself, as well as similar future cases.

I have been writing articles and blog posts about Iran's nuclear program and related international legal questions for over ten years. At a conference several years ago, a friend said to me, "You've already written so much on this topic, you've basically got half a book written already. Why not just finish the book?" That made a lot of sense to me.

As a bit of an aside, the development of my ideas on this subject I think interestingly demonstrates how changes in technology have affected the scholarly endeavor. We can now develop ideas through blog posts and other shorter online pieces, inclusive of engagement with peers through comments in those fora, and through that process mature and ferment our thinking for a while, before we sit down to write a formal article or book on the subject. In years past, one could try out one's ideas at conferences and in private discussion with peers, but opportunities to engage with essentially the entire epistemic community were simply not readily available. The Internet and the blogging revolution now give us this opportunity. For me, the process of blogging and writing shorter online pieces for the past several years has been invaluable in developing, testing out, and reforming my thoughts on the subject of this book.

In the course of that development, I have had a range of responses to my analysis and arguments concerning Iran's nuclear program. Some from my scholarly colleagues have been most constructive and useful. This includes the comments I received from colleagues at Hebrew University in Jerusalem, who very kindly invited me to share my ideas with them on this subject of intense interest and import in Israel in particular.

Certainly the most colorful responses, though, have come from other quarters, and particularly from members of what I like to call the "nonproliferation expert community"; a Washington, D.C.–centric collection of think tanks and nongovernmental organizations (NGOs), focused on weapons of mass destruction (WMD) nonproliferation issues. Members of this community have various professional backgrounds. Very few are lawyers—a fact which does not, however, tend to dissuade them from confidently expressing their views on complex legal questions.

As with many issue-specialist policy communities, the nonproliferation expert community tends to be quite a cliquish, professionally incestuous, and self-referential little village. But unlike many other civil society groups, I have found that the nonproliferation expert community, in by far most cases, is very closely aligned in its views and emphases with the core narratives and emphases of powerful Western governments, and in particular with those of the U.S. government, with only the smallest amounts of quibbling around the edges. The reasons for this coincidence of effort and views appears to have greatly to do with the members of this expert community having been previously, or hoping to be in the future, employed by Western governments, and being either directly or indirectly dependent upon those governments for funding and favor.[1] As a result, this expert community, which exercises a perversely disproportionate influence on government policy makers, has very little time for, and indeed is quite hostile to, anyone who challenges the core narratives of those governments' policies, including particularly the U.S. government's view that Iran's nuclear program is among the foremost international threats to the interests and security of the United States.

Since in my work over the years I have concluded that Iran's international legal arguments with regard to its nuclear program are in many instances persuasive and worthy of serious consideration, and that those arguments are, in fact, frequently more objectively correct that those of Iran's Western detractors on the nuclear issue, and even than those of the IAEA itself, the nonproliferation expert community has overall reacted quite hostilely to my work, and on multiple occasions it has been expressed to me that I am in essence providing aid and comfort to the enemy of the free world through my international legal analysis.[2] A rather strange position for a humble international law academic to be placed in.

1. *See, e.g.*, Daniel Joyner, *The Revolving Door between the USG and Wonkdom Turns Yet Again*, ARMS CONTROL LAW, Nov. 21, 2014.

2. *See, e.g.*, David Albright et al., *Understanding the IAEA's Mandate in Iran: Avoiding Misinterpretations*, ISIS Report, Nov. 27, 2010; Daniel H. Joyner, *A Whole ISIS Report Devoted to Little Ol' Me*, ARMS CONTROL LAW (blog), Nov. 27, 2012; James Fry, Book Review of Daniel H. Joyner & Marco Roscini, *Nonproliferation Law as a Special Regime: A Contribution to Fragmentation Theory in International Law*, 108 AM. J. INT'L L. 146, 152–153 (Jan. 2014) ("Perhaps the book's most important contribution is that it represents another step in Joyner's ongoing effort . . . to establish nonproliferation law as its own bona fide field within international law. Despite that effort, specialists in nonproliferation law largely continue to identify themselves as specialists in other fields, such as international trade law, space law, the law of the sea and international environmental law. Not many of them even teach courses on nonproliferation law . . . To help understand the general reticence to identify oneself as a nonproliferation law specialist, one might want to look at the vitriolic criticism that international relations–oriented realists have levied at Joyner, essentially for arguing that certain nonproliferation laws actually limit the actions of states and international organizations.").

The reason I mention these particular responses to my work on my blog and in other online fora is that I would like to address at the beginning of this book a few of the questions that this nonproliferation expert community have put to me over the years, that have caused me to do some soul-searching, and to come to my own understanding of why I work in this area, which I would like to briefly share. These questions often take something like the following form:

> Are you an Iran apologist?
>
> Are you on the payroll of the Iranian government?
>
> Aren't you afraid that, in making these arguments, you are giving aid and comfort to Iran?
>
> Why do you spend so much time and effort pushing your analysis and conclusions on this subject?

Let's take these in turn. First, am I an Iran apologist, or on the payroll of the Iranian government? The answer is absolutely in the negative to both questions. I have no particular sympathies or positive biases toward the Iranian government whatsoever. I view Iran's actions in international relations neutrally, as I would view those of any other state; agreeing and sympathizing with some, and opposing others. I certainly have never received a penny from the Iranian government, nor have I advised or represented the Iranian government on any of the legal matters relevant to this book. I value my objectivity and independence as a legal scholar above everything else in my professional life.

I have long thought that the most important contribution that university-based international legal scholars can make to discourse on important issues of international relations flows from our ability to independently and objectively analyze legal questions, free from particular bias toward the interests of any of the parties to the issue. Now, I am neither so naïve nor so arrogant as to think that biases and prejudices do not exist among university-based international legal scholars, myself most certainly included. However, when we are at our best and most objective, it is *because* we are financially and institutionally independent of the government powers that are party to a dispute. The same cannot be said of the majority of the NGO-based nonproliferation experts who write and speak on the topic of Iran's nuclear program in the United States and in other Western states, whose personal and professional fortunes, as I have noted above, are all too often either directly or indirectly tied to a party to the dispute.

Thus, one of the primary reasons I continue to work and write in this area is that there are few independent, university-based international lawyers writing on international arms control law topics, inclusive of the topic of Iran's nuclear program, and I think that it is important to have independent voices evaluating the legal arguments of the states parties to this dispute, as in any other area of international law. Indeed, the need for independent scholarly analysis only increases in areas of heightened political sensitivity. And there are few areas of greater sensitivity to states than the area of nuclear weapons development, possession, and proliferation. Within that context, Iran's nuclear program is at the forefront of international concern.

Second, am I not afraid of somehow aiding and abetting Iran through my work? Returning to the issue of academic independence, I think that this is a wholly inappropriate question to ask of a legal academic. It assumes that one's scholarly research program and analysis should somehow be influenced by politics and ideology, and that due to these considerations, some issues or questions are outside of the proper or prudential scope of independent scholarly inquiry. I think that this is a rather fundamental mistake. Would you ask a university-based physical scientist studying the theory of evolution by natural selection, whether he is concerned about the impact his work may have in providing support to one position or another in political debates between creationists and evolutionists regarding public education—and if he is not, shouldn't he be? Of course not. The scientist must approach research topics in a dispassionate manner, and must assess data collected in an objective and independent fashion, letting the results of his analysis fall where they may, without any thought or regard concerning the ideological or policy positions his work may or may not support. This, in my view, is the most important role of the independent, university-based scholar or scientist; to apply his disciplinary tools rigorously to arrive at analytical conclusions, and to keep his discipline free from concern for or regard to political or ideological considerations or implications. On this basis, therefore, my answer to this question is categorically no. I am not concerned.

Third, so why *have* I spent so much of my time and effort on this subject? In addition to the other reasons mentioned above, the honest truth is that I have a deep and abiding frustration with bad international legal argumentation made by states, and especially by powerful states, that goes unchallenged. And in the international dispute regarding Iran's nuclear program, I have found erroneous legal analysis and argumentation by concerned states parties to be ubiquitous.

While international law is by no means the central concern of the parties to the ongoing dispute over Iran's nuclear program, international legal arguments have been made and continue to be made by all interested parties, both states and international organizations, in an attempt to provide support for and legitimacy to their respective policy approaches and efforts relative to the dispute. Thus, international law plays a significant, if not central, role in the larger international relations and security dispute over Iran's nuclear program *because the parties to the dispute recognize that it does*. And in an international legal system in which resolution of high-politics disputes by international judicial bodies, especially in the international security realm, is rare, I think there is a particularly needful role for international legal scholars to play, in providing independent analysis of the international legal issues raised in such disputes; i.e., playing a role of neutral arbiters to the self-interested legal arguments of all parties to the dispute.

Scoffs of incredulity will no doubt attend the expression of the following sentiment, but I am someone who actually does deeply care about the integrity and credibility of international law and the international legal system. This is at the root of my concern that incorrect legal arguments, particularly those made by powerful states (i.e., those states able to withstand the horizontal, issue-linkaging compliance pressure forces on which enforcement of international law depends) that are employed as justification for state action, do not go unchallenged and are shown persuasively to be erroneous, lest it be verified, as many developing states already believe, that international law is simply a tool of power, exercised by powerful states for the furtherance of their own interests. If developing states, representing as they do the majority of states and peoples of the world, do generally become convinced that international law is simply one more tool of powerful, Western states to exercise their power over weaker states, through incorrect interpretation and politicization of the law, I think that international law will increasingly lose its credibility, and with it its power and influence in international relations.

My general theoretical approach to international law may accurately be termed a formalist approach. I think international law serves its purposes best when it provides for an even juridical playing field for states, and for predictable and orderly relations among states that consent to rules that are subsequently applied objectively, consistently, and universally. Powerful states, of course, are typically formalists themselves when it comes to their own legal obligations, and will invariably vehemently oppose attempts by others to assert that they are bound by obligations to which they did not clearly consent. Nevertheless, in their relations with weaker, developing states, powerful states often manifest an extraordinary ability to forget the advisability of this state-sovereigntist view of international legal obligation, and to quickly turn into legal realists, arguing that even if established legal sources do not clearly impose an obligation on a weaker state, normative and practical considerations, supplemented increasingly by the practice of international organizations over which powerful states have disproportionate influence, support an extension of legal obligation nevertheless.

It is this sort of legal realism, employed by powerful states to allow them to modify their own legal obligations ex post facto, and to impose legal obligations upon weaker states in a less-than-consensual manner, that allows their power and discretion to better serve their own interests, at the expense of orderly, predictable, and consistent relations among states, and frequently at the expense of the interests of developing states.[3]

In my opinion, international law only has a future of usefulness and value to international relations if its integrity and credibility as a proper legal system, which eschews the disproportionate influence of power, is preserved. The future usefulness and relevance of international law depends very much upon its present treatment by powerful states in particular.

Powerful states will, of course, rationally seek to use their power in furtherance of their own interests in international affairs. This is understandable, and normative debate of this proposition is largely useless. However, the ability of powerful states to hijack the sources and institutions of international law, to provide a veneer of legitimacy to what are, in fact, naked uses of power in self-interest, prejudicial to the interests of weaker states should, in my opinion, be vigorously opposed by those who care about the credibility of international law as a legal system.

Part of the preservation of the integrity of international law lies in demonstrating when powerful states' and powerful international organizations' legal arguments are incorrect—a job that indeed would ideally be done by properly authorized international judicial tribunals. But in the practical absence of such dispute resolution on most issues of high-politics and international security, in my view independent, university-based international legal scholars must fill in this gap and provide objective, rigorous legal analysis. While this will not have the same effect, or serve as useful a role, as would meaningful and predictable resort to proper international adjudication, at the least it will demonstrate to developing states that the international law scholarly community wants to uphold the integrity of international law. This may help them to continue investing in and engaging with the international legal system.

3. *See, e.g.*, Monica Hakimi, *Unfriendly Unilateralism*, 55 HARV. INT'L L.J. 105–150 (2014).

I know that I have waxed quite grandiose in this introduction. But I wanted to provide readers with a sense of my motivations for writing this book, and the concerns that have animated me in spending so much time and effort on this subject.

A word now on how this book fits in with my previous work and publications. This is my third monograph on the overall topic of arms control law, and in particular nuclear energy and nuclear nonproliferation law. In my previous two books, *International Law and the Proliferation of Weapons of Mass Destruction* (2009), and *Interpreting the Nuclear Nonproliferation Treaty* (2011), I have provided explication and analysis of the international legal and normative regime governing state possession and proliferation of nuclear energy materials and technologies, including nuclear weapons. In brief, the present book is an attempt to apply the law of that regime, as I have developed an understanding of it in my previous two books, to the concrete case study of the Iranian nuclear program.

Having written these previous two books, I am keen to keep redundancy of material in the present book to a minimum, while also of course constructing this book to be a stand-alone volume. In implementing this balance, I will provide in this book all of the material necessary to the legal analyses involved. I will also, however, at times make reference to and point the reader to analysis contained in my earlier two books, when I think that the full explication of a concept here would produce excessive redundancy of text. In those instances, I will provide a summary of the relevant analysis here, while directing readers to the more full analysis elsewhere, should they wish to reference it.

On the case itself. Iran's nuclear program and the international dispute concerning it is, I believe, an important case study of the application of international law to a complex international dispute in the issue area of nuclear energy and nuclear nonproliferation. This is a dispute which is ongoing at the diplomatic level, even with the conclusion of the Joint Comprehensive Plan of Action among Iran, the European Union, and the P5+1 (the United States, the United Kingdom, France, Germany, Russia, China) in July 2015. And it is of course impossible to predict what further diplomatic or other developments lay in store. No matter how this dispute further evolves going forward, however, an analysis of the legal issues that have been raised in the context of the Iran nuclear dispute since its inception in 2002 can, I believe, provide an important instructional case study of the application of international law to a complex international dispute involving the development of peaceful nuclear energy capabilities and concerns regarding nuclear weapons proliferation. It is my hope that the analysis herein will provide a current understanding of the application of international law to the Iran nuclear case—which will also provide the legal context for understanding the implications of the Joint Comprehensive Plan of Action (JCPOA)—as well as an enduring understanding of the legal issues that have been raised in the Iran case, that can be applied to similar future cases.

Finally, a note on the framing of the legal analysis in this book. As I wrote in the Preface, as I finish this manuscript in January 2016, the JCPOA has been agreed among Iran, the European Union, and the P5+1, and endorsed by the U.N. Security Council. As I will explain more fully in Chapter 7, the JCPOA is not itself a source of international law. It is explicitly legally nonbinding. However, it does comprise detailed and important political commitments undertaken by its parties. Some of these commitments, when implemented, will have legal implications: for example, Iran's commitment to provisionally apply the IAEA Additional Protocol. The JCPOA itself, however, is simply a diplomatic accord that provides a path forward for a peaceful resolution of the concerns of the various actors that have given rise to the legal disputes considered in this book.

In Chapters 1–6, therefore, I will provide a review of the historical and diplomatic background of the Iran nuclear dispute, and an explanation of the dispute itself beginning in August 2002 and lasting until the date of the agreement of the JCPOA in July 2015. I will also provide international legal analysis of the chief legal questions that have been raised in the context of this dispute. I will conduct this legal analysis as a historical case study and will provide assessments and conclusions regarding these legal questions, that I consider to be correct as of July 2015, at the time of the agreement of the JCPOA. Chapters 1–6 will therefore comprise Part I of the book, covering this thirteen-year period of confrontation between Iran and its critics regarding its nuclear program.

In Chapter 7, which comprises Part II of this book, I will consider the legal situation on the eve of the adoption of the JCPOA. I will then proceed to review this momentous diplomatic and legal accord reached between the various parties to this dispute, as well as the other relevant legal and political developments that have occurred since July 2015 and will consider their legal and political implications for the context of Iran's nuclear program.

PART I

CONFRONTATION

Chapter 1

Iran's Nuclear Program and the Period of Confrontation from 2002 to 2015

This is, of course, primarily a book about international law and its application to the Iranian nuclear case. And the balance of the book's chapters will identify and analyze these international legal questions. However, as with any legal analysis, one must start with an understanding of the factual context in which the law is to be applied. To that end, I will provide in this first chapter an overview of the history and constituent elements of Iran's nuclear program, along with important related historical context. I will also provide an account of the political and diplomatic crisis that ensued between Iran and the West from August 2002 through to July 2015, when the Joint Comprehensive Plan of Action was agreed among Iran, the European Union, and the P5+1 states (the United States, the United Kingdom, France, Germany, Russia, China)—i.e., through the years of confrontation leading up to the political and legal accord between these parties which the JCPOA represents.

After the legal analysis of this period of confrontation contained in Chapters 2–6, I will pick up the historical and diplomatic narrative in Chapter 7 by reviewing the JCPOA itself, and the other legal and diplomatic developments that have occurred since July 2015, along with their legal implications.

More complete and detailed histories of these subjects are available elsewhere, and I do not intend for the following to be an exhaustive account.[1] However, I do think it is important to include this necessarily brief and selective narrative here, in order to provide the essential historical and factual context on which the primary legal analysis of the succeeding chapters of the book will be based.

I. HISTORY, ORIGIN, DEVELOPMENT, AND STRUCTURE OF IRAN'S NUCLEAR PROGRAM

A. Birth of Iran's Nuclear Program

In the 1950s Shah Mohammad Reza Pahlavi became motivated to develop nuclear technology in Iran for a number of reasons. One of these was generally to develop Iranian independence and strength. As with many countries in the Middle East, Iran viewed itself as having been historically exploited by stronger Western powers, particularly with regard to its natural oil wealth. In light of this history, and particularly in light of the overthrow of the democratically elected prime minister of Iran, Mohammed Mossadegh, in a coup orchestrated by the United States and the United Kingdom in 1953, many Iranians at the time felt that Iran was "a weak country that must do what it can to protect itself against stronger and more aggressive ones to achieve some kind of 'independence' within a Western-dominated world that is historically hostile."[2]

For the Shah, developing nuclear technology presented one means by which Iran could break from this history of exploitation and "modernize" itself.[3] The Shah did not view rebelling against Western ideas to be an effective means of breaking away from Western dominance, but instead believed that "modernization and Westernization were synonymous" and that by emulating the West, he could modernize

1. *See, e.g.*, David Patrikarakos, Nuclear Iran: The Birth of an Atomic State (2012).

2. *Id.* at 9–12.

3. *Id.* at 13.

Iran and help it join the ranks of the most powerful countries in the world.[4]

In 1956, Iran established the Atomic Center of Tehran University, and shortly thereafter began negotiating with the United States to purchase a 5 megawatt (MW) reactor for this center.[5] In 1957, the United States and Iran signed a bilateral agreement entitled "Cooperation Concerning Civil Uses of Atoms."[6] This agreement laid the framework for Iran's pursuit of nuclear technology for peaceful purposes, with Western assistance.[7] The agreement provided for U.S. technical assistance, the lease of U.S. origin uranium, and the delivery from the United States of a light-water research reactor.[8] That same year, the International Atomic Energy Agency was created, in implementation the goals outlined in U.S. President Eisenhower's 1953 "Atoms for Peace" speech, including positive international assistance particularly to developing states in their acquisition of nuclear technology for civilian purposes.[9] Beginning with the 1957 bilateral agreement, the United States was to play a central role in the successful development of Iran's nuclear program. In the words of David Patrikarakos, "[n]uclear power was born in Iran; the USA was its midwife."[10]

In 1967, the Tehran Research Reactor (TRR), a pool-type, water-moderated reactor, was supplied to Iran by the United States firm GA Technologies. The United States also supplied Iran with 5.54 kilograms (kg) of enriched uranium to use in this reactor, along with

4. *Id.* at 15.

5. Ali Asghar Soltanieh, *Lecture at the University of Vienna* (Apr. 18, 2007), *available at* http://afa.at/sispr/v20070418-text.pdf; Muhammad Sahimi, *Atoms for Peace*, CAIRO REV. OF GLOBAL AFF., July 21, 2013.

6. *Id.*

7. DAVID PATRIKARAKOS, NUCLEAR IRAN: THE BIRTH OF AN ATOMIC STATE, at 15 (2012).

8. *Id.* at 15–16.

9. *Id.* at 4. *See also* DANIEL JOYNER, INTERPRETING THE NUCLEAR NONPROLIFERATION TREATY 9–13 (2011).

10. DAVID PATRIKARAKOS, NUCLEAR IRAN: THE BIRTH OF AN ATOMIC STATE, at 16 (2012).

112 grams of plutonium.[11] The Atomic Center of Tehran University was soon renamed the Tehran Nuclear Research Center (TNRC). During this time, Iran was eager to cooperate with other states, and to show that it intended to pursue nuclear energy for peaceful purposes. It signed the Limited Test Ban Treaty in 1963 and the Nuclear Nonproliferation Treaty (NPT) on the first day that it was open for signatures, July 1, 1968.[12] The NPT was subsequently ratified by the Iranian parliament, the Majlis, on February 2, 1970.[13] Iran further signed a comprehensive safeguards agreement with the International Atomic Energy Agency (INFCIRC/214), which came into force on May 15, 1974.

On March 13, 1969, the U.S.-Iran nuclear cooperation agreement was extended for another ten years. On December 18, 1972, Iran announced its intention to begin constructing nuclear power plants, and its ministry of water and power began researching the feasibility of constructing a nuclear reactor in southern Iran.[14]

B. Development during the Shah's Reign

The Shah continued to push for nuclear energy development in Iran throughout the 1970s, thinking that this would be one of the quickest ways to modernize Iran. Money was no object. With the country's booming oil export trade, the Shah was willing to invest almost unlimited resources in Iran's nuclear energy program.[15] At the peak of Iran's economic development during the Shah's reign, Iran was actively cooperating with the United States, China, Brazil, Japan, and

11. Contract between the International Atomic Energy Agency, Iran and the United States of America for the transfer of Enriched Uranium and Plutonium for a Research Reactor in Iran, U.S.-Iran, Dec. 22, 1967, 1967 U.N.T.S. 112.

12. David Patrikarakos, Nuclear Iran: The Birth of an Atomic State, at 53 (2012).

13. Muhammad Sahimi, *Atoms for Peace*, Cairo Rev. of Global Aff., July 21, 2013.

14. *Id.*

15. *Id.* at 20–21.

other countries, arranging visits and exchanges.[16] Relations were especially good between the United States and Iran during this period. U.S. President Richard Nixon and the Shah were close friends, and Nixon approved of the idea of Iran acting as a "regional policeman" of the Middle East.[17]

In the early 1970s, Iran's nuclear program continued to grow and develop with the support of the United States and other Western powers. In 1973, the U.S.-based Stanford Research Institute assessed Iran's nuclear energy needs and "recommended the building of nuclear plants capable of generating 20,000 megawatts of electricity before 1994."[18] In 1974, France helped Iran to establish the Esfahan Nuclear Technology Center (ENTEC), which would work to develop the complete nuclear fuel cycle, including uranium enrichment, inside of Iran.[19] Also in 1974, the Shah established the Atomic Energy Organization of Iran (AEOI) and made substantial plans for development of the Iranian nuclear program and completion of the fuel cycle, including plans for the construction of twenty-three nuclear plants, which would generate around 23,000 megawatts of energy over a twenty-year period.[20]

Western support during this period included specific support for Iran's uranium enrichment program. On March 14, 1975, in a National Security Study Memorandum 219, U.S. President Gerald

16. *Id.* at 36.

17. *Id.* at 49.

18. Mohammad Javad Zarif, *Tackling the Iran-U.S. Crisis: The Need for a Paradigm Shift*, 60 J. INT'L AFF. 73, 80 (2007).

19. Muhammad Sahimi, *Atoms for Peace*, CAIRO REV. OF GLOBAL AFF., July 21, 2013; *see also* Mark Hibbs, *U.S. in 1983 Stopped IAEA from Helping Iran Make UF6*, 28 BONN NUCLEAR FUEL 16 (Aug. 4, 2003). U.S. President Jimmy Carter opposed this bilateral agreement between Iran and France, and objected to France's plans to help Iran produce nuclear material. Facing U.S. opposition, France stopped assisting Iran with enrichment activities but did continue to help with production of UO2 fuel and had plans to help Iran with purifying uranium until the time that work was halted at ENTEC because of the Iranian Revolution. *Id.*

20. *Solving the Iranian Nuclear Puzzle*, ARMS CONTROL ASSOCIATION 33 (September 2013).

R. Ford directed "a study of the issues involved in reaching an acceptable agreement with the Government of Iran which would allow nuclear commerce between the countries—specifically, the sale of the U.S. nuclear reactors and materials, Iranian investment in the U.S. enrichment facilities, and other appropriate nuclear transactions in the future."[21] In National Security Decision Memorandum 292, dated April 22, 1975, President Ford further determined that the United States would "permit U.S. materials to be fabricated into fuel in Iran for use in its own reactors and for pass-through to third countries with whom we have agreements."[22] In addition, the United States offered Iran uranium enrichment and reprocessing technologies, as well as the opportunity to invest in U.S. enrichment facilities.[23]

During this period of cooperation, Iran also contracted with a German firm, Kraftwerk, to build two 1,196 MW nuclear power reactors at Bushehr, on Iran's southwest coast.[24] Construction on the Bushehr reactors began that same year, with a German subcontractor, ThyssenKrupp AG, carrying out the construction.[25] Kraftwerk estimated that the first reactor would be completed by 1980 and the second reactor by 1981.[26] At the time of the 1979 Revolution, the first reactor was 85 percent complete.[27]

Iran had nuclear cooperation agreements in place with a number of other countries as well during this period. In June 1974, Iran struck a deal with France for two 900 MW reactors, a supply of uranium, and the future construction of a nuclear research center.[28]

21. Muhammad Sahimi, *Iran Has a Right to Enrich—And America Already Recognized It*, NAT'L INTEREST, Nov. 19, 2013.

22. *Id.*

23. *Id.*

24. William O. Beeman, *Does Iran Have the Right to Enrich Uranium? The Answer Is Yes*, HUFFINGTON POST, Oct. 31, 2013.

25. DAVID PATRIKARAKOS, NUCLEAR IRAN: THE BIRTH OF AN ATOMIC STATE, at 36–37 (2012).

26. *Id.* at 38.

27. *Id.*

28. *Id.* at 39; *see also* Mohammad Javad Zarif, *Tackling the Iran-U.S. Crisis: The Need for a Paradigm Shift*, 60 J. INT'L AFF. 73, 80, at 80 (2007).

Additionally, Iran purchased a 10 percent share in Eurodif, a French uranium enrichment enterprise.[29] Iran also decided to source uranium from abroad, contracting with South African companies Nufcor and Rossing to supply 13,000 tons of uranium between 1978 and 1990.[30] Iran further contracted with a Belgian company, Belgonucleaire, for a 30 MW research reactor.[31]

The official U.S. posture toward Iran during this time was generally hopeful and cooperative. A 1978 U.S. State Department memorandum stated regarding Iran's nuclear ambitions: "we have been encouraged by Iran's efforts to broaden its non-oil energy base. We are hopeful that the U.S.-Iran Nuclear Energy Agreement will be finalized soon and that American companies will be able to play a role in Iran's nuclear energy program."[32]

Throughout the 1970s the Shah publicly maintained that he was pursuing nuclear technology for peaceful purposes.[33] In his autobiography, *Mission for My Country*, the Shah contends that he was developing the nuclear program "for a future of prosperity and peace, not of war and devastation."[34] He stated that his chief goals for the program were economic and industrial. He saw nuclear energy as a source of cheap power that could improve his country's economy and meet its growing energy demands. He further saw nuclear power as a means of aligning Iran with the industrialized countries of the West.[35]

29. *Id.* at 80.

30. David Patrikarakos, Nuclear Iran: The Birth of an Atomic State, at 44 (2012).

31. *Id.* at 46.

32. Mohammad Javad Zarif, *Tackling the Iran-U.S. Crisis: The Need for a Paradigm Shift*, 60 J. Int'l Aff. 73, 80, at 80 (2007).

33. David Patrikarakos, Nuclear Iran: The Birth of an Atomic State, at 51 (2012).

34. *Id.*

35. *Id.* at 28–29. Critics of Iran's current nuclear program have alleged that Iran's facilities far exceed its energy needs. For example, in the *Washington Post* in 2005, former U.S. Secretary of State Henry Kissinger wrote that "for a major oil producer such as Iran, nuclear energy is a wasteful use of resources." Mohammad Javad Zarif, *Tackling the Iran-U.S. Crisis: The Need for a Paradigm Shift*, 60 J. Int'l Aff. 73, 80, at 81

Privately, however, the Shah may also have wanted to at least keep a nuclear weapons option on the table. After the 1974 nuclear weapon test by India, the Shah began to question the prudence of remaining in the NPT and wondered if Iran, too, should pursue nuclear weapons. When the French news source *Les Informations* asked the Shah shortly thereafter if Iran would pursue nuclear weapons, the Shah responded, "without any doubt, and sooner than one would also think."[36] The Iranian embassy in France downplayed this statement and stated that the French media had fabricated it. But the statement, if essentially accurate, does seem to suggest that the Shah was at least considering the possibility of nuclear weapons development, as of course were many other countries during this period.[37] Nevertheless, the Shah continued to state publicly that it was unnecessary for Iran to develop a nuclear bomb due to the country's strong conventional military capabilities. In 1975, he told the *Washington Post* that "[t]he best guarantee that I do not want nuclear weapons is the program I have launched in conventional weapons. I want to be able to take care of anything by non-nuclear arms."[38]

(2007). However, Mohammad Zarif contends that nuclear reactors would provide a necessary substitute for Iran's diminishing stock of oil and natural gas. He suggests that "Iran's nuclear program is neither ambitious nor economically unjustifiable. Diversification—including the development of nuclear energy—is the only sound and responsible energy strategy for Iran." *Id.* at 79–80. Interestingly, when Kissinger was secretary of state for President Ford, he wrote that "introduction of nuclear power will both provide for the growing needs of Iran's economy and free remaining oil reserves for export or conversion to petrochemicals." *Id.* at 81. Kissinger further explained that the issue of proliferation did not come up at this time because Iran was an ally of the United States. The change in Kissinger's view over the succeeding decades strongly suggests that U.S. concern with Iran's nuclear expansion is neither based on a lack of energy demand nor on proliferation concerns, but rather on the ebbing of political relations between the United States and Iran. *Id.*

36. David Patrikarakos, Nuclear Iran: The Birth of an Atomic State, at 59 (2012).

37. *See* Joseph Cirincione et al., Deadly Arsenals, Nuclear, Biological and Chemical Threats 333 (2d ed. Carnegie Endowment 2005); Ariel Levite, *Never Say Never Again: Nuclear Reversal Revisited*, 27.3 Int'l Security 59–88 (2002–2003); Carey Sublette, Nuclear Weapons Archive, http://nuclearweaponarchive.org/.

38. David Patrikarakos, Nuclear Iran: The Birth of an Atomic State, at 65 (2012).

C. Shift in Attitude after the Revolution

The Iranian Revolution in 1979 brought about a dramatic shift in attitude toward Iran's nuclear program, both inside Iran and in the West. The Islamic revolutionaries in Iran generally rejected all things Western and sought to distance themselves from "the Shah's Western 'subservience' [which] had emasculated the country."[39]

Relations between the United States and Iran significantly worsened with the Hostage Crisis of 1979.[40] President Jimmy Carter described the event as "unprecedented in 600 years of recorded diplomatic history." In response, the United States froze Iranian assets, imposed financial sanctions, and ended all nuclear cooperation with Iran. When Ronald Reagan took office in 1981, he maintained the view that any possibility of nuclear cooperation with Iran had been destroyed by its actions during the Hostage Crisis.[41]

Initially, the new revolutionary government in Iran itself opposed further development of the country's nuclear program. Since the nuclear program was seen as a source of Western technology and excessive spending, Ayatollah Khomeini wanted to distance Iran from this technology as much as possible. In April 1979, Fereydun Sahabi, the new head of the AEOI, announced that the entire nuclear program was under review and began making significant cuts. In June 1979, the AEOI announced that all nuclear projects other than the Bushehr reactors would be canceled. In July 1979, the deal with Kraftwerk for completion of the Bushehr reactors fell apart. Kraftwerk canceled the contract based on the large debts Iran owed to the company for the parts and construction services that had been performed thus far.[42] A year after this cancellation, the AEOI stated its official position on Bushehr, saying:

> The construction of these reactors, started by the former regime *on the basis of colonialist and imposed treaties,* was harmful for

39. *Id.* at 92–93.
40. *Id.* at 106.
41. *Id.*
42. *Id.* at 95–98.

> the country from the economic, political and technical points of view, and *was a cause of greater dependence on imperialist countries*. These contracts were stopped after the victory of the revolution.[43]

Iran soon, however, was faced with an electricity shortage and returned to nuclear power as a possible solution. Iran began arbitrating its disputes with Kraftwerk and agreed to settle its debts and have Kraftwerk complete the Bushehr reactors. Iran also began trying to negotiate with France again. While the French company Eurodif refused to refund the $1 billion Iran had invested in it, Eurodif and Iran did reach an agreement in which Iran would be supplied with 35,000 tons of equipment and half of the fuel necessary for the reactors.[44]

D. Influence of the Iran-Iraq War

With U.S.-Iran relations strained, the United States began looking for another ally in the Middle East. As Kenneth R. Timmerman writes:

> The Islamic revolution in Iran upset the entire strategic equation in the region. America's principal ally in the Persian Gulf, the Shah, was swept aside overnight, and no one else on the horizon could replace him as the guarantor of U.S. interests in the region.[45]

The United States eventually found its desired ally in Iraq and its leader, Saddam Hussein. Hussein sought to capitalize on Iranian weakness in the wake of the revolution by invading Iran. It appears that the United States at least tacitly assented to Iraq's plans to invade Iran from the very beginning. Former National Security Council staff member Gary Sick has been quoted as saying that the National Security Council "was letting Saddam assume there was a

43. *Id.* at 98–99.
44. *Id.* at 102–105.
45. Kenneth R. Timmerman, The Death Lobby: How the West Armed Iraq (1991).

U.S. green light for his invasion of Iran, because there was no explicit red light."[46]

When the Iran-Iraq War began in 1980, Iran faced not only a military threat but also decreasing oil revenues and increased domestic energy demand, including for its war effort. This led some Iranian officials to turn to Iran's nuclear energy program as a possible solution.[47] A 2009 International Atomic Energy Agency (IAEA) internal report shows that in April 1984, then Iranian President Ali Khamenei officially announced that Iran would "reactivate the nuclear program as the only way to secure the Islamic Revolution from the schemes of its enemies, especially the United States and Israel."[48]

In 1983, Iran asked the IAEA for assistance in setting up a plant for production of uranium hexafluoride, to be used in the enrichment process.[49] In October 1983, the IAEA sent a team to Iran to visit ENTEC and discuss the assistance requested.[50] The team recommended to Hans Blix, the director general of the IAEA, that the IAEA provide assistance in the development of Iran's nuclear research program.[51] The subsequent IAEA report stated that "'a timely cooperation of the IAEA (with ENTEC) is highly recommendable' to overcome 'a lack of practical experience and perhaps . . . a lack of contact with other scientists in more advanced institutes.'"[52] However, this assistance was never provided. It appears that this was due in large part to U.S. opposition. Mark Hibbs has written:

> Four years after the Islamic revolution, and two years after Iran's new leaders dusted off the nuclear program of the deposed Reza

46. *Id.*

47. Muhammad Sahimi, *Atoms for Peace*, CAIRO REV. OF GLOBAL AFF., July 21, 2013.

48. David Morrison & Peter Oborne, *Does the BBC Not Trust US Intelligence on Iran?*, OPEN DEMOCRACY, Aug. 8, 2013.

49. Muhammad Sahimi, *Atoms for Peace*, CAIRO REV. OF GLOBAL AFF., July 21, 2013.

50. *Id.*

51. *Id.*; *see also* Mark Hibbs, *U.S. in 1983 Stopped IAEA from Helping Iran Make UF6*, 28 BONN NUCLEAR FUEL 16 (Aug. 4, 2003).

52. *Id.*

> Shah Pahlavi, IAEA officials were keen to assist Iran in reactivating a research program to learn how to process U3O8 into UO2 pellets and then set up a pilot plant to produce UF6, according to IAEA documents obtained by *Nuclear Fuel*.
>
> Sources said that when in 1983 the recommendations of an IAEA mission to Iran were passed on to the IAEA's technical cooperation program, the U.S. government then "directly intervened" to discourage the IAEA from assisting Iran in production of UO2 and UF6. "We stopped that in its tracks," said a former U.S. official.[53]

Thus, as early as 1983, Iran informed the IAEA of its intentions to renew its development of civilian nuclear technology and attempted to operate ENTEC with assistance from and under the supervision of the IAEA; however, as in this first instance, it would face Western opposition at every step.[54]

During this period, the Iranian government continued to maintain that it was pursuing nuclear technology for peaceful purposes. In 1984, Ayatollah Khomeini, Iran's supreme leader and the "guardian jurist" of the Islamic Republic, issued a *fatwa*, or religious injunction, against nuclear weapons, declaring them "un-Islamic."[55] In the U.N. General Assembly, Iran spoke out against the insanity of the Cold War arms race. It also consistently voted in favor of disarmament and nonproliferation measures. Yet Western suspicions concerning Iran's intentions remained. With the emergence of nuclear weapons in India and Pakistan, many thought that Iran might soon similarly turn to the development of a nuclear weapon as a security measure.[56]

53. *Id.*

54. Muhammad Sahimi, *Atoms for Peace*, CAIRO REV. OF GLOBAL AFF., July 21, 2013.

55. DAVID PATRIKARAKOS, NUCLEAR IRAN: THE BIRTH OF AN ATOMIC STATE, at 117 (2012); Gareth Porter, *When the Ayatollah Said No to Nukes*, FOREIGN POL'Y, Oct. 16, 2014.

56. DAVID PATRIKARAKOS, NUCLEAR IRAN: THE BIRTH OF AN ATOMIC STATE, at 118–120 (2012).

Despite the 1982 arbitration agreement in which Kraftwerk had agreed to continue work at Bushehr, in 1984 Kraftwerk said that it would only continue construction on the Bushehr reactor when the Iran-Iraq War was over.[57] The Bushehr plant was attacked several times during the war, resulting in damage to the dome of the reactor and creating problems for the supporting infrastructure.[58] Iranian officials were unhappy with the IAEA's failure to act in response to Iraq's attacks on Iran's nuclear facilities. Ali Akbar Velayati, then Iran's Foreign Minister, sharply criticized the IAEA, claiming that its inactions showed:

> The harsh reality that an august international body such as the IAEA is either totally impotent in observing and/or implementing its own adopted resolutions or else, and here more disturbingly, is strongly biased in its dealings with the relevant affairs of its various member states.[59]

The IAEA's inaction during the Iran-Iraq War reinforced Iran's belief that international organizations, such as the IAEA, acted as tools of powerful Western countries. This strengthened Iran's resolve to proceed in furtherance of its interests, in a manner which it characterized as the "defiance of a modernizing state overtly confronting the system that denied it justice."[60]

In 1984, the United States urged a worldwide ban on the sale of nuclear materials to and nuclear cooperation with Iran. In 1986, the U.S.-Iranian relationship was further weakened by the Iran-Contra Affair, wherein it was revealed that the United States had secretly assisted in the sale of arms to Iran in exchange for the release of U.S. hostages held in Lebanon. Americans were outraged. Iran was again dubbed an enemy of the United States, making it

57. *Id.* at 108.
58. *Id.*
59. *Id.* at 110.
60. *Id.* at 111.

nearly impossible for diplomatic relations to exist between the two countries.[61]

As the Iran-Iraq War progressed, the United States began to make its support for Iraq more pronounced. In a 1995 statement to the U.S. District Court in the Southern District of Florida, Howard Teicher, former Director of Political-Military Affairs for the National Security Council, stated:

> [T]he United States actively supported the Iraqi war effort by supplying the Iraqis with billions of dollars of credits, by providing U.S. military intelligence and advice to the Iraqis, and by closely monitoring third country arms sales to Iraq to make sure that Iraq had the military weaponry required. The United States also provided strategic operational advice to the Iraqis to better use their assets in combat.[62]

The most controversial exercise of U.S. support during this time is the use of U.S. military intelligence to facilitate Iraqi chemical attacks against Iran.[63] Shane Harris and Matthew Aid have written:

> In 1988, during the waning days of Iraq's war with Iran, the United States learned through satellite imagery that Iran was about to gain a major strategic advantage by exploiting a hole in Iraqi defenses. U.S. intelligence officials conveyed the location of the Iranian troops to Iraq, fully aware that Hussein's military would attack with chemical weapons, including sarin, a lethal nerve agent.[64]

61. *Id.* at 114–115, 128.

62. Statement by former NSC official Howard Teicher to the U.S. District Court, Southern District of Florida (Jan. 31, 1995), *available at* http://www.webcitation.org/5flvP0UgC.

63. Shane Harris & Matthew M. Aid, *Exclusive: CIA Files Prove America Helped Saddam as He Gassed Iran*, FOREIGN POL'Y, Aug. 23, 2013.

64. *Id.*

The intelligence supplied to Iraq included imagery and maps providing details about Iranian troop movements, the locations of Iranian logistics facilities, and information about Iranian air defenses. Relying on this U.S. intelligence, Iraq used mustard gas and sarin in four chemical weapons attacks in early 1988. While U.S. officials have denied knowledge of Iraq's intent to engage in chemical weapons attacks, numerous sources suggest that the United States was well aware of Hussein's plans. Retired Air Force Colonel Rick Francona, who was a military attaché during the Iran-Iraq War, stated that "[t]he Iraqis never told us that they intended to use nerve gas. They didn't have to. We already knew."[65]

Recently declassified CIA files show that the United States had hard evidence of Iraqi chemical attacks as early as 1983. At this time, Iran was trying to gather evidence of Iraq's chemical attacks to present to the United Nations. The declassified CIA files show that the United States determined that Iran might not find evidence of the chemical attacks and that it would be to the United States' advantage to allow the attacks to continue. Harris and Aid write that "the United States applied a cold calculus three decades ago to Hussein's widespread use of chemical weapons against his enemies and his own people. The Reagan administration decided that it was better to let the attacks continue if they might turn the tide of the war."[66]

Iraq went on to use weaponized sarin in massive quantities against Iranian forces three more times in the months that followed.[67] The effects of these chemical attacks were catastrophic and have lived long in the collective memory of Iranians to the present day. Mohammad Javad Zarif, who would later become Iran's Minister of Foreign Affairs, wrote in a 2007 article that "[t]he Iranian people experienced war and destruction on the battlefields and in their homes, thanks to Saddam's doctrine of total war. Massive diplomatic, financial and military support for the aggressor from every corner of

65. *Id.*
66. *Id.*
67. *Id.*

the world added insult to injury."[68] He specifically criticized the U.S., Soviet, French, and German support of Iraq through provision of military intelligence and supplies, including the materials that were used to create chemical and biological weapons.[69] Additionally, he alleged that the U.N. Security Council, facing pressure from powerful Western states, turned a blind eye to the use of chemical weapons by Iraq despite Iran's pleas to consider the mounting evidence.[70]

In the wake of the devastation caused by the Iran-Iraq War, and the international community's lack of response to this destruction and to Iraq's aggression, Iranian officials resolved to do whatever was necessary to protect the country in the future. In a 1988 speech, Ali Akbar Rafsanjani, who was then speaker of the Iranian parliament and Iran's commander-in-chief, said:

> With regard to chemical, bacteriological, and radiological weapons training, it was made very clear during the war that these weapons are very decisive. It was also made clear that the moral teachings of the world are not very effective when war reaches a serious stage and the world does not respect is own resolutions and closes its eyes to the violations and all the aggressions which are committed in the battlefield. We should fully equip ourselves both in the offense and defensive use of chemical, bacteriological, and radiological weapons.[71]

However, Zarif further writes that because of its experience with such weapons, an important part of Iran's security doctrine has become "the elimination of weapons of mass destruction, strengthening and universalization of the Non-Proliferation Treaty and

68. Mohammad Javad Zarif, *Tackling the Iran-U.S. Crisis: The Need for a Paradigm Shift*, 60 J. Int'l Aff. 73, 80, at 73–74 (2007).

69. *Id.*

70. *Id.*

71. David Patrikarakos, Nuclear Iran: The Birth of an Atomic State, at 130 (2012).

the establishment of a zone free from such weapons in the Middle East."[72] This apparently schizophrenic attitude toward weapons of mass destruction, caused by the selfsame experience of the trauma of the Iran-Iraq War, is perhaps understandable.

E. Developments in the 1990s

Faced with opposition from many states to its efforts to develop its nuclear energy program further, in the 1990s Iran turned to more covert means of development. Muhammad Sahimi writes that through its earlier attempts to develop its nuclear research program,

> Iran learned a lesson: it could not set up the enrichment facilities with full transparency, because the United States would stop the effort at their inception. Beginning in 1987, while it was pursuing its nuclear power program openly, Iran also began quietly developing a uranium enrichment program based on whatever design it could obtain.[73]

As many other countries now refused to work with Iran, Iran turned increasingly to China and Russia for nuclear cooperation. In 1990, Iran signed a nuclear cooperation agreement with China, and the next year imported one metric ton of uranium hexafluoride.[74] On January 8, 1995, Iran signed an agreement with Russia for the completion of one of the Bushehr light-water reactors, which was left incomplete at the time of the Iranian Revolution and was subsequently significantly damaged in the Iran-Iraq War.[75]

In 1997, facing U.S. pressure to withdraw, China dropped out of most of its agreements with Iran, including its agreement to construct

72. Mohammad Javad Zarif, *Tackling the Iran-U.S. Crisis: The Need for a Paradigm Shift*, 60 J. Int'l Aff. 73, 80, at 75 (2007).

73. *Id.*

74. *Id.*

75. Muhammad Sahimi, *Atoms for Peace*, Cairo Rev. of Global Aff., July 21, 2013.

the uranium hexafluoride plant at ENTEC.[76] The AEOI reiterated to the IAEA that it would continue with construction of the ENTEC facility regardless of whether it had Chinese support. While it appears that China stuck to its agreement that it would no longer build the plant in Iran, it did sell the blueprints for the facility to the AEOI, thus allowing Iran to construct the plant on its own. Thereafter, construction began on the uranium hexafluoride plant at ENTEC in 1997, facilitated by the Chinese blueprints and possible Russian support. The UF6 plant at ENTEC was declared to the IAEA in 2000.[77]

With the United States' policy of pressuring other countries not to assist Iran in developing its nuclear program firmly in place and consistently applied, Mohammad Zarif contends that "Iran was left with no option but to be discreet in its peaceful activities."[78]

F. 9/11 Responses

In the aftermath of the September 11, 2001, attacks on the United States, Iran provided significant support for U.S. efforts against the Taliban in Afghanistan. The United States joined Iran's already existing coalition against the Taliban, and Iran offered support for U.S. efforts including the offer of air bases for U.S. use, offering to perform search-and-rescue efforts in the case of failed aviation missions and providing intelligence information regarding the location of important al-Qaeda leaders.[79] The United States and Iran momentarily joined together in pursuit of their common interest in unseating the Taliban from power. Iran was highly influential in the December 2001 Bonn Conference, in which prominent Afghan leaders met along with various U.N. leaders, to develop a plan for governing Afghanistan, leading to the signing of the historic Bonn Agreement.[80]

76. Mark Hibbs, *U.S. in 1983 Stopped IAEA from Helping Iran Make UF6*, 28 Bonn Nuclear Fuel 16 (Aug. 4, 2003).

77. *Id.*

78. Mohammad Javad Zarif, *Tackling the Iran-U.S. Crisis: The Need for a Paradigm Shift*, 60 J. Int'l Aff. 73, 80, at 81 (2007).

79. *Id.*

80. *Id.* at 40.

The U.S.-Iranian cooperation at the Bonn Conference seemed like a positive step in relations. Nevertheless, only weeks later at President George W. Bush's January 2002 State of the Union address, Iran's support in Afghanistan seemed long forgotten. In his speech, Bush infamously branded Iran, along with Iraq and North Korea, as part of a dangerous group of states comprising an "Axis of Evil."[81] Iranian officials were outraged. This incident sent a clear message to Iran in the perception of many: America was untrustworthy. Iranian hard-liners suggested that "[i]f you give in, if you help from a position of weakness, then you get negative results."[82] As Trita Parsi writes in *A Single Roll of the Dice: Obama's Diplomacy with Iran*, "The experience in Afghanistan negated what little trust existed between Washington and Tehran, and rendered any future cooperation more difficult."[83]

Former IAEA Director Mohamed ElBaradei has since sharply criticized the Bush administration's approach to dealing with Iran, stating that "[a]nytime you try to isolate a country, the situation gets much, much worse."[84] ElBaradei attributed the failures in the Bush administration's relations with Iran to "a combination of ignorance and arrogance."[85]

G. Discovery of the Natanz Facility

In mid-2002, the IAEA began receiving intelligence information about the possible existence of a uranium enrichment plant in Natanz, near the city of Esfahan.[86] In August 2002, the National Council of Resistance of Iran, an Iranian opposition group based in Paris, announced its allegation of a secret enrichment facility at Natanz at

81. *Id.*

82. *Id.* at 41 (quoting Scott Peterson, *Pragmatism May Trump Zeal as Iran's Power Grows*, Christian Science Monitor, July 6, 2006).

83. Trita Parsi, A Single Roll of the Dice: Obama's Diplomacy with Iran, at 41 (2012).

84. *Id.* at 43–44.

85. *Id.* at 44.

86. *See* Mohamed ElBaradei, The Age of Deception: Nuclear Diplomacy in Treacherous Times, at 112 (2011).

a press conference in Washington.[87] ElBaradei and the IAEA immediately began investigating these allegations. At the IAEA General Conference in Vienna, ElBaradei confronted Gholamreza Aghazadeh, the vice president of Iran and head of the AEOI. ElBaradei asked Aghazadeh to "[t]ell [him] about this Natanz facility . . . Is [it] for enrichment, as the satellite photos suggest? Perhaps we should make a visit."[88] Aghazadeh's response was vague and ambiguous—simply stating that the IAEA would be able to visit soon and that everything would be explained then.[89] Satellite photos taken in December 2002 identified undeclared facilities being constructed at both Natanz and Arak.

On February 9, 2003, Iranian President Mohammad Khatami confirmed the existence of a nuclear research facility at Natanz. On February 21, 2003, ElBaradei and a team of IAEA inspectors visited Iran.[90] At the initial meeting with the IAEA, Aghazadeh and his AEOI colleagues admitted that the facility at Natanz was meant to be a uranium enrichment plant.[91] The Iranians maintained that they had not meant to hide the plant from the Agency and that they had not violated their obligations under the NPT.[92] They promised that no nuclear material had been introduced into Natanz, so that, in their opinion, they were not in violation of their commitment, pursuant to the subsidiary arrangements under their safeguards agreement, to inform the IAEA 180 days before the introduction of nuclear material into the facility.[93]

When the IAEA team visited the facility, they were shocked by its size. First, they entered the pilot enrichment facility, which

87. *Id.*

88. *Id.*

89. *Id.* at 113.

90. Muhammad Sahimi, *Atoms for Peace*, CAIRO REV. OF GLOBAL AFF., July 21, 2013.

91. *See* MOHAMED ELBARADEI, THE AGE OF DECEPTION: NUCLEAR DIPLOMACY IN TREACHEROUS TIMES, at 114 (2011).

92. Muhammad Sahimi, *Atoms for Peace*, CAIRO REV. OF GLOBAL AFF., July 21, 2013.

93. *Id.*

contained 20 centrifuges, but had space for six blocks of 164 centrifuges, coming to a potential total of slightly fewer than 1,000 centrifuges. When they went to the underground portion of the facility, they found that, although it was currently empty, the underground hall had the potential to hold more than 50,000 centrifuges.[94]

ElBaradei has suggested that the Iranians may have thought it was necessary to conceal the facility at Natanz for as long as possible:

> Given the size of the Natanz facility, it is likely that the Iranians were not intending to "hide" it per se. Their aim, I believe, was to delay its reporting as far as legally permissible under their safeguards agreement and to delay IAEA inspection until they had completed their construction and received all the needed knowledge and technology, which were being obtained through clandestine channels due to sanctions. I was later told they were worried that declaring the Natanz facilities would expose their supply network.[95]

Aghazadeh, head of the AEOI, claimed that the centrifuge program at Natanz was entirely indigenous and that no nuclear material had been used in this site or at any other Iranian sites. However, the IAEA had its doubts.[96] The IAEA received intelligence information that possible nuclear testing had been done at the Kalaye Electric Company on the southern outskirts of Tehran. The Iranians insisted that they had only done "simulation studies" at this workshop and that they had not used nuclear material in these experiments. When the IAEA was eventually able to overcome Iranian resistance and was allowed to visit the Kalaye site, the inspectors discovered that nuclear material had indeed been used in the centrifuges at Kalaye. At this point, Iran's story began to change. The AEOI no longer clung

94. *Id.*

95. *See* MOHAMED ELBARADEI, THE AGE OF DECEPTION: NUCLEAR DIPLOMACY IN TREACHEROUS TIMES, at 114 n.3 (2011).

96. *Id.* at 115.

to its assertion that their nuclear program was entirely indigenous, but now admitted that components of their centrifuges had been imported from other countries and explained that contaminated parts must have been the source of the uranium particles found at the Kalaye facility—a claim later proved correct. The IAEA also discovered undeclared natural uranium imported from China at the Jabr Ibn Hayan Multipurpose Laboratories (JHL) at the Tehran Nuclear Research Center. Neither the uranium nor the existence of the JHL had been reported to the IAEA. Much of the uranium that the IAEA discovered had been converted into uranium metal. Three cylinders of UF6 uranium gas were discovered in storage, but one of the containers was missing some of its uranium gas. When questioned about the missing gas, the Iranians said that it must have leaked.[97]

The concealment of the Natanz facility and the inconsistencies found in the IAEA inspections of Iran's facilities, caused ElBaradei to come to the conclusion that he was "dealing with people who were willing to deceive to achieve their goals and that we should not accept any attestation without physical verification."[98] Nevertheless, Iranian leaders continued to insist that Iran's nuclear program was only for peaceful purposes. Ali Akbar Rafsanjani, the former president of Iran and then head of the Guardian Council, explained his reasoning for pursuing only a peaceful program, stating, "I have seen so many of our people killed with chemical weapons during the Iran-Iraq War. I cannot be the one advocating dialogue among civilizations and at the same time developing nuclear weapons."[99] Still, ElBaradei reminded the Iranian leaders that they had hurt their credibility with the international community by their concealment of the Natanz facility and that they were thus "starting out with a confidence deficit."[100]

Even after the IAEA uncovered evidence of Iran's covert nuclear facility development, Iran maintained that its actions were justified.

97. *Id.* at 115–117.
98. *Id.*
99. *Id.* at 118.
100. *Id.*

Iranian officials based this belief on a history of "double dealings with the West."[101] They felt that they had been repeatedly treated unjustly in their past experiences with the West with regard to their nuclear program. Under the Shah, the United States, Germany, France, and other Western countries had pledged their support to Iran's nuclear programs. Iran had signed a contract with a German firm to build the first plant at Bushehr. Iran had also acquired a 10 percent share in a French uranium enrichment plant. However, after the 1979 Revolution, the West's attitude toward Iran's nuclear program dramatically changed, for purely political reasons. The German firm refused to finish construction of the Bushehr plant, the United States stopped supplying fuel to Iran's research reactor, and France refused to provide Iran with enriched uranium, despite Iran's share in the French plant.[102]

Furthermore, sanctions imposed on Iran by the United States and its allies had prohibited the import of any nuclear materials, so it became necessary for Iran to import the materials and technology covertly. In addition, Russia, as Iran's only fuel supplier, was charging Iran exorbitant prices for fuel and supplies.[103] Thus, Iran desperately wanted to develop its own fuel cycle to break its dependence on Russia and on the Western countries now refusing to support its nuclear ambitions. The United States was unreceptive to these arguments, though, and considered that the concealment was "proof positive that Tehran intended to produce nuclear weapons."[104] Other Western countries began to support the U.S. position, while developing countries were generally more sympathetic to Iran's view that it was necessary to develop its program in secret.[105]

Discrepancies in the Iranian story continued to appear. The IAEA inspectors were skeptical that Iran's nuclear program could have

101. *Id.* at 118–119.
102. *Id.*
103. *Id.* at 119.
104. *Id.*
105. *Id.*

reached this advanced stage without more experimentation and testing than the country was admitting.[106] IAEA inspectors visited a laser facility at Lashkar Ab'ad, equipped with vapor lasers that could be used in uranium enrichment. However, Iran denied that the lasers were used for this purpose. Also, inconsistencies appeared regarding the construction plans for Arak. Iran had plans to construct an IR-40 heavy-water reactor at Arak beginning in 2004, but the plans did not include "hot cells," which are special chambers for the processing of radioactive material and separation of plutonium. Yet the IAEA knew Iran had made attempts to procure the materials necessary to create hot cells from abroad.[107] The Iranians insisted that no experiments involving nuclear material had taken place, and only when they were confronted with sample results that contradicted this claim did Iranian officials eventually admit to experiments with almost every phase of the uranium conversion process.[108]

Reactions to Iran's concealment of the Natanz facility have been varied. A May 28, 2013, BBC Radio Broadcast entitled *Iran's Nuclear Standoff* frames the discovery of Natanz as a gross violation of Iran's international obligations, stating:

> The Agency went to Iran and they saw the [Natanz] facility and were flummoxed. They were not anticipating seeing this. During the course of the next twelve months, the IAEA then was able to confirm that over a period of eighteen years, the IAEA was systematically lied to and deceived by Iran, because Iran had imported nuclear materials from places which it did not declare. It was processing some of this material into sensitive forms, such as uranium metal, which could be used for nuclear weapons research.[109]

106. *Id.* at 119–120.
107. *Id.* at 120.
108. *Id.*
109. David Morrison & Peter Oborne, *Does the BBC Not Trust US Intelligence on Iran?*, Open Democracy, Aug. 8, 2013.

Others have characterized this rhetoric as overblown and contend that Iran's noncompliance consists only, at the worst, of failing to timely report its activities to the IAEA, maintaining that none of the hidden activities "were related to a nuclear weapons programme."[110] As Hassan Rouhani, the recently elected president of Iran, who was head of Iran's nuclear negotiating team from 2003 to 2005, has explained:

> What is often cited by American officials as 20 years of Iranian secret nuclear military program turned out to be, as declared by the IAEA, nothing more than the failure to declare, in a timely manner, some experiments and receiving some material and equipment. Such failures to declare are not uncommon among the NPT members. Remedial steps are envisioned in the Safeguards Agreement to address them, and Iran has done so. Moreover, it was no secret that we were in the European, Russian and Asian markets to purchase enrichment technology in the late '80s and '90s. Therefore, an Iranian secret weapon program is only hype, and the sense of urgency about Iran's nuclear program is rather tendentious. The world should not allow itself to be dragged into another conflict on false pretenses in this region again.[111]

II. HISTORY OF DIPLOMACY AND RELATIONS AMONG IRAN, THE IAEA, AND WESTERN POWERS

A. 2003 IAEA Resolution

On September 12, 2003, the IAEA Board of Governors adopted a resolution (GOV/2003/69) calling for Iran to suspend all enrichment-related activities and make full declarations of all activities relevant to its uranium enrichment program. The resolution also asked Iran

110. *Id.*
111. *Id.* (citing *Iran's Nuclear Program: The Way Out*, TIME, May 9, 2006).

to allow IAEA inspectors to take additional samples at any suspected locations and encouraged Iran to adopt the Additional Protocol to its safeguards agreement. This resolution required Iran to meet these conditions by October 31, 2003.[112]

On October 16, 2003, IAEA Director General ElBaradei met with Hassan Rouhani, then secretary of Iran's Nuclear Security Council, to discuss the inconsistences discovered in the inspections following the revelation of Natanz.[113] Iran agreed to meet the IAEA's October 31 deadline and also agreed to a voluntary suspension of uranium enrichment, ahead of upcoming negotiations with European foreign ministers.[114] This commitment to cooperate with the IAEA, and to implement the Additional Protocol, was reaffirmed in the October 21 Tehran Declaration made between France, Germany, and the United Kingdom (the EU-3), and Iran.[115] In this declaration, Iran agreed to cooperate with IAEA inspections, implement the Additional Protocol, and voluntarily and temporarily suspend enrichment and reprocessing activities. In exchange, the EU-3 agreed to recognize "the right of Iran to enjoy peaceful use of nuclear energy in accordance with the NPT."[116]

On October 23, the IAEA received a letter from Iran admitting to many of the activities Iran had not previously reported, including testing of centrifuges at Kalaye using the UF6 gas that was found to be missing from one of the cylinders at the JHL in the IAEA inspections, conducting laser enrichment experiments in the 1990s, small amounts of plutonium separation experiments, and a number of other previously unreported uranium conversion experiments.[117]

112. *Solving the Iranian Nuclear Puzzle*, Arms Control Association 33, at 34 (Sept. 2013).

113. *See* Mohamed ElBaradei, The Age of Deception: Nuclear Diplomacy in Treacherous Times, at 120 (2011).

114. *Solving the Iranian Nuclear Puzzle*, Arms Control Association 33, at 34 (Sept. 2013).

115. *See* Mohamed ElBaradei, The Age of Deception: Nuclear Diplomacy in Treacherous Times, at 121 (2011).

116. *Iranian Nuclear Energy Program Negotiations*, http://nuclearenergy.ir.

117. *See* Mohamed ElBaradei, The Age of Deception: Nuclear Diplomacy in Treacherous Times, at 121 (2011).

On November 10, 2003, ElBaradei submitted his report (GOV/ 2003/75) to the IAEA Board of Governors, detailing the new discoveries in Iran's nuclear program and chastising Iran for maintaining a "policy of concealment" and for only providing limited cooperation to the IAEA, while at the same time acknowledging Iran's promises of future cooperation, along with its voluntary uranium suspension and its decision to implement an Additional Protocol.[118] In paragraph 47, the report stated:

> Based on all information currently available to the Agency, it is clear that Iran has failed in a number of instances over an extended period of time to meet its obligations under its Safeguards Agreement with respect to the reporting of nuclear material and its processing and use, as well as the declaration of facilities where such material has been processed and stored.

The final conclusion of the report stated, however:

> [T]here is no evidence that the previously undeclared nuclear material and activities referred to above were related to a nuclear weapons programme. However, given Iran's past pattern of concealment, it will take some time before the Agency is able to conclude that Iran's nuclear programme is exclusively for peaceful purposes.[119]

This conclusion provoked a negative response from the United States, which criticized ElBaradei for not taking a harsher position against Iran.[120]

On December 18, 2003, Iran signed the Additional Protocol (INFCIRC/540) to its IAEA comprehensive safeguards agreement, which had been in force since 1974, and further voluntarily agreed to

118. *Id.* at 121–122.
119. *Id.* at 122.
120. *Id.* at 122.

implement the Additional Protocol's procedures, including the filing of declarations to the IAEA, while the treaty was presented to the Majlis for consent to ratification.[121] Despite progress in some areas, inconsistencies remained in Iran's account of its nuclear program. In January 2004, Iran admitted that it had received design plans for the more advanced P-2 centrifuge models from the illicit A.Q. Khan network.[122] When evidence of the extent of the Khan network surfaced in 2004, the IAEA discovered that Iran had purchased the components for a centrifuge and design plans as early as 1987.[123]

In March 2004, ElBaradei traveled to New York to meet with President George W. Bush. Despite the U.S. hard-line public approach toward Iran, ElBaradei found Bush to be receptive to diplomatic solutions to the Iranian nuclear problem.[124] In response to ElBaradei's suggestion that a diplomatic solution was the best response, Bush replied, "It's not only the best solution . . . [I]t's the only solution—other than the Israeli solution. You know there is concern . . . that the Israelis might want to use force."[125] However, despite ElBaradei's pleas for diplomacy, and what seemed to be considerable progress on both the Iranian and U.S. fronts, in June 2004 the IAEA Board of Governors adopted a resolution (GOV/2004/49) critical of the continued delays and of Iranian deception.[126] The report criticized Iran for failing to provide "full, timely, and proactive cooperation" to the IAEA.[127] Clearly unhappy with this report, Iran responded by withdrawing its commitment to suspend its enrichment activities.[128]

121. *Solving the Iranian Nuclear Puzzle*, ARMS CONTROL ASSOCIATION 33, at 34 (Sept. 2013). The Majlis never consented to the ratification of the Additional Protocol, however, and Iran has not ratified the treaty.

122. *See* MOHAMED ELBARADEI, THE AGE OF DECEPTION: NUCLEAR DIPLOMACY IN TREACHEROUS TIMES, at 126–127 (2011).

123. *Id.* at 167.

124. *Id.* at 130–131.

125. *Id.* at 131.

126. *Id.* at 136.

127. *Id.* at 136.

128. *Solving the Iranian Nuclear Puzzle*, ARMS CONTROL ASSOCIATION 33, at 34 (Sept. 2013).

B. EU-3 Negotiations and the Paris Agreement

The October 2003 Tehran Declaration provided the basis for ongoing talks between Iran and the EU-3.[129] In February 2004, the EU-3 and Iran met in Brussels to continue negotiations. Here the parties signed the Brussels Agreement, in which Iran again agreed to voluntarily accept a suspension of uranium enrichment, including halting the manufacturing and assembling of centrifuge parts. The EU-3 in return agreed to push for normalization of relations between Iran and the IAEA, as well as for Iran's nuclear file to be closed in the June 2004 IAEA Board of Governors meeting. Pursuant to this agreement, Iran suspended its manufacturing and assembling of centrifuge parts in mid-April. The EU-3, however, failed to deliver diplomatic results, and with the collapse of the Brussels Agreement, Iran ended its suspension on the manufacturing and assembling of centrifuge parts.[130]

In an effort to move forward with negotiations, representatives from Iran and the EU-3 signed the Paris Agreement on November 14, 2004. [131] The Paris Agreement stated:

> [T]he E3/EU and Iran have agreed to begin negotiations, with a view to reaching a mutually acceptable agreement on long-term arrangements. The agreement will provide objective guarantees that Iran's nuclear program is exclusively for peaceful purposes. It will equally provide firm guarantees on nuclear, technological, and economic cooperation and firm commitments on security issues.[132]

Initially the Paris Agreement had positive effects. IAEA inspectors confirmed that a full suspension was in place one week after

129. Mary Kaszynski, *Talking with Tehran: An Overview of U.S.-Iran Nuclear Negotiations*, American Security Project (July 2012).

130. *Iranian Nuclear Energy Program Negotiations*, http://nuclearenergy.ir.

131. Muhammad Sahimi, *Atoms for Peace*, Cairo Rev. of Global Aff., July 21, 2013.

132. *Id.*

the agreement was made.[133] At the March 2005 IAEA Board meeting, Iran's nuclear program did not seem to be of immediate concern and was not on the meeting's agenda for the first time in almost two years.[134] However, the EU-3 negotiations would ultimately fail because Iran and the EU-3 were unable to come to an agreement on long-term arrangements. In March 2005, Iran submitted a proposal to the EU-3 that proposed allowing Iran to resume some of its uranium enrichment activities under close monitoring, along with incentives of Western technology and trade agreements.[135] The EU-3 significantly delayed responding to this proposal, and when it finally did submit a proposal to Tehran in August 2005, the proposal contained only vague language and no guarantee that Iran would not be attacked, yet asked for Iran to eliminate its nuclear facilities entirely.[136] Iran rejected the August EU-3 proposal.[137]

In retrospect, some view the failure of the EU-3 negotiations as a missed opportunity. A group of former European ambassadors to Tehran wrote in 2011:

> In 2005 Iran was ready to discuss an upper limit for the number of its centrifuges and to maintain its rate of enrichment far below the high levels necessary for weapons. Tehran also expressed its readiness to allow intrusive inspections, even in non-declared sites. But at that time Europe and the US wanted to compel Iran to ditch its enrichment programme entirely. Iranians assume that this is still the European and US goal, and that for this reason the Security Council insists on suspension of all Iranian enrichment activities. But the goal of "zero centrifuges operating

133. *See* Mohamed ElBaradei, The Age of Deception: Nuclear Diplomacy in Treacherous Times, at 141 (2011).

134. *Id.* at 143.

135. *Id.* at 143.

136. Muhammad Sahimi, *Atoms for Peace*, Cairo Rev. of Global Aff., July 21, 2013.

137. *Id.*

> in Iran, permanently or temporarily" is unrealistic, and has contributed greatly to the present standoff.[138]

While Iran was attempting to negotiate with the EU-3, it was continuing to develop its nuclear program in other respects. On February 27, 2005, Russia and Iran entered into an agreement under which Russia would supply fuel for the Bushehr reactor, and Iran would return the spent fuel to Russia.[139]

C. 2006 Referral to the Security Council

After the EU-3 negotiations failed, the IAEA Board of Governors adopted resolution GOV/2005/77 on September 24, 2005, in which it decided:

> Iran's many failures and breaches of its obligations to comply with its NPT Safeguards Agreement, as detailed in GOV/2003/75, constitute noncompliance in the context of Article XII.C of the Agency's Statute.

This was the Board of Governors' first formal finding that Iran was in noncompliance with its obligations under its safeguards agreement with the IAEA. On January 3, 2006, in response to this finding, Iran informed the IAEA that it would resume its uranium enrichment research and development.[140]

This sequence of events led to IAEA Board of Governors' referral of Iran's case to the U.N. Security Council on February 4, 2006.[141]

138. David Morrison & Peter Oborne, *Does the BBC Not Trust US Intelligence on Iran?*, Open Democracy, Aug. 8, 2013.

139. *Solving the Iranian Nuclear Puzzle*, Arms Control Association 33, at 35 (Sept. 2013).

140. *See* Mohamed ElBaradei, The Age of Deception: Nuclear Diplomacy in Treacherous Times, at 191 (2011).

141. Muhammad Sahimi, *Atoms for Peace*, Cairo Rev. of Global Aff., July 21, 2013.

In response, Iran withdrew its voluntary implementation of its Additional Protocol (which the Majlis had not consented to and therefore had not been ratified by Iran) in accordance with a 2005 law that had been passed by the Majlis, directing the government to suspend the implementation of the Additional Protocol in the event that Iran were to be referred to the Security Council.[142] In late 2005 to early 2006, U.S. hopes for diplomacy with Iran had been replaced with the hard-line stance that "not one centrifuge" should be spinning in Iran.[143]

D. U.N. Sanctions

In June 2006, the Europeans began working on a new proposal with Iran, which would follow a two-track approach: a set of incentives in exchange for Iran limiting its enrichment program; or conversely, a set of sanctions if Iran failed to accept the proposal. ElBaradei feared that such an approach would not work since Iran generally was not receptive to offers to negotiate under threat. However, Iran did consider the proposal. Contrary to the previous EU-3 proposal, the incentives offered in this new proposal were generous, but Iran said it wanted until August 22 to respond. The West viewed Iran's request for more time with suspicion, and the United States, the United Kingdom, and other Western powers were unwilling to wait for an answer.[144]

In July 2006—only three weeks before the date Iran had said it would respond to the proposal—the Security Council issued Resolution 1696, in which it acted under Article 40 of Chapter VII of the U.N. Charter to demand the suspension of all uranium enrichment activities in Iran. The resolution requested the IAEA to report

142. *See* Mohamed ElBaradei, The Age of Deception: Nuclear Diplomacy in Treacherous Times, at 193 (2011).

143. *Id.* at 195.

144. *Id.* at 195–199.

back to the Security Council by the end of August to confirm that Iran had suspended its enrichment activities.[145]

Iran's response to Resolution 1696 was, unsurprisingly, critical. Among its expressed concerns were, first, that the timing of the resolution seemed inappropriate, with an answer from Iran expected so soon. Second, the legality of the resolution was questionable, they argued, since the IAEA's inspections had not shown any evidence of an Iranian nuclear weapons program. On the contrary, the director general of the IAEA had reported that the IAEA had found no evidence of such a program. Ali Larijani, secretary of Iran's Supreme National Security Council, stated that the Islamic Republic of Iran would never again agree to suspension of its uranium enrichment activities.[146] For his part, IAEA Director General ElBaradei believed that Resolution 1696 was a misstep by the Security Council, later writing:

> In my view, Resolution 1696 was not only counterproductive from a policy perspective, but also a misuse of the council's authority under Chapter VII of the UN Charter. It was staggering to compare the difference in treatment of North Korea and Iran. North Korea had walked out of the NPT and made explicit threats about developing nuclear weapons . . . yet the Americans were ready to join them in direct dialogue, and Chris Hill seemed to be in Pyongyang every other day. By contrast, Iran, which remained under safeguards and party to the NPT, was penalized for possibly having future intentions to develop nuclear weapons, and the Americans refused to talk to them without preconditions.[147]

Despite Iran's rhetoric suggesting it would no longer be open to negotiations, it submitted a response to the European proposal as scheduled on August 22, 2006.[148] The response suggested that Iran

145. *Id.* at 199.
146. *Id.* at 201.
147. *Id.* at 203.
148. *Id.* at 204.

was still open to the possibility of a diplomatic resolution.[149] Over the next month, Javier Solana, on behalf of the P5+1, attempted to negotiate with Iranian representative Ali Larijani.[150] The P5+1 agreed that they would give Iran until early October to reach an agreement on the terms of its uranium suspension.[151] However, no agreement was reached by October, and on December 23, 2006, the U.N. Security Council passed Resolution 1737, in which it acted under Article 41 of the Charter and made binding the demands of Resolution 1696, and further implemented sanctions that, for the most part, simply reaffirmed measures already in place, including "a ban on supplying Iran with nuclear-related technology and materials and a freeze of the assets of specific individuals and companies who had supported Iran's enrichment program."[152] Iran's response to the resolution was also fairly tame, reiterating its belief that it was "being punished for exercising its inalienable rights" to civil nuclear technology under the NPT.[153]

In January 2007, the European powers made some efforts to continue negotiations with Iran regarding its enrichment activities, but these negotiations were met with U.S. opposition.[154] Hardliners in Washington continued to insist that Iran must give up all enrichment capability.[155] France proposed the idea of working toward a "double-suspension" deal with Iran, in which Iran would suspend its enrichment in exchange for the Security Council's suspension of sanctions.[156] ElBaradei began to push for this idea of a "double time-out" as he had now termed it, but this proposal alone did not present an acceptable solution to the P5+1.[157] Their collective position was to support the idea of a double time-out deal, but

149. *Id.*
150. *Id.* at 204–208.
151. *Id.* at 208.
152. *Id.* at 210, 244.
153. *Id.* at 210.
154. *Id.* at 241.
155. *Id.* at 242.
156. *Id.* at 243.
157. *Id.* at 244–247.

they planned to pursue a dual-track approach in which negotiations would occur alongside Security Council resolutions and continued sanctions.[158] The Iranian response to this dual approach was clear: If the Security Council issued a new round of sanctions, that would "be the end of the negotiating process."[159] Thus, when the Security Council adopted Resolution 1747 on March 24, 2007, calling again for the suspension the Iran's uranium enrichment program, this action effectively curtailed any negotiations regarding a double time-out.[160] The additional sanctions in this resolution included "banning Iran's arms imports and exports, freezing assets, and restricting the travel of individuals engaged in the country's nuclear activities."[161] While some criticized the sanctions for their effect in stifling a diplomatic resolution, others believed that sanctions and force were the only solution to the Iranian nuclear crisis.[162] For example, John Bolton, former U.S. ambassador to the United Nations, said in a 2007 interview:

> If you believe, as I do, that Iran is never going to be chatted out of its nuclear weapons, because it sees the nuclear weapons program as its trump card, then the only recourse is to dramatically ratchet up the economic and political pressure on Iran and keep open the option of regime change or even military force.[163]

In August 2007, with other diplomatic options failing, the IAEA sought to come to an agreement with Iran regarding lingering inspections issues.[164] On August 27, 2007, Olli Heinonen, then the IAEA deputy director general for safeguards, announced that he had reached an agreement with Iran whereby Iran would resolve all

158. *Id.* at 246–247.
159. *Id.* at 247.
160. *Id.* at 250.
161. *Id.*
162. *Id.* at 250–253.
163. *Id.* at 253 n.9.
164. *Id.* at 257.

the remaining inspections issues within a three-month period.[165] Western media vigorously attacked ElBaradei and the IAEA for this deal, calling ElBaradei a "Rogue Regulator," and criticizing the IAEA for "striking its own deal with the Iranian regime."[166]

In late 2007, the Bush administration continued to express its harsh disapproval of the Iranian nuclear program. In a speech to the American Legion in Reno, Nevada, Bush stated that "Iran's active pursuit of technology that could lead to nuclear weapons threatens to put a region already known for instability and violence under the shadow of a nuclear holocaust."[167] President Bush also remarked in an October 17 press conference that "if you're interested in avoiding World War III, it seems like you ought to be interested in preventing [the Iranians] from having the knowledge necessary to make a nuclear weapon."[168]

In late 2007, a new U.S. National Intelligence Estimate (NIE) on Iran was released. It concluded that, while Iran appeared to have pursued at least some nuclear weaponization research and development work prior to the autumn of 2003, "in fall 2003, Tehran halted its nuclear weapons program."[169] ElBaradei supplemented this report with a press release in which he stated that "the Agency has no concrete evidence of an ongoing nuclear weapons program or undeclared nuclear facilities in Iran."[170]

President Bush has since written that he was "angry" when the NIE report came out because this "tied [his] hands on the military side" and did not allow him to reasonably pursue the use of a military force as a response to a country that had been declared to not possess nuclear weapons.[171] As recently as April 18, 2013, U.S. Director

165. *Id.* at 257.
166. *Id.* at 258.
167. *Id.* at 263.
168. *Id.* (substitution in original).
169. *Id.* at 268.
170. *Id.*
171. David Morrison & Peter Oborne, *Does the BBC Not Trust US Intelligence on Iran?*, Open Democracy, Aug. 8, 2013.

of National Intelligence James Clapper confirmed that the 2007 NIE report still represented the United States' assessment of Iran's nuclear program.[172]

From 2003 to 2013, the U.N. Security Council issued six resolutions applying an increasingly harsh multilateral economic/financial sanctions regime against Iran.[173] Unilateral U.S. and E.U. sanctions have additionally targeted Iran's energy and banking sectors in an attempt to isolate Iran financially and pressure it to cease its uranium enrichment program.[174] The United States in particular has implemented extremely broad and damaging unilateral sanctions against Iran. The United States has issued a full trade ban on Iran that prohibits all commercial exchanges between the United States and Iran, except for limited exchanges of a humanitarian nature.[175] Since 2008, U.S. financial institutions have been prohibited from conducting "U-turn" transactions, i.e., transactions completed through a foreign bank acting on behalf of an Iranian company. The United States has also prohibited Iran from conducting transactions in U.S. currency, which is particularly detrimental since this is the common currency of international oil markets.[176]

E. ElBaradei's 2008 Report to the IAEA

The IAEA's investigation of Iran's nuclear program continued, and a number of specific instances of past noncompliance with Iran's safeguards obligations over the preceding decade were determined. These included Iran's failure to declare to the IAEA the existence, transfer, and location of nuclear materials in a number of instances, its failure to declare experiments conducted using those nuclear materials,

172. *Id.*

173. *Solving the Iranian Nuclear Puzzle*, ARMS CONTROL ASSOCIATION 33, at 1 (Sept. 2013).

174. *Id.*

175. *Id.* at 14.

176. *Id.*

and its failure to declare design details of certain facilities related to nuclear materials. These instances included *inter alia* the following:

- Iran's failure in 1991 to declare the importation from China of 1.8 tons (0.13 effective kg) of natural uranium compounds (UF4, UF6, and UO2), their transfer for further processing, their use in experiments to test its conversion processes, as well as the facilities in which these materials were kept;
- Iran's additional undeclared use in 1999 and 2002 of a small amount of its imported UF6 in the P1 centrifuges at the Kalaye Electric Company centrifuge workshop;
- Undeclared experiments carried out between 1989 and 1993 that produced Polonium-210, a highly radioactive but unstable material with a short half-life;
- Iran's failure in 1994 to declare the importation of 50 kg of natural uranium metal; 8 kg of which were used at the TNRC in experiments involving atomic vapor laser isotope separation; and
- Undeclared experiments carried out by Iran between 1988 and 1993 involving plutonium separation using UO2.[177]

In his February 22, 2008, report to the IAEA Board of Governors (GOV/2008/4), however, Director General ElBaradei importantly concluded:

52. The Agency has been able to continue to verify the non-diversion of declared nuclear material in Iran . . . Iran has also responded to questions and provided clarifications and amplifications on the issues raised in the context of the work plan, with the exception of the alleged studies. . .
53. The Agency has been able to conclude that answers provided by Iran, in accordance with the work plan, are consistent

177. Muhammad Sahimi, *Atoms for Peace*, Cairo Rev. of Global Aff., July 21, 2013.

with its findings—in the case of the polonium-210 experiments and the Gchine mine—or are not inconsistent with its findings—in the case of the contamination at the technical university and the procurement activities of the former Head of PHRC. Therefore, the Agency considers those questions no longer outstanding at this stage...

54. The one major remaining issue relevant to the nature of Iran's nuclear programme is the alleged studies on the green salt project, high explosives testing and the missile re-entry vehicle. This is a matter of serious concern and critical to an assessment of a possible military dimension to Iran's nuclear programme.

The importance of this conclusion was that it represented the director general's determination that all declared nuclear material in Iran was in peaceful use, and that all prior concerns the IAEA had registered involving nuclear materials and related facilities in Iran had been resolved through dialogue with Iranian authorities.

The remaining issues that ElBaradei flagged as of continuing, unresolved concern to the IAEA were not issues involving nuclear materials, but rather related to the question of possible military dimensions to Iran's nuclear program—i.e., issues potentially related to research and development of a nuclear explosive device.

From 2008 onward, the original 2003 findings of safeguards noncompliance regarding nuclear materials having been resolved, the IAEA's and Western governments' concerns about unresolved issues relevant to Iran's nuclear program would focus exclusively on such possible military dimensions issues, as well as on some states' lingering yet unsubstantiated suspicions regarding nuclear materials and related facilities that had remained undeclared by Iran.

F. Obama's Election in 2008

Many hoped that Barack Obama's election to the U.S. presidency in 2008 would provide an opportunity for more meaningful engagement with Iran than had been possible under the Bush administration. In seeking the Democratic presidential bid and later in campaigning for the presidency, Obama sought to distinguish himself from other candidates by demonstrating a willingness to negotiate with Iran. In an interview with the *New York Times*, Obama expressed his intent to talk to Iran without imposing preconditions. He said, "We are willing to talk about certain assurances in the context of them showing some good faith. . . . I think it is important for us to send a signal that we are not hellbent on regime change, just for the sake of regime change, but expect changes in behavior."[178]

After Obama's election, Mahmoud Ahmadinejad, then president of Iran, sent a congratulatory message to Obama, stating that he hoped for "major, fair and real changes, in policies and actions."[179] This was the first congratulatory message from an Iranian president to a newly elected American president since the Iranian Revolution.[180] Ayatollah Khamenei additionally expressed a willingness to engage in dialogue with the United States.[181]

However, not everyone thought that Obama's approach to diplomacy was a change for the better. Some officials inside the U.S. government were concerned that Obama would "seek too quick a deal and make too many compromises," implicating many potential nonproliferation concerns.[182] Israel in particular maintained that if Obama was going to pursue diplomacy, it should be under the "stick of military pressure."[183]

Throughout the period of crisis concerning Iran's nuclear program, Israel has consistently tried to emphasize the divide between Iran and the Western world, and to cast Iran as the enemy of the

178. Michael R. Gordon & Jeff Zeleny, *If Elected . . . Obama Envisions New Iran Approach*, N.Y. Times, Nov. 2, 2007.

179. *See* Mohamed ElBaradei, The Age of Deception: Nuclear Diplomacy in Treacherous Times, at 286 (2011).

180. *Id.*

181. *Id.* at 35.

182. *Id.* at 45.

183. *Id.* at 51.

West, while casting itself as the United States' one democratic ally in the Middle East.[184] For Israeli officials, Iran's potential possession of a nuclear weapons capability is typically perceived as an existential threat, in addition to a threat to Israel's power and influence in the region. As stated by Israel's former deputy minister of defense, Ephraim Sneh, "We cannot afford a nuclear bomb in the hands of our enemies, period. They don't have to use it; the fact that they have it is enough."[185]

Nevertheless, despite opposition from both Israel and within the U.S. government, attempts at diplomacy persisted throughout the beginning of Obama's presidency. In early spring 2008, several high-level representatives of the Iranian government as well as top American foreign policy experts, including many who were associated with the Obama campaign, met in The Hague to see if progress could be made.[186] These discussions took place as part of the renowned Pugwash Conferences on Science and World Affairs.[187]

President Obama took an unprecedented step toward diplomacy in 2009 when he released a three-and-a-half-minute statement of congratulations on the occasion of the Iranian New Year celebration.[188] In this message, President Obama stated that he "would like to speak directly to the people and leaders of the Islamic Republic of Iran" and that his "administration is now committed to diplomacy that addresses the full range of issues before us, and to pursuing constructive ties among the United States, Iran and the international community."[189] The video was released on YouTube and on the White House website, in an effort to reach the Iranian people directly and avoid censorship by the Iranian government.[190] Obama's message

184. *Id.* at 25.

185. *Id.* at 26.

186. *Id.* at 31.

187. *Id.*

188. *Id.* at 62; Ian Black, *Barack Obama Offers Iran "New Beginning" with Video Message*, THE GUARDIAN, Mar. 20, 2009.

189. TRITA PARSI, A SINGLE ROLL OF THE DICE: OBAMA'S DIPLOMACY WITH IRAN, at 62 (2012).

190. *Id.* at 63.

further expressed his belief that U.S.-Iranian problems would "not be advanced by threats," signaling a marked departure from the approach taken by the Bush administration.[191]

A day later, Iran's Supreme Leader, Ayatollah Ali Khamenei, gave a speech addressing Obama's message. Khamenei expressed skepticism regarding Obama's overtures, citing a long list of Iranian suffering inflicted by the hand of the American government, including sanctions issued by the United States, U.S. support of Saddam Hussein in the Iran-Iraq War, and U.S. support for Iranian opposition groups.[192] Khamenei's response made clear that it would take more than kind words to repair the broken relationship between the United States and Iran, and to truly open the door for diplomacy.

G. The TRR Fuel Deal

The Tehran Research Reactor (obtained from the United States in 1967) runs on uranium that is enriched to a level of 19.8 percent U235. This reactor is used for research and in the production of radioactive isotopes for medical applications. In June 2009, Iran informed the IAEA that it was seeking to resupply fuel for this reactor, but could not do so under normal commercial terms due to the sanctions that had been applied to its nuclear program.[193] In September 2009, the United States and Russia proffered a proposal to the IAEA under which Tehran would receive fuel for the research reactor in exchange for 1,200 kg of Iran's stockpile of LEU, representing roughly 80 percent of the then existing stockpile. The LEU would be sent out of Iran, converted to fuel in Russia and France, and then returned to Iran in the form of a reactor core that could be used to power the Tehran Research Reactor.[194] This plan would remove a significant

191. *Id.* at 62–64.

192. *Id.* at 64–65.

193. Muhammad Sahimi, *Atoms for Peace*, CAIRO REV. OF GLOBAL AFF., July 21, 2013.

194. *Id.*

portion of the LEU from inside Iran and, at least temporarily, alleviate Western concerns of Iran further enriching this LEU for use in a nuclear weapon, while also supplying Iran with the fuel needed for its research reactor.[195]

Finding a way to get a significant portion of Iran's LEU out of the country was a key goal of the Obama administration, and the TRR fuel swap proposal seemed to provide the perfect solution to this problem.[196] The proposal appeared promising at first, with Ahmadinejad expressing his approval and stating that he was "ready to engage in bilateral negotiations, without conditions and on the basis of mutual respect."[197] This deal would also have been positive for Iran in that it would implicitly recognize the legitimacy of Iran's enrichment activities.[198]

However, negotiation efforts would soon be stalled as the result of a statement from U.S. Secretary of State Hillary Clinton. Two weeks before the meeting to discuss the fuel proposal was set to take place, Clinton spoke out against Iran in particularly critical statements, saying that "[t]he international community will not wait indefinitely for evidence that Iran is prepared to live up to its international obligations" and

> [w]ith Iran, it is tragic that a country with such a great history, with so much to give to the rest of the world, is so afraid of their own people. The way that they are utilizing secret prisons and detentions, show trials, is a reflection of the discontent that they know people feel toward the current leadership.[199]

195. *Id.*

196. Trita Parsi, A Single Roll of the Dice: Obama's Diplomacy with Iran, at 114–115 (2012).

197. *See* Mohamed ElBaradei, The Age of Deception: Nuclear Diplomacy in Treacherous Times, at 295 (2011).

198. Trita Parsi, A Single Roll of the Dice: Obama's Diplomacy with Iran, at 117 (2012).

199. *See* Mohamed ElBaradei, The Age of Deception: Nuclear Diplomacy in Treacherous Times, at 304–305 (2011).

Clinton's statements enraged Iranian leaders and hindered negotiation efforts.[200] Clinton later toned down her remarks, but Iranian officials continued to disagree with other aspects of the TRR fuel deal. Iran objected, for example, to France being a part of the agreement, due to France's failure to deliver fifty tons of uranium that Iran had bought from France before the 1979 Revolution.[201] Iran was also distrustful that the United States and Russia would hold up their ends of their bargain and supply Iran with the fuel core once Iran shipped its LEU out of the country. Iran therefore insisted on receiving the fuel core for the TRR first, after which Iran would ship out the agreed amount of LEU, in two separate batches.[202] The IAEA suggested that it could maintain custody over Iran's LEU from the time it was shipped out until the fuel core was provided to Iran, providing it a guarantee that the promises would be fulfilled.[203] However, Iran and the United States could not agree on the timing and amount of LEU to be shipped out under the deal, and negotiations stalled.[204]

Both Iran and the United States grew frustrated with the lack of progress being made. Michael Ratney of the U.S. State Department questioned, "What is the value of us investing that energy [in negotiations] both internally and with our allies—the president's political capital—if the sense is that the Iranians, to be glib about it, don't have their act together?"[205] Since negotiations seemed like they were going nowhere with the TRR deal, the United States concluded that "[d]iplomacy was not dead, but it was abandoned."[206]

With no solution to its fuel problem, on February 9, 2010, Iran announced that it would begin enriching LEU up to 20 percent U235

200. *Id.* at 305.
201. *Id.* at 306.
202. *Id.* at 307.
203. *Id.*
204. *Id.* at 307–310.
205. Trita Parsi, A Single Roll of the Dice: Obama's Diplomacy with Iran, at 151 (2012).
206. *Id.*

in order to indigenously produce fuel for the TRR.[207] On February 11, Ahmadinejad declared that Iran had become a "nuclear state."[208] IAEA inspections that month confirmed that Iran was enriching uranium to 19.8 percent in its Natanz facility.[209]

Despite this failure of overt diplomacy between the United States and Iran, President Obama continued to quietly encourage Turkey and Brazil to further pursue negotiations with Iran on the TRR fuel deal.[210] Presidents Lula and Erdogan of Brazil and Turkey, respectively, had received a letter from Obama dated April 20, 2010, spelling out the elements that would have to be present for the United States to accept a potential TRR fuel deal.[211] In this letter, Obama stated that the purpose of the exchange was "for both sides to gain trust and confidence."[212] Obama reiterated that an acceptable deal could be reached if Iran agreed to: (1) ship out 1,200 kg of its LEU; (2) immediately; (3) to a third country—specifically Turkey—to be held in escrow.[213] With the understanding that a deal could and would be accepted by the United States if Iran met these terms, Lula and Erdogan continued to negotiate with Iran, hoping to successfully reach an agreement on the fuel swap.[214]

On May 17, 2010, Iran, Turkey, and Brazil announced that they had reached an agreement on the fuel exchange.[215] Iran would send 1,200 kg of its LEU to Turkey in exchange for 120 kg of uranium fuel rods for the TRR.[216] Turkish Minister of Foreign Affairs Ahmet

207. *See* MOHAMED ELBARADEI, THE AGE OF DECEPTION: NUCLEAR DIPLOMACY IN TREACHEROUS TIMES, at 312 (2011).

208. *Id.*

209. *Id.* at 312.

210. *Id.*

211. TRITA PARSI, A SINGLE ROLL OF THE DICE: OBAMA'S DIPLOMACY WITH IRAN, at 187 (2012).

212. *Id.*

213. *Id.*

214. *Id.* at 188–189.

215. *See* MOHAMED ELBARADEI, THE AGE OF DECEPTION: NUCLEAR DIPLOMACY IN TREACHEROUS TIMES, at 312 (2011); TRITA PARSI, A SINGLE ROLL OF THE DICE: OBAMA'S DIPLOMACY WITH IRAN, at 173 (2012).

216. Muhammad Sahimi, *Atoms for Peace*, CAIRO REV. OF GLOBAL AFF., July 21, 2013.

Davutoglu proclaimed the deal was a "historic turning point."[217] Presidents Lula and Erdogan maintained that there was no need to pursue another round of sanctions since an agreement had been reached and Iran was cooperating. The United States, however, rejected this agreement, claiming it was merely a ploy on Iran's part to delay further sanctions.[218] While Turkey and Brazil had been working on reaching an agreement with Iran, the United States had been lobbying the permanent members of the Security Council to issue a new set of sanctions against Iran.[219] Essentially, "the fight for diplomacy was a race against sanctions."[220] The time for a diplomatic solution had passed—it was too late for the United States to turn back now.

Although the deal did contain the key elements that President Obama had emphasized as necessary in his letter to Lula and Erdogan only weeks before, members of the U.S. Department of State continued to be skeptical of the deal, claiming that it represented nothing "fundamentally new."[221] U.S. officials condemned the deal for failing to address the suspension of uranium enrichment in Iran—although this had never been on the table in the initial fall 2009 fuel swap negotiations.[222] State Department spokesperson P. J. Crowley criticized the deal sharply, stating, "The joint declaration doesn't address the core concerns of the international community. Iran remains in defiance of five U.N. Security Council resolutions, including its unwillingness to suspend enrichment operations."[223] A day later, Hillary Clinton announced before the U.S. Senate that the deal would not be accepted and that an agreement on a U.N. sanctions resolution had been reached.[224] Clinton announced, "We plan to circulate that

217. TRITA PARSI, A SINGLE ROLL OF THE DICE: OBAMA'S DIPLOMACY WITH IRAN, at 192 (2012).

218. *See* MOHAMED ELBARADEI, THE AGE OF DECEPTION: NUCLEAR DIPLOMACY IN TREACHEROUS TIMES, at 312 (2011).

219. TRITA PARSI, A SINGLE ROLL OF THE DICE: OBAMA'S DIPLOMACY WITH IRAN, at 183 (2012).

220. *Id.*

221. *Id.* at 193.

222. *Id.*

223. *Id.* at 193–194.

224. *Id.* at 194.

draft resolution to the entire Security Council today. And let me say, Mr. Chairman, I think this announcement is as convincing an answer to the efforts undertaken in Tehran over the last few days as any we could provide."[225]

On the technical side, the United States made the argument that in October 2009, when the deal had originally been presented, 1,200 kg of LEU represented around 75 percent of Iran's total stockpile, but in May 2010, when the Turkey and Brazil deal was presented, 1,200 kg of LEU was only around 50 percent of Iran's total stockpile. If Iran had exported 1,200 kg of LEU in October 2009, they argued, Iran would not have been left with enough LEU to make a bomb. However, by May 2010, if Iran exported 1,200 kg of LEU, it would in theory still have enough uranium for one bomb. Thus, they argued, the benefits of the deal had been significantly reduced.[226] In short, Washington had not expected Turkey and Brazil to succeed in negotiations with Iran, and when they did, it was too late for the United States to accept a deal.[227] The sanctions route was now the more attractive option.

On June 9, 2010, the Vienna Group (France, Russia, the United States, and the IAEA) formally rejected the Tehran Declaration as presented by Brazil, Turkey, and Iran.[228] Five hours later, the Security Council met to vote on a new round of sanctions against Iran. The following day, Resolution 1929 was passed, with Brazil and Turkey voting against it and Lebanon abstaining.[229] Two weeks later, the United States passed gasoline sanctions on Iran by an overwhelming majority—a vote of 408–8 in the House, and 99–0 in the Senate. President Obama signed the gasoline sanctions bill into law on July 1.[230]

In the wake of the failed TRR fuel swap negotiations, Iran continued to expand its production of highly enriched uranium. As the

225. *Id.*
226. *Id.* at 197.
227. *Id.* at 194–195.
228. *Id.* at 204.
229. *Id.* at 204–205.
230. *Id.* at 206.

stock increased, so did pressure on the West to drop suspension as a precondition for negotiations. The P5+1 met with Iran in Geneva in December 2010 and in Istanbul in January 2011.[231] These talks ultimately failed because neither Iran nor the United States was willing to compromise on its preconditions. The United States insisted that Iran suspend enrichment as a precondition to negotiations, while Iran asserted that it had a sovereign right to enrich uranium. Iran's chief nuclear negotiator, Saeed Jalili, stated, "Any kinds of talks and cooperation, as I underlined during the talks with Mrs. Ashton [the European Union's foreign policy chief], should be based on respecting the nation's rights . . . including Iran's right to nuclear technology." Ashton stated that during the meetings in Istanbul, "it became clear that the Iranian side was not ready for this unless we agree to preconditions related to enrichment and sanctions. Both these preconditions are not the way to proceed."[232]

H. The Fordow Facility

In the midst of negotiations concerning the TRR, on September 21, 2009, Iran informed the IAEA that it was constructing a uranium enrichment facility at Fordow, outside of the holy city of Qom.[233] The Fordow site was of particular concern to Western powers because it is underground and would be very difficult to destroy by bombing.[234] Iran claimed that the Fordow facility was "conceived as a backup enrichment facility during the Bush administration, when the threat of a military strike at Natanz seemed serious."[235] The revelation of the

231. *See, e.g.*, Julian Borger, *Iran Nuclear Talks Under Way in Geneva*, The Guardian, Dec. 6, 2010; Julia Damianova, *Nuclear Negotiations with Iran End in Failure*, L.A. Times, Jan. 23, 2011.

232. *Id.*

233. Muhammad Sahimi, *Atoms for Peace*, Cairo Rev. of Global Aff., July 21, 2013; Mark Hibbs, *Iran Plant Disclosure May Prompt IAEA to Focus on Weapons Data*, 50 Nucleonics Week 39 (Oct. 1, 2009).

234. *Id.*

235. *See* Mohamed ElBaradei, The Age of Deception: Nuclear Diplomacy in Treacherous Times, at 299 (2011).

Fordow facility did not help to assuage Western fears regarding Iran's concealment of its nuclear operations. Western officials alleged, as they had regarding the Natanz facility, that Iran had failed to declare the Fordow facility in a timely manner, pursuant to its safeguards commitments. ElBaradei spoke of the revelation of the new facility "as an unfortunate 'setback to the principle of transparency, and to the effort by the international community to build confidence about the Iranian nuclear program.' "[236] The Fordow facility was designed to hold 2,976 centrifuges and sixteen cascades.[237]

The Iranians described this facility as a "pilot plant"; however, Iran already had a pilot plant at Natanz, so this description seemed suspicious to the United States and other Western countries.[238] The West suggested that the plant instead was either a parallel military-run program or an attempt to create a backup plant in case of military strikes on Iran's other nuclear facilities.[239] Ali Asghar Soltanieh, Iran's ambassador to the IAEA, argued that threats from the United States and Israel had forced Iran to keep the Fordow facility secret.[240] He stated, "We had to be cautious and show vigilance and to take precautions . . . to make sure that the enrichment process would not be suspended even a second."[241]

I. New IAEA Director General

When Yukiya Amano succeeded Mohamed ElBaradei as the director general of the IAEA in December 2009, he demonstrated a markedly different approach to the Iranian nuclear situation from that of ElBaradei. Since taking office, Amano has overall been far more

236. *Id.* at 300.

237. Muhammad Sahimi, *Atoms for Peace*, CAIRO REV. OF GLOBAL AFF., July 21, 2013.

238. TRITA PARSI, A SINGLE ROLL OF THE DICE: OBAMA'S DIPLOMACY WITH IRAN, at 123 (2012).

239. *Id.*

240. *Id.*

241. *Id.*

aggressive than ElBaradei in pursuing the possible military dimensions issue in particular. This change of tack under Amano's leadership did not come as a surprise to many, however, since Amano was described in internal U.S. diplomatic cables, subsequently revealed by WikiLeaks, as "solidly in the U.S. court on every key strategic decision, from high-level personnel appointments to the handling of Iran's alleged nuclear weapons program."[242] Once in office, Amano removed IAEA experts who had not been "helpful to U.S. positions."[243]

J. 2011 IAEA Report

On November 8, 2011, the IAEA issued a report described by Western media as "game changing" and "landmark."[244] However, for the most part, the report repeated concerns expressed in previous IAEA reports, adding some considerable detail to them.[245] Again, these concerns focused not on nuclear material or related facilities in Iran, but rather on possible military dimensions to Iran's nuclear program—i.e., activities potentially related to research and development of a nuclear explosive device. The allegations contained in the report included:

- Iran's possession of a document which "describes, inter alia, processes for the conversion of uranium compounds into uranium metal and the production of hemispherical enriched uranium metallic components";
- the development of "safe, fast-acting detonators, and equipment suitable for firing the detonators";

242. Julian Borger, *Nuclear Wikileaks: Cables Show Cosy US Relationship with IAEA Chief*, THE GUARDIAN, Nov. 30, 2010.

243. Muhammad Sahimi, *Atoms for Peace*, CAIRO REV. OF GLOBAL AFF., July 21, 2013; Julian Borger, *Nuclear Watchdog Chief Accused of Pro-Western Bias over Iran*, THE GUARDIAN, Mar. 22, 2012.

244. Muhammad Sahimi, *Atoms for Peace*, CAIRO REV. OF GLOBAL AFF., July 21, 2013.

245. *Id.*

- Iran's possession of "information on the design concept of a multipoint initiation system that can be used to initiate effectively and simultaneously a high explosive charge over its surface";
- "experimental research involving a scaled down version of [a] hemispherical initiation system and high explosive charge";
- the construction of "a large explosives containment vessel in which to conduct hydrodynamic experiments"; and
- the conduct of "studies involv[ing] the modeling of spherical geometries, consisting of components of the core of an HEU nuclear device subjected to shock compression, for their neutronic behaviour at high density, and a determination of the subsequent nuclear explosive yield."

The report also alluded to an unnamed foreign scientist who had allegedly helped with the development of Iran's nuclear program, and reiterated long-standing allegations about Parchin, a military facility in Iran used to produce ammunition and explosives.[246] The IAEA report stated:

> The Agency has strong indications that the development by Iran of the high explosives initiation system, and its development of the high speed diagnostic configuration used to monitor related experiments, were assisted by the work of a foreign expert who was not only knowledgeable in these technologies, but who, a Member State has informed the Agency, worked for much of his career with this technology in the nuclear weapon program of the country of his origin. The Agency has reviewed publications by this foreign expert and has met with him. The Agency has been able to verify through three separate routes, including the expert himself, that this person was in Iran from about 1996 to about 2002, ostensibly to assist Iran in the development of a facility

246. *Id.*

and techniques for making ultra-dispersed diamonds, where he also lectured on explosion physics and its applications.[247]

The IAEA report further alleged that Iran had built a containment chamber at the Parchin site for experiments with high explosives relevant to initiating a nuclear reaction. The IAEA had investigated the Parchin site in 2004 and had found no evidence of any nuclear-related activity at the site. Nevertheless, Iran allowed the IAEA to visit the Parchin site two more times—once in January 2005 and once again in November 2005. The IAEA visited five locations within the complex, along with a "surprise" sixth location, and found no evidence to support any of the allegations regarding nuclear experimentation. It is unclear what revived the suspicions surrounding the Parchin facility in the November 2011 IAEA report, but the subject continued to be a source of allegations regarding Iran's nuclear program. Regarding the IAEA's Parchin allegations, Robert Kelley, a former IAEA inspector, has written:

> In the case of Parchin, the IAEA is relying upon secret information provided by unspecified states or parties. A great deal of the information has been selectively leaked to create an impression that the agency has significant reason to want to visit a particular building, among hundreds at the site. The IAEA bases its request upon a suspicion that that the building was used for experiments involving explosives and uranium to understand the hydrodynamic behavior of a neutron initiator for a nuclear explosive. Such experiments, if they occurred, would use a few grams of uranium in a huge chamber. They would probably be a violation of Iran's nuclear safeguards undertakings. However the IAEA has failed to make a convincing case that these experiments took place. And it has added confusion by saying the most important experiments involving test explosions took place at an Iranian town called Marivan, 500 kilometers away.[248]

247. *Id.*

248. Daniel Joyner, *Robert Kelley—Next Steps Forward for the IAEA and Iran*, ARMS CONTROL LAW, Jan. 31, 2013.

As Kelley observes, the allegations regarding possible military dimensions in Iran contained in the November 2011 IAEA report, and in other IAEA reports, are the product of intelligence information in the IAEA's possession, much of which was provided to the IAEA by third-party national intelligence agencies. The potential for politicization and forgery in such intelligence sharing activities, and the fact that the IAEA did not divulge the sources of the intelligence on which it relied in these reports, emerged as a major concern relating to the IAEA's allegations concerning possible military dimensions to Iran's nuclear program.

Many of the allegations concerning possible military dimensions to Iran's nuclear program stem from documents supposedly found on a laptop computer that was stolen in Iran and made available to Western intelligence agencies, and from them to the IAEA—popularly nicknamed the "laptop of death."[249] Kelley and other independent technical experts have called into question the authenticity of the documents contained on the laptop and other documents provided to the IAEA by foreign governments.[250]

K. The Post-2011 State of Iran's Nuclear Program

Iran refused to respond in detail to the allegations of the November 2011 IAEA report, claiming the report's allegations are baseless.[251] Iran also continued to expand its uranium enrichment program. In its report on August 27, 2015, the IAEA determined that Iran possessed 7,845 kg of LEU enriched to 5 percent, and had 15,420 IR-1 centrifuges operating at Natanz and 2,710 IR-1 centrifuges operating at Fordow. As of this report, construction work was also

249. Julian Borger, *US Iran Intelligence "Is Incorrect,"* THE GUARDIAN, Feb. 22, 2007.

250. Scott Peterson, *Iran Nuclear Report: Why It May Not Be a Game-Changer after All*, CHRISTIAN SCIENCE MONITOR, Nov. 9, 2011; Yousef Butt, *IAEA Conduct Complicates Iran Nuclear Deal*, REUTERS, Feb. 22, 2014.

251. Muhammad Sahimi, *Atoms for Peace*, CAIRO REV. OF GLOBAL AFF., July 21, 2013.

proceeding on the heavy-water reactor at Arak.[252] Iran has claimed that the heavy-water reactor at Arak is being built to produce medical isotopes.[253] The Arak reactor has the potential, however, to produce enough plutonium for one or two nuclear weapons a year once fully operational.[254] However, in order for Iran to use the plutonium from Arak in a nuclear weapon, it would also need a reprocessing facility to separate the plutonium from the spent fuel. It does not appear that Iran is currently working on such a facility.[255]

Diplomacy also continued between the P5+1 and Iran. The parties met for negotiations in Istanbul in April 2012. Additional meetings were also held in Baghdad in May 2012 and in Moscow of June 2012.[256] The P5+1 retreated somewhat from their initially inflexible position that Iran must shut down the Fordow site completely and permanently stop enriching uranium to 19.75 percent, and asked instead only for a temporary suspension. Iran has also retreated somewhat from its prior positions. Where it had previously declared that it would never agree to a suspension in its enrichment activities, it suggested in early 2013 negotiations in Almaty, Kazakhstan, that it might be amenable to stopping enrichment for six months.[257] However, after a March 2013 meeting in Istanbul and an April 2013 meeting in Kazakhstan, the parties were unable to reconcile their differences and come to an agreement.[258]

The inauguration of Iranian President Hassan Rouhani on August 3, 2013, presented a potential opportunity for continued negotiations between Iran and the West.[259] Shortly after Rouhani's inauguration,

252. GOV/2015/50.

253. *Solving the Iranian Nuclear Puzzle*, ARMS CONTROL ASSOCIATION 33, at 7 (September 2013).

254. *Id.* at 8.

255. *Id.*

256. *Id.* at 25.

257. Muhammad Sahimi, *Atoms for Peace*, CAIRO REV. OF GLOBAL AFF., July 21, 2013.

258. *Solving the Iranian Nuclear Puzzle*, ARMS CONTROL ASSOCIATION 33, at 25 (Sept. 2013).

259. *Id.* at 1.

the White House expressed its desire to come to a peaceful resolution with Iran, stating:

> The inauguration of President Rouhani presents an opportunity for Iran to act quickly to resolve the international community's deep concerns over Iran's nuclear program. Should this new government choose to engage substantively and seriously to meet its international obligations and find a peaceful solution to this issue, it will find a willing partner in the United States.[260]

President Rouhani also expressed his interest in arriving at a peaceful solution, stating that "Iran has a serious political will to solve the nuclear problem while protecting the rights of the Iranian people at the same time as it seeks to remove concerns of the other party."[261] Iran continues to maintain that it is not pursuing nuclear weapons. Iran's Foreign Minister Mohammad Javad Zarif stated in an August 19, 2013, interview that "nuclear weapons have no place in our national security doctrine and are even detrimental to our national security."[262]

L. Targeted Killings, Sabotage, and Cyberwarfare

At the same time as this diplomatic history has been unfolding, the United States and Israel, in particular, have reportedly resorted to new forms of technological sabotage of Iran's nuclear program and to direct targeted killing of Iranian nuclear scientists.[263] Since 2007, at least five Iranian nuclear scientists have been assassinated.[264]

260. *Id.* at 2.

261. *Id.* at 2.

262. *Id.*

263. *See generally* DAVID SANGER, CONFRONT AND CONCEAL: OBAMA'S SECRET WARS AND SURPRISING USE OF AMERICAN POWER, chs. 6–9 (2012).

264. David Blair, *Iran's Newest Nuclear Facility Struck by "Saboteurs,"* THE TELEGRAPH, Sept. 17, 2012.

Fereydoun Abbasi, then head of the Iranian Atomic Energy Organization, was wounded when a motorcyclist attached a bomb to his car in November 2010.[265] Iran has investigated these attacks and arrested several people it believes were linked to the January 2010 killing of scientist Masout Alimohammadi.[266] After interrogating these arrested suspects, the Iranian interior minister announced that the suspects were trained and charged by the U.S., U.K., and Israeli intelligence agencies.[267] Following these assassinations, President Ahmadinejad stated, "I swear to God, if this act of assassination is once more repeated, I will bring every member of the U.N. Security Council to trial."[268] U.S. officials have largely responded to the killings of Iranian scientists with approval and with insensitivity to Iranian concerns.

An August 17, 2012, an explosion temporarily disabled the Fordow plant when it severed electricity cables running from the city of Qom.[269] Deliberate sabotage is suspected by Iranian officials in this incident. However, the IAEA inspected the Fordow site the day after the incident and did not report any damage, thus suggesting that the Fordow facility's backup power system kicked in and prevented damage to the facility.[270] This method of sabotage had previously been employed at Natanz, with one power outage destroying 50 centrifuges.[271] Each of these covert attacks is believed to be a part of a strategic sabotage campaign, code-named "Olympic Games," begun under the Bush administration.[272]

The most significant of these attacks was the introduction of the Stuxnet computer virus into the Natanz facility in 2009. This virus

265. *Id.*

266. Seyed Hossein Mousavian, The Iranian Nuclear Crisis: A Memoir 25–26 (2012).

267. *Id.* at 26.

268. *Id.* at 26.

269. David Blair, *Iran's Newest Nuclear Facility Struck by "Saboteurs,"* The Telegraph, Sept. 17, 2012.

270. *Id.*

271. *Id.*

272. *Id.*

caused the centrifuges in the facility to spin out of control and destroy themselves.[273] David Blair estimates that this attack alone set Iran's nuclear development back by up to a year;[274] Ralph Langer estimates that the virus set the program back by two years.[275] It has been well established that the Stuxnet virus was created by the United States and intentionally introduced into the Natanz facility.[276] The Stuxnet virus operated by causing increases in the rotor speed of the target centrifuges, thereby increasing the rotor wall pressure and causing centrifuges to break.[277] The Stuxnet virus did not target all centrifuges at once and cause a one-time hit of catastrophic damage, however. Rather, the attack was meant to cause continuous damage to the facility. Langer writes: "Stuxnet is a low-yield weapon with the overall intention of reducing the lifetime of Iran's centrifuges and making the Iranians' fancy control systems appear beyond their understanding."[278] Iran kept a stockpile of spare centrifuges to replace at least 50 percent of its inventory. Thus, Iran likely would have been able to recover from simultaneous catastrophic destruction of its centrifuges quicker than it was able to recover from this ongoing attack.[279] Langer further suggests that the operation of the Stuxnet virus at Natanz sends a clear message that "[d]igital weapons work" and that "cyberwarfare is here to stay."[280] Hossein Mousavian contends that Stuxnet was the "first unattributed act of war against Iran" and that in choosing such forms of cyberwarfare, the United States is setting the stage for future military action and choosing its short-term interests over long-term goals.[281]

273. *Id.*
274. *Id.*
275. Ralph Langer, *Stuxnet's Secret Twin*, FOREIGN POL'Y, Nov. 19, 2013.
276. David E. Sanger, *Obama Ordered Wave of Cyberattacks against Iran*, N.Y. TIMES, June 1, 2012.
277. Ralph Langer, *Stuxnet's Secret Twin*, FOREIGN POL'Y, Nov. 19, 2013.
278. *Id.*
279. *Id.*
280. *Id.*
281. SEYED HOSSEIN MOUSAVIAN, THE IRANIAN NUCLEAR CRISIS: A MEMOIR, at 28 (2012).

M. The 2013 Joint Plan of Action

A unique opportunity for a diplomatic breakthrough emerged in late 2013. On November 24, 2013, after long and tense negotiations, Iran and the P5+1 concluded a Joint Plan of Action (JPOA).[282] In this interim agreement, Iran agreed to cease enrichment of uranium beyond 5 percent U235. It also agreed that it would not install any new centrifuges, start up any that were not already operating, or build any new enrichment facilities.[283] Iran also agreed to halt work on its heavy-water reactor and to allow U.N. inspectors daily access to its facilities.[284] Iran did not agree, however, to stop enriching uranium to a level of 3.5 percent or to dismantle any of its existing centrifuges. In return for these Iranian concessions, the United States agreed to provide $6–7 billion in sanctions relief. Roughly $4.2 billion of this would come from Iranian oil revenue frozen in foreign banks.[285]

Iranian officials stated that the interim deal acknowledged Iran's right to enrich. President Rouhani said, "Let anyone make his own reading, but this right is clearly stated in the text of the agreement that Iran can continue its enrichment, and I announce to our people that our enrichment activities will continue as before."[286] U.S. officials disagreed with this interpretation. Secretary of State John Kerry stated, "There is no inherent right to enrich. And everywhere in this particular agreement it states that they could only do that by mutual agreement, and nothing is agreed on until everything is agreed on."[287]

282. *Joint Plan of Action on Iran's Nuclear Program* (Nov. 24, 2013).

283. Michael R. Gordon, *Accord Reached with Iran to Halt Nuclear Program*, N.Y. Times, Nov. 23, 2013.

284. Anne Gearan & Joby Warrick, *World Powers Reach Nuclear Deal with Iran to Freeze Its Nuclear Program*, Wash. Post, Nov. 24, 2013.

285. Michael R. Gordon, *Accord Reached with Iran to Halt Nuclear Program*, N.Y. Times, Nov. 23, 2013.

286. Anne Gearan & Joby Warrick, *World Powers Reach Nuclear Deal with Iran to Freeze Its Nuclear Program*, Wash. Post, Nov. 24, 2013.

287. *Id.*

Iran's commitments under the 2013 JPOA comprised a more significant list of concessions than was expected by most observers.[288] Some experts pointed to Iran's acceptance of the JPOA as evidence that economic sanctions had contributed to a shift in Iran's nuclear policies. Iranian officials have sharply contested this belief. In a November 19, 2013, piece in the *Financial Times*, Hossein Mousavian wrote:

> [T]he idea that it is sanctions that have brought Tehran to the table is wrong. The real cause is the desire of new President Hassan Rouhani to reach a rapprochement with the US, the EU, its neighbours and other world powers, alongside the fact that the US red line has changed from "no enrichment of uranium" to "no nuclear bomb."[289]

Nevertheless, numerous officials praised the interim deal as a landmark step toward reaching a final diplomatic resolution. Regarding the agreement, President Obama stated, "While today's announcement is just a first step, it achieves a great deal. For the first time in nearly a decade, we have halted the progress of the Iranian nuclear program, and key parts of the program will be rolled back."[290]

Greg Thielmann, a Senior Fellow at the Arms Control Association, suggested that the JPOA was successful in alleviating the most acute proliferation concerns.[291] Trita Parsi, president of the National Iranian American Council, praised diplomacy for "deliver[ing] the U.S. and Iran from the brink of a disastrous war and plac[ing] the two countries at the beginning of a brighter, more sustainable path forward."[292]

288. Daniel Joyner, *The New Deal Between the P5+1 and Iran*, EJIL: TALK!, Nov. 26, 2013.

289. Hossein Mousavian, *It Was Not Sanctions that Brought Iran to the Table*, FIN. TIMES, Nov. 19, 2013.

290. *Id.*

291. Greg Thielmann, *Sorry, Skeptics: The Iran Nuclear Deal Is Working*, NAT'L INTEREST, Aug. 7, 2014.

292. Anne Gearan & Joby Warrick, *World Powers Reach Nuclear Deal with Iran to Freeze Its Nuclear Program*, WASH. POST, Nov. 24, 2013.

N. The 2015 Joint Comprehensive Plan of Action

Following the 2013 agreement on a JPOA, negotiations continued off and on between Iran and the P5+1 for the next two and a half years. Finally, on July 14, 2015, it was announced that a Joint Comprehensive Plan of Action (JCPOA) had been agreed among the P5+1 states and Iran, together with a "Roadmap Agreement" reached between Iran and the IAEA. These agreements were the culmination of the twenty months of negotiations between the P5+1 and Iran since the initial JPOA was agreed, and represented the first time that a comprehensive agreement had been reached for ending the international dispute over Iran's nuclear program.

The JCPOA is by any measure a watershed moment in international relations. The document itself comprises 159 total pages of text, consisting of 18 pages of the JCPOA itself, with a further 141 pages divided among five annexes. It was carefully constructed to address in impressive detail all aspects of dispute related to Iran's nuclear program, including both the concerns of the West and the IAEA regarding the peaceful nature of Iran's nuclear program, and Iran's concerns regarding economic sanctions applied against it by both the U.N. Security Council and Western states acting unilaterally.

The JCPOA was deliberately framed as a legally nonbinding agreement among its parties, and as such is not a treaty. However, it does comprise a comprehensive set of political commitments among its parties, additionally inclusive of commitments of action by the European Union and the U.N. Security Council, which are designed to resolve the legal and diplomatic crisis concerning Iran's nuclear program.

Under the terms of the JCPOA, Iran has agreed to significant limits on its civilian nuclear energy program, including limits on its uranium enrichment activities, and to an enhanced inspection regime by the IAEA, including provisional application by Iran of the IAEA Additional Protocol. In return, the P5+1, along with the European

Union, have agreed to a coordinated lifting of the economic and financial sanctions that have been applied against Iran since 2006.

On July 20, 2015, the U.N. Security Council adopted Resolution 2231, in which it unanimously endorsed the JCPOA and brought into force the measures relating to the Security Council that were agreed in the JCPOA.

In essence, the JCPOA and Resolution 2231 together provide for an approximately ten-year period of implementation of the various commitments of the parties. If the envisioned program of commitments is fully and successfully implemented, then at the end of that ten-year period all resolutions of the Security Council relative to Iran's nuclear program will be terminated, and all nuclear-related economic sanctions against Iran, whether imposed multilaterally by the Security Council or unilaterally by states, will be lifted.

I will devote Chapter 7 of this book to a more fulsome consideration of the JCPOA, its contents, and implications. But it is impossible to understand the JCPOA, and the gauntlet of legal and political disputes that ultimately shaped it, without a consideration of the essential sources of international nuclear law and their application to the Iran case. It is this consideration which Chapters 2–6 of this book will provide.

Chapter 2

Summary of Arguments

With this historical sketch in place, we can now move on to the relevant sources of international law and their applicability to the case study of the international confrontation over Iran's nuclear program, beginning in August 2002 and continuing until the conclusion of the Joint Comprehensive Plan of Action (JCPOA) in July 2015. In the succeeding chapters, I will consider questions arising during the dispute over Iran's nuclear program, that are based in sources of international nuclear law, with the 1968 Nuclear Nonproliferation Treaty (NPT) as its cornerstone.

I have thought it best to organize these chapters by beginning with a brief summary of the legal arguments maintained by the two sides to this legal dispute. On the one side is, of course, Iran. On the other side are primarily the United States and its European allies (the United Kingdom, France, and Germany—sometimes referred to as the EU3). These four states have been Iran's chief detractors on the nuclear issue, and while their respective national policy positions toward the issue have of course differed on details, yet I think it is fair to lump them together as states that have made relatively similar legal arguments regarding Iran's nuclear program. I will therefore consider them—at some times along with the International Atomic Energy Agency (IAEA) itself—as the opposing side in this legal dispute and will refer to the four states alternately as Western states, the West, etc.

The positions of Russia and China, the other two states comprising the P5+1 negotiating group (i.e., the permanent five members of the U.N. Security Council plus Germany), have been more nuanced on the Iran nuclear issue. Both of these countries have very different historical relationships with Iran than do the United States and the EU3, and this in turn has made them view the subject of Iran's nuclear program quite differently. Both have at times voted along with the Security Council in condemning Iran's actions and in seeking to compel Iran to cease its uranium enrichment program. However, both have also resisted on a number of occasions further sanctions resolutions against Iran on the issue, and Russia in particular has at times voiced solidarity with some of Iran's legal positions.[1] I will therefore leave these two states out of the opposing group.

In this chapter, I will present a description of the legal positions of both sides to the dispute in a brief, summary manner only, in order to make a succinct statement of these positions, which can then guide the reader and serve as a reference as the book progresses. Sources of law mentioned in this summary will be explained and analyzed in much greater detail in the succeeding chapters, which will evaluate the legal arguments on each particular question in dispute. Throughout this chapter, and the rest of the book, IAEA documents will be identified by the IAEA's internal system of reference, including Information Circulars published openly by the IAEA (INFCIRCs), and reports adopted by the IAEA's Board of Governors (GOVs), which are sometimes restricted in their initial distribution.

I. LEGAL ARGUMENTS OF WESTERN STATES AND THE IAEA

Let us begin with a summary of the legal arguments of Western states, some of which are joined in by the IAEA itself. The legal arguments of

1. *See, e.g.*, *Russia Says Geneva Deal Confirms Iran's Enrichment Right*, TASNIM NEWS AGENCY, Dec. 11, 2013, http://www.tasnimnews.com/English/Home/Single/217735 ("Speaking in a joint press conference with his Iranian counterpart Mohammad Javad Zarif here in Tehran on Wednesday, Lavrov stressed that one of the results brought by the November nuclear deal in Geneva was Iran's right to enjoy peaceful nuclear energy, particularly its right to enrich uranium.").

Western states can be organized according to the sources of law they reference.[2]

Firstly, and most prominently, Western legal arguments critical of Iran's nuclear program during the period of confrontation focused on Iran's noncompliance with its comprehensive safeguards agreement with the IAEA (INFCIRC/214), and the subsidiary arrangements entered into pursuant to that safeguards agreement. In summary, Western states and the IAEA argued that Iran failed to comply with its safeguards agreement obligations in a number of respects, beginning principally with the 2002 disclosure of the Natanz and Arak facilities. These breaches of obligation, as they are termed by Western arguments, relate to Iran's failure to timely

2. For reference for this section, *see, e.g.*, Paul Kerr, *Iran's Nuclear Program: Tehran's Compliance with International Obligations*, Congressional Research Service Report, Dec. 21, 2011; United States Department of State, *Adherence to and Compliance with Arms Control, Nonproliferation, and Disarmament Agreements and Commitments Report*, July 2013, http://www.state.gov/documents/organization/212096.pdf ("Iran is in violation of obligations under the NPT, its IAEA Safeguards Agreement, and relevant UN Security Council resolutions."); Permanent Mission of France to the United Nations in New York official website, *Iran*, http://www.franceonu.org/france-at-the-united-nations/geographic-files/middle-east/iran-non-proliferation-472/article/iran (viewed June 24, 2014) ("Iran's secret development of a nuclear program in violation of the Non-Proliferation Treaty constitutes a major, international security crisis that is liable to seriously undermine the nuclear nonproliferation regime."); German Foreign Ministry Website, *The Conflict Surrounding Iran's Nuclear Program*, http://www.auswaertiges-amt.de/EN/Aussenpolitik/RegionaleSchwerpunkte/NaherMittlererOsten/Iran/Iranisches-Nuklearprogramm_node.html ("To date, Iran has failed to fulfil the conditions stipulated by the United Nations Security Council and the International Atomic Energy Agency (IAEA) on the suspension of its nuclear programme and failed to cooperate comprehensively with the IAEA to clarify questions regarding the possible military dimension of the programme."); UK Government Website, *Leading International Efforts to Resolve Concerns about Iran's Nuclear Programme*, https://www.gov.uk/government/policies/leading-international-efforts-to-resolve-concerns-about-irans-nuclear-programme ("The UK, along with the international community, remains deeply concerned about the possible military dimensions of Iran's nuclear programme. Iran continues to develop its nuclear programme in direct violation of six UNSC resolutions and in defiance of several IAEA Board of Governors resolutions.").

disclose and declare to the IAEA the existence of these two facilities, as well as to subsequently determined failures to declare some nuclear materials on the territory of Iran, the facilities in which these materials were located, and certain experiments conducted with these materials.

Specifically, the failure by Iran to timely declare the existence of the Natanz and Arak facilities has been argued to comprise a violation of Iran's obligations under its subsidiary arrangements agreement with the IAEA, signed pursuant to its comprehensive safeguards agreement. These allegations are outlined in the 2003 IAEA report GOV/2003/75. The failure by Iran to declare nuclear materials and related facilities and experiments has been argued to violate the terms of Iran's IAEA comprehensive safeguards agreement itself. A summary of these arguments can be found in the 2008 IAEA report GOV/2008/4.

The West and the IAEA further argued that, in accordance with the IAEA's standards for investigation and assessment of Iran's compliance with it safeguards obligations, Iran remained in noncompliance with its safeguards obligations throughout the period of confrontation, up to the agreement of the JCPOA in July 2015. The essence of this legal argument was that, since Iran had failed to adequately cooperate with the IAEA to answer the IAEA's remaining concerns focused on the possible existence of undeclared nuclear material and related facilities in Iran, the IAEA had been unable to determine with confidence that all nuclear material in Iran was in exclusively peaceful uses. As the IAEA report from August 2012 (GOV/2012/37) concluded:

> While the Agency continues to verify the non-diversion of declared nuclear material at the nuclear facilities and LOFs declared by Iran under its Safeguards Agreement, as Iran is not providing the necessary cooperation, including by not implementing its Additional Protocol, the Agency is unable to provide credible assurance about the absence of undeclared nuclear material and

activities in Iran, and therefore to conclude that all nuclear material in Iran is in peaceful activities.

Additionally, there was a further implication of Iran's safeguards obligation violations, argued Western officials. Since the obligation to conclude and to abide by a safeguards agreement with the IAEA has its source in Article III, paragraph 1, of the NPT, it followed that a violation of Iran's safeguards obligations per se implicated Iran's responsibility for breach of Article III of the NPT. And since Article IV, paragraph 1, of the NPT makes the exercise of Iran's right to peaceful use of nuclear materials and technology conditional on Iran's compliance with its nonproliferation obligations, inclusive of Article III, Iran's safeguards violations had the yet further implication of negating Iran's Article IV right to peaceful uses of nuclear energy, inclusive of uranium enrichment.

The final NPT-based legal argument made by Western states against Iran focuses on Article II of the NPT, which requires NNWS parties to the treaty such as Iran "not to manufacture or otherwise acquire nuclear weapons or other nuclear explosive devices . . ." According to this argument, Western officials claimed that Iran's alleged research and development work on a nuclear explosive device (i.e., the possible military dimensions activities referred to in Chapter 1) were included in the prohibitive scope of the term "manufacture" of nuclear explosive devices in NPT Article II.

Finally, Western states and the IAEA insisted that Iran had violated its international legal obligations arising from the resolutions of the U.N. Security Council, and in particular the Security Council's demand in Resolution 1737 that Iran suspend all uranium enrichment activities.

Thus, if all of the Western legal arguments were to be accepted as correct, the legal conclusion as of July 2015 would have been that Iran had violated, and continued to be in violation of, the terms of the NPT as well as its safeguards agreement with the IAEA, and that Iran was further in violation of the legally binding resolutions of the U.N. Security Council—all of which implicated Iran's state responsibility.

II. IRAN'S LEGAL ARGUMENTS

Iran's legal arguments in response to the allegations of Western states and the IAEA were in summary as follows, in the same order according to legal source.[3]

With regard to pre-2003 questions concerning disclosure of the Natanz and Arak facilities and the discovery of undeclared nuclear materials and related facilities and experiments, Iran argued that it was in compliance with its safeguards obligations in not declaring the existence of the Natanz and Arak facilities and that any issues with nondeclaration of nuclear materials and related facilities and experiments were relatively minor and were resolved by 2008 through cooperation with the IAEA.

Specifically, Iran has argued that the version of its commitments in its subsidiary arrangements agreement current as of 2003 did not require Iran to disclose design details of, or the existence of, the Natanz and Arak facilities, because at the time of their discovery, nuclear material had not yet been introduced into these facilities. This position was maintained, *inter alia*, in Iran's communication with the IAEA in INFCIRC/660, of October 9, 2005.

With regard to the undeclared nuclear materials and related facilities and experiments, Iran emphasized that these issues came to light through Iran's voluntary efforts of cooperation with the IAEA to increase the transparency of its nuclear program and that where inconsistencies between Iran's declaration, and its actual nuclear material stocks had been found, Iran had cooperated with the IAEA to correct its declaration, resulting in the IAEA's determination in 2008 that all outstanding issues relating to these nuclear materials and related facilities and experiments had been resolved. These

3. For reference for this section, *see, e.g.*, a listing of Iran's communications with the IAEA at the IAEA's website, under Member States Communications, Iran, http://www.iaea.org/newscenter/focus/iaeairan/ms_communications.shtml, including in particular INFCIRC/853, of July 23, 2013; also legal arguments on Iran's nuclear program website, http://nuclearenergy.ir/legal-aspects/.

arguments are contained in Iran's communications to the IAEA, beginning with document INFCIRC/648 on August 1, 2005.

With regard to the argument that Iran was in continuing violation of its safeguards obligations throughout the period of confrontation and up to July 2015 due to the IAEA's inability to confidently determine the nonexistence of undeclared nuclear materials or related facilities in Iran, Iran argued that the IAEA had misstated the Agency's legal standard of investigation and assessment and that the IAEA's only proper standard for assessment was a determination of whether all declared nuclear materials in a safeguarded state are in peaceful uses. Iran thus argued that, pursuant to this correct understanding of the IAEA's lawful standard for investigation and assessment, the IAEA had determined consistently since 2008 that all declared nuclear materials in Iran are in peaceful uses and that therefore Iran was in compliance with its safeguards obligations as of July 2015. These arguments can be found in Iran's communication to the IAEA in document INFCIRC/866, of June 13, 2014.

In response to arguments that Iran's alleged safeguards obligation violations also *per se* constituted a violation of Article III of the NPT, as well as arguments that Iran's research and development activities connected to nuclear weaponization constituted a violation of Article II of the NPT, Iran maintained that no nuclear material within Iran has ever been diverted to nonpeaceful uses and that no authenticated evidence of weaponization work within Iran has ever been presented by the IAEA. Iran emphasized its "inalienable right" pursuant to Article IV of the NPT to maintain a peaceful nuclear energy program. Thus, Iran argued that it had not at any point violated the terms of the NPT. These arguments can be found in document INFCIRC/853, of July 23, 2013.

Finally, on the subject of U.N. Security Council resolutions concerning Iran's nuclear program, Iran argued that the IAEA Board of Governors' referral of Iran's case to the Security Council was itself illegal and improper and that because of procedural and substantive improprieties, the resolutions adopted by the Security Council against Iran were likewise illegal. These arguments can be found in document INFCIRC/853, of July 23, 2013.

Thus, if all of Iran's legal arguments were to be accepted as correct, the legal conclusion as of July 2015 would have been that Iran was in full compliance with its safeguards obligations, that Iran had never violated the provisions of the NPT, and that U.N. Security Council resolutions purporting to require Iran to cease its uranium enrichment program were illegal, and therefore null and void.

III. KEY LEGAL QUESTIONS IN DISPUTE

Obviously, there is quite a wide gulf separating the two sides in their understanding of the correct application of principles of international nuclear law to the case of Iran's nuclear program.

I think that the best way to proceed in considering which side has had the better of these widely divergent arguments is to identify the key legal questions in dispute between the parties and then to examine them in turn. I propose to do so in the succeeding chapters, providing legal analysis and conclusions.

Thus, Chapter 3 will consider the disputed question of whether Iran has been in violation of the NPT at any point. Chapter 4 will then consider the question of whether Iran was in violation of its safeguards obligations in 2003 and the question of the legal implications of Iran's alleged failures to timely declare nuclear facilities. Chapter 5 will then consider whether Iran was in violation of its safeguards obligations as of July 2015 and whether the IAEA has used proper legal standards in its assessments of Iran's compliance. Finally, Chapter 6 will be devoted to considering the implications of the U.N. Security Council's actions regarding Iran's nuclear program during the period of confrontation.

Chapter 3

Has Iran Violated the NPT?

There are two reasons for addressing this question first, even though I mentioned this source of law last in the summary of legal arguments. First, the Nuclear Nonproliferation Treaty (NPT) is by far the most important source of international law involved in the dispute over Iran's nuclear program. The NPT, for all of its shortcomings and all of the justified criticism leveled against it (including by me in my previous writings), is still the *lex lata* cornerstone treaty of the international nuclear energy and nuclear weapons nonproliferation normative regime, and the rest of the legal architecture of this existing regime is built upon it. So the question of whether Iran's actions with regard to its nuclear program have at any time violated the provisions of the NPT carries with it the highest potential implications, both for Iran's state responsibility, and for the effect of this determination upon the broader regime.

Second, and this is fortunate for Iran in this case, this question is the simplest of the key legal questions in dispute to answer. Arguments by the West that Iran has violated the NPT itself through actions related to its nuclear program are the weakest among the legal arguments they have advanced against Iran.

For both of these reasons, I think it makes sense to deal with this question first and clearly resolve it, so that more space and time can be devoted to the more controversial and complex arguments concerning International Atomic Energy Agency (IAEA) safeguards and related subsidiary arrangements.

I. THE NPT REGIME

I will try to avoid redundancy at this point and refer the reader to my earlier books for a more fulsome description of the origins and history of the NPT's establishment, its structure and content, and the verification and export control normative regimes that have been created to implement and to supplement it.

In brief, however, the NPT was agreed in 1968, at the height of the Cold War, to constitute a grand bargain between its signatory states, covering the topics of peaceful nuclear energy use, nuclear weapons nonproliferation, and the disarmament of existing nuclear weapons stockpiles. It comprises a structure of *quid pro quo* differential obligations, undertaken by two distinct categories of states parties: the five Nuclear Weapons States (NWS) (the United States, the United Kingdom, France, China, Russia) on the one hand; and all other states parties, collectively categorized as Non-Nuclear Weapon States (NNWS), on the other.

Under the NPT's terms, the five NWS are allowed to maintain possession of nuclear weapons, but in return take upon themselves obligations to assist NNWS in developing peaceful nuclear energy programs and to move toward disarmament of their existing nuclear weapons stockpiles in good faith.

For their part, the NNWS undertake in Article II of the NPT not to acquire nuclear weapons by any means. They further agree in Article III to conclude a separate bilateral treaty with the IAEA, referred to as a safeguards agreement. More on the substance of IAEA safeguards agreements later.

Rounding out the normative architecture related to the NPT, the Nuclear Suppliers Group (NSG) is an informal (i.e., legally nonbinding) group of nuclear technology supplier states, formed in 1975 for the purpose of coordinating and harmonizing nuclear export control laws and policies among the group. The NSG Guidelines reference both the NPT and IAEA safeguards in their agreed determinations on export control standards. However, the NSG is not formally related to either the NPT or the IAEA.

A point which should be borne in mind, and to which I shall return at intervals, is that the prohibition on NNWS parties to the NPT, such as Iran, acquiring nuclear weapons is contained exclusively in the NPT itself, in the terms of Article II. Article III of the NPT and the IAEA safeguards agreements bilaterally entered into between NNWS and the IAEA pursuant to Article III(4), on the other hand, are verification provisions related to nuclear materials generally. One must not confuse the NPT Article III nuclear material verification provisions, and the IAEA safeguards agreements implementing them, with the obligation contained in Article II of the NPT mandating that NNWS not acquire nuclear weapons by any means. These are distinct legal obligations that are only indirectly related. The IAEA is not, as it is commonly expressed in the media, a "nuclear weapons watchdog." The IAEA and its safeguards agreements with NPT NNWS are directly related only to the Article III obligation concerning nuclear materials accounting and verification. They are related only very indirectly with the Article II prohibition on NNWS acquisition of nuclear weapons.

II. SAFEGUARDS NONCOMPLIANCE = NPT VIOLATION?

This brings us to the first of the NPT-related legal arguments made by Western states against Iran; i.e., the argument that because Iran has violated its safeguards agreement, it has also per se violated NPT Article III. As stated in a report prepared by the U.S. Congressional Research Service:

> Iran's violations of its safeguards agreement appear to constitute violations of Article III, which requires NPT non-nuclear-weapon states-parties to accept IAEA safeguards, in accordance with the agency's statue, "for the exclusive purpose of verification of the fulfillment of its obligations assumed under this Treaty with a view to preventing diversion of nuclear energy

from peaceful uses to nuclear weapons or other nuclear explosive devices."[1]

This is an argument which, as a matter of law, I examined carefully in my book *Interpreting the Nuclear Nonproliferation Treaty*.[2] I concluded there that the operative obligation in NPT Article III(4) for NNWS to enter into a safeguards agreement with the IAEA, of a type described in Article III(1–3), is the extent of the legal relationship between the NPT on the one hand, and the IAEA and its safeguards agreements with states on the other.

The reasoning for this conclusion is as follows. The IAEA is its own self-enclosed treaty-based international organization. Its existence predates that of the NPT by more than a decade. It has its own constitutional treaty—the IAEA Statute—and its own separate membership as an international organization. Its statute contains detailed rules and procedures regarding its functioning and authority. The IAEA's only legal connection to the NPT is the obligation in Article III(4) of the NPT for all NNWS parties to "conclude agreements with the International Atomic Energy Agency to meet the requirements of this Article."

Some have argued that the operative legal obligation for NNWS in Article III is contained in Article III(1). They point to the language in Article III(1) stating that each NNWS "undertakes to accept safeguards as set forth in an agreement to be negotiated and concluded with the International Atomic Energy Agency. . . ," and to the phrases "Procedures for the safeguards required by this Article shall be followed with respect to source or special fissionable material. . ." and "The safeguards required by this Article shall be applied on all source or special fissionable material . . ." They see in these terms an obligation in Article III(1) not only to enter into a safeguards agreement

1. *Iran's Nuclear Program: Tehran's Compliance with International Obligations*, Congressional Research Service, 11, Apr. 28, 2014.

2. *See* Daniel H. Joyner, Interpreting the Nuclear Nonproliferation Treaty 87–93 (2011).

with the IAEA but also an obligation *to comply with* the terms of that safeguards agreement.[3]

However, a closer reading of the whole of Article III renders this interpretation unpersuasive. Article III does contain an obligation for NNWS to enter into a safeguards agreement with the IAEA. That obligation is discussed in Article III(1), but is stated with even more clarity and specificity in Article III(4), which states: "Non-nuclear-weapon States Party to the Treaty shall conclude agreements with the International Atomic Energy Agency to meet the requirements of this Article . . ."

Additionally, reading into Article III(1)'s provisions an independent obligation to comply with the terms of the safeguards agreement to be negotiated with the IAEA produces a redundancy from a normative system perspective. One of the fundamental system rules of international law is contained in the customary international law rule of *pacta sunt servanda* ("treaties are to be observed"), which holds that parties to a treaty are under an obligation to perform their treaty undertakings in good faith.[4] *Pacta sunt servanda* is an omnipresent rule of customary international law, binding all states and all treaties made.

Therefore, to interpret Article III(1) of the NPT as comprising an operative legal obligation would be to make its provisions redundant with the obligation clearly spelled out in Article III(4). Furthermore, to interpret Article III(1)'s terms as containing an obligation to comply with the terms of another treaty (a safeguards agreement) would render the terms of Article III(1) redundant and superfluous in light of the rule of *pacta sunt servanda*. An interpretation of a treaty which renders some of its terms redundant or superfluous internally,

3. *See, e.g.*, John Carlson, *Defining Noncompliance: NPT Safeguards Agreements*, 29 Arms Control Today 22 (May 2009) ("Noncompliance with an NPT safeguards agreement constitutes violation of Article III of the NPT, the obligation to accept safeguards on all nuclear material. . .").

4. *See* VCLT Article 26; *Gabcikovo-Nagymaros Project* (Hung v. Slov.), 1997 I.C.J. Rep. 7, para. 114.

or redundant with regard to other system rules of international law, is to be avoided.[5]

The terms of Article III(1) are better interpreted in their context within Article III as describing, along with Article III(2) and Article III(3), the sort of safeguards agreement which NNWS are to enter into with the IAEA. Under this interpretation, Article III makes sense holistically, and redundancy is avoided. Paragraphs 1–3 of Article III lay out in detail the type of safeguards agreement which paragraph 4 requires NNWS to enter into with the IAEA. Indeed this is precisely what the terms of Article III(4) provide: "Non-nuclear-weapon States Party to the Treaty shall conclude agreements with the International Atomic Energy Agency *to meet the requirements of this Article*."[6]

Interpreted correctly, then, it is clear that the operative obligation in Article III(4) for NNWS to enter into a safeguards agreement with the IAEA, of a type described in Article III(1–3), is the extent of the legal relationship between the NPT on the one hand, and the IAEA and its safeguards agreements with states on the other.

What this means is that an IAEA determination of safeguards agreement noncompliance by a safeguarded state does not *per se* constitute a determination of a violation of NPT Article III by that state. This conclusion is supported by several additional interpretive considerations that I developed in *Interpreting the Nuclear Nonproliferation Treaty*, including the conclusion that noncompliance with an IAEA safeguards agreement is not *per se* equivalent to a material breach, or even a violation, of a state's safeguards agreement, but rather constitutes only a preliminary technical finding of treaty noncompliance short of breach, which results in explicitly detailed rights and responsibilities of the IAEA under Article XII of the IAEA Statute. This is in harmony with the nonjudicial nature of the powers

5. *See* Ulf Linderfalk, On the Interpretation of Treaties: The Modern International Law as Expressed in the 1969 Vienna Convention on the Law of Treaties 109–110 (2007).

6. Emphasis added.

of the IAEA Board of Governors, an essentially political body which makes such findings of IAEA safeguards agreement noncompliance.

To be clear, I do not intend to address at this point the controversy concerning whether Iran has at any time acted, or continues to act, in noncompliance with its IAEA safeguards agreement. That is a discussion for later chapters. What I am saying here is that, regardless of the outcome of that determination of safeguards agreement compliance, *as a matter of law, noncompliance with an IAEA safeguards agreement does not per se constitute a violation of NPT Article III.* This relationship between the two legal sources simply does not exist. Iran has in force with the IAEA a comprehensive safeguards agreement (INFCIRC/214), which it entered into on December 13, 1974. That fact alone establishes Iran's compliance with NPT Article III. So the argument by the West that Iran's safeguards agreement noncompliance constitutes a violation of NPT Article III is incorrect as a matter of law, regardless of factual considerations.

III. NPT ARTICLE II AND "MANUFACTURE"

The more interesting NPT-related legal argument made against Iran by the West is that Iran's research and development activities related to nuclear weaponization, i.e., studies related to a nuclear explosive device purposed for military use, constitute a violation of Article II of the NPT, and specifically of that article's prohibition on the "manufacture" of nuclear weapons. As provided in Article II, all NNWS undertake "not to manufacture or otherwise acquire nuclear weapons or other nuclear explosive devices; and not to seek or receive any assistance in the manufacture of nuclear weapons or other nuclear explosive devices." This legal argument by the West is stated in a 2005 U.S. State Department report:

> The breadth of Iran's nuclear development efforts, the secrecy and deceptions with which they have been conducted for nearly 20 years, its redundant and surreptitious procurement channels,

> Iran's persistent failure to comply with its obligations to report to the IAEA and to apply safeguards to such activities, and the lack of a reasonable economic justification for this program leads us to conclude that Iran is pursuing an effort to manufacture nuclear weapons, and has sought and received assistance in this effort in violation of Article II of the NPT.[7]

Commenting on this report, a later U.S. Congressional Research Service report observed:

> The State Department's reasoning appears to be based on an interpretation of the NPT which holds that a wide scope of nuclear activities could constitute violations of Article II. The 2005 report states that assessments regarding Article II compliance "must look at the totality of the facts, including judgments as to" a state-party's "purpose in undertaking the nuclear activities in question"... It is worth noting that the 2005 State Department report's arguments appear to rely heavily on the notion that a state's apparent intentions underlying certain nuclear-related activities can be used to determine violations of Article II.[8]

From these statements concerning the interpretation of the Article II prohibition on the manufacture of nuclear weapons, we can see that the U.S. view is that the term "manufacture" in this context should be interpreted broadly, to include within its scope not only the actual physical construction of a nuclear explosive device but also a range of activities short of such final construction which, alone or in combination, reveal a purpose or intent to construct a nuclear

7. Adherence to and Compliance with Arms Control, Nonproliferation and Disarmament Agreements and Commitments, Department of State, Aug. 2005, *available at* http://www.state.gov/documents/organization/52113.pdf.

8. *Iran's Nuclear Program: Tehran's Compliance with International Obligations*, Congressional Research Service, 12, Apr. 28, 2014.

weapon. Such activities, according to the 2005 State Department Report, can include:

> (1) the presence of undeclared nuclear facilities; (2) procurement patterns inconsistent with a civil nuclear program (e.g., clandestine procurement networks, possibly including the use of front companies, false end-use information, and fraudulent documentation); (3) security measures beyond what would be appropriate for peaceful, civil nuclear installations; (4) a pattern of Article III safeguards violations suggestive not of mere mistake or incompetence, but of willful violation and/or systematic deception and denial efforts aimed at concealing nuclear activities from the IAEA; and (5) a nuclear program with little (or no) coherence for peaceful purposes, but great coherence for weapons purposes.[9]

This broad, purposive interpretation of the Article II "manufacture" term, is of long-standing provenance among U.S. officials. In testimony before the U.S. Senate Foreign Relations Committee in 1968, the head of the U.S. delegation to the NPT negotiations, William Foster, gave his view of Article II as follows:

> Facts indicating that the purpose of a particular activity was the acquisition of a nuclear explosive device would tend to show non-compliance. (Thus, the construction of an experimental prototype nuclear explosive device would be covered by the term "manufacture" as would be the production of components which would only have relevance to a nuclear explosive device.)[10]

The problem with this purposive interpretation of the term "manufacture" in NPT Article II, however, is that it is not supported

9. *Iran's Nuclear Program: Tehran's Compliance with International Obligations*, Congressional Research Service, 12, n. 50, Apr. 28, 2014.

10. Senate Committee on Foreign Relations, *Remarks Submitted by William C. Foster*, 89th Cong., 2d sess., July 10, 1968.

by either the plain meaning of the terms of Article II, or the negotiating history of Article II.

A. Interpreting NPT Article II

Beginning, as a treaty interpreter must, with the plain meaning of the term in its context, the plain meaning of the term "manufacture," by reference to dictionary definitions, can be expressed as the making or production of goods or wares from raw materials by manual labor or by machinery. This definition is typically accompanied in a dictionary setting by a listing of synonyms, including "assemble" and "fabricate." The plain meaning of the term "manufacture" as it appears in NPT Article II, therefore, can be deduced to refer to the physical construction, fabrication, assembly, or production of a nuclear explosive device.

Taken in its context within Article II, and within the rest of the NPT, this definition of the term "manufacture" makes sense. In the first clause of Article II, NNWS undertake not to receive the transfer of a nuclear explosive device, or control over a nuclear explosive device, "from any transferor whatsoever." This clause would seem to be focused on the transfer from another state of a completed nuclear explosive device.

But the drafters of Article II clearly wanted to expand the scope of the prohibition to include means of acquisition other than the receipt of a nuclear explosive device from another state. Thus, in its second clause, Article II forbids both self-manufacture of a nuclear explosive device by the obliged state, receipt of assistance in self-manufacture, and any other means of acquisition of a nuclear explosive device. The "manufacture" term within this clause, then, seems to go to indigenous construction of a nuclear explosive device, or assistance in such construction, while the "otherwise acquire" term seems to fill the role of a "catch-all" clause, prohibiting any other means whereby possession of a nuclear weapon might be realized.

In all of these *modi operandi* of acquiring a nuclear explosive device described in Article II, however, there is one common denominator. That is that there is never any deviation from the concept that it is a completed nuclear explosive device that is the subject of the various prohibitions. Nowhere in either Article I or Article II of the NPT is there language which can reasonably be interpreted in its plain meaning to apply to anything short of a completed nuclear explosive device, which has been either transferred from or to, manufactured by (with or without assistance), or otherwise acquired by, an obligated state.[11]

Having arrived at an interpretation of the plain meaning of a treaty term, taken in its context, a treaty interpreter may consult the negotiating history of the treaty in order to confirm this interpretation of the term.[12] In his seminal treatise on the negotiating history of the NPT, Mohamed Shaker offers this interesting vignette about the drafting of Article II, and in particular the term "manufacture":

> The prohibition on manufacture was envisaged in all the previous treaty drafts. The Soviet draft of 24 September 1965 also envisaged the undertaking by the States "not possessing nuclear weapons" not to "prepare for the manufacture" of nuclear weapons. The American draft as amended on 21 March 1966 included the preparations for the manufacture but only with respect to the prohibition on assistance. This means that non-nuclear-weapon States would have been allowed, under the American draft, to prepare for the manufacture of nuclear weapons as long as no assistance was provided from outside.[13]

11. *See* David S. Jonas, *Ambiguity Defines the NPT: What Does "Manufacture" Mean?*, 36 Loy. L.A. Int'l & Comp. L. Rev. (2014); Steven G. Stransky, *The Nuclear Non-Proliferation Treaty and Pakistan: Interpreting Nuclear Security Assistance Prohibitions*, 23 Fla. J. Int'l L. 1, 34–35 (2011); Michael Spies, *Iran and the Limits of the Nuclear Non-Proliferation Regime*, 22 Am. U. Int'l L. Rev. 401, 402 (2007).

12. *See* the Vienna Convention on the Law of Treaties, Articles 31 and 32. I have not included a consideration of the object and purpose of the NPT in performing this interpretation, because I think the NPT's object and purpose provides no interpretive insight in the case of this particular treaty term. *See* my discussion of the NPT's object and purpose on pages 29–32 of Interpreting the Nuclear Nonproliferation Treaty.

13. Mohamed Shaker, The Nuclear Non-proliferation Treaty: Origin and Implementation 1959–1979 Vol. 1, at 249 (1980).

There are at least two instructive points arising from this account by Shaker that can serve as evidence confirming the limited meaning of "manufacture" in NPT Article II, as I have interpreted it. The first point is Shaker's observation that in the early U.S. and Soviet drafts of the NPT, there was a distinction clearly drawn between the terms "manufacture" and "prepare for the manufacture." These were separate terms of different scope and meaning and were selected intentionally by different drafters for inclusion in different drafts. "Manufacture" was clearly of a more limited scope than "prepare for the manufacture," and looked more to the later steps of actual fabrication, construction, assembly, and production of the component parts of a nuclear weapon and to the completion of the full device from those component parts. "Prepare for the manufacture" clearly sought to include earlier steps on the ladder of development of a nuclear weapon, including the concept, capacity building, design, research, and experimentation steps. The fact that both terms had been considered by the drafters, and that the term "manufacture" was the term eventually agreed upon by all NPT treaty parties, tends to confirm the limited meaning of the term.

The second instructive point arising from this negotiating history account is that it was the American draft of 1966 that apparently initiated the use of the term "manufacture," as opposed to the term "prepare to manufacture," in the text of what eventually became Article II. This fact seems to belie later statements by U.S. officials seeking to expand the meaning of the agreed term "manufacture" to include actions that would have much more persuasively been included in the term "prepare to manufacture," which was proposed by the Soviet Union for inclusion in Article II and ultimately rejected by U.S. drafters.

For purposes of interpretive persuasion, let us consider the practical prudence of a limited interpretation of the manufacture term of Article II and the practical difficulties that would attend a broader, purposive definition. These considerations are in fact closely analogous to the considerations which prompted the drafters of the U.N. Charter, in its Article 51, to make the unilateral right of self-defense exercisable only "if an armed attack occurs." In both NPT Article II and U.N. Charter Article 51, what the treaty drafters were after was a bright line rule: a rule the satisfaction of which would be objectively clear. The actual attack of an enemy's military, instead of simply their perceived preparations to attack. The actual construction of a nuclear weapon, instead of the perceived preparation to manufacture one. Facts which can be objectively established to exist, instead of interpretations of the subjective intent of others to act in the future.

Arguments favoring a purposive interpretation of NPT Article II are in this sense analogous to arguments favoring the interpretation of U.N. Charter Article 51 to include a right of anticipatory or preemptive self-defense. In both contexts, such arguments wish to expand the principle in question to include facts which do not yet exist, but with regard to which an intent to establish them in the future is argued to be capable of discernment from the current behavior of another. In both contexts, the argument is that the subjective intent, plans, and purposes of another actor can be augured and predicted, as by so many pigeon entrails, through an observation of precursor behaviors.

In both NPT Article II and U.N. Charter Article 51, the drafters chose to reject this attempt to predict future facts not yet objectively existing, through a discernment of the subjective intent of others. In doing so they acted in harmony with general principles of domestic law which, by analogy only, in criminal law, for example, typically require more than just a *mens rea* of intent to commit a crime in the future. *Mens rea* must typically be supplemented by some *actus reus* objectively satisfying a definite legal standard. NPT Article II and U.N. Charter Article 51 were drafted with just such *actus reus* requirements, objectively determinable actions the commission of which will trigger legal consequences. The alternative choice to prohibit "preparations to manufacture" in NPT Article II, or to allow self-defense when another state is "preparing to attack" you, would not only have made these principles determinant on the discernment of subjective intent but would also have made them unworkably broad, without additional criteria for satisfaction or limitations on scope. Where would "preparations to manufacture" a nuclear weapon begin? Once begun, could they ever be stopped? How could either fact be determined? Again, fortunately the drafters of both the NPT and the U.N. Charter avoided such indeterminacy by selecting the bright line, objective formulations they did.

To restate, then, the term "manufacture" in NPT Article II should be understood to have a meaning limiting the attached prohibition to the physical construction, fabrication, assembly, or production of a completed nuclear explosive device.

B. Application to the Iran Case

Having arrived at this restrictive interpretation of Article II and the prohibition on manufacturing nuclear weapons, I could wrap up the application of this legal rule to the facts of the Iran case pretty quickly by stating, truthfully, that none of the Western states critical of Iran's nuclear program, nor the IAEA itself, have alleged that Iran has ever constructed a completed nuclear explosive device, and therefore that there is no factual basis for arriving at the conclusion that Iran has breached NPT Article II. While this is, in fact, the correct legal conclusion, I will at least review the factual claims that have been made about past possible military dimensions of Iran's nuclear program, as they have been made by both the IAEA and the West.

There is a widespread assumption in the West, and particularly in the United States, among both state officials and the nuclear nonproliferation expert community, that at least some elements of the Iranian government (whether centrally directed or not) desire to acquire nuclear weapons. It is difficult to pinpoint exactly the source of this assumption. Iranian officials have repeatedly stated since the 1979 Revolution that Iran does not wish to acquire nuclear weapons. The Supreme Leader of Iran, Ayatollah Khamenei, has gone so far as to issue a *fatwah*, or religious injunction, against the development or possession of nuclear weapons and other weapons of mass destruction.[14] However, the suspicion persists in the West that Iran

14. Http://nuclearenergy.ir/legal-aspects/#Fatwa_against_Nuclear_Weapons ("Ayatollah Khomeini's successor as Iran's Leader, Ayatollah Ali Khamenei, has also

nevertheless maintains—perhaps only previously actively, but nevertheless certainly presently latently—desires to obtain nuclear weapons. The root of this suspicion is likely the mutual antipathy which has subsisted between Iran and particularly the United States since the Iranian Revolution of 1979, as well as the even greater mutual antipathy between Iran and Israel, a key regional ally of the United States. There is a tendency, therefore, for Western officials and observers to view Iranian actions relative to its nuclear program through glasses tinged with this suspicion. *La vie en bombe.*

In Chapter 1, I detailed the allegations made by the IAEA in a November 8, 2011, report by Director General Yukiya Amano to the Board of Governors, which summarized a number of allegations previously made by Western states, adding considerable detail to them. These allegations essentially charged that Iran had, beginning in the late 1980s and continuing until at least 2003, engaged in research and development efforts best explainable as efforts purposed in establishing a capacity to indigenously construct a nuclear explosive device. Evidence of these efforts, collectively termed "possible military dimensions" (PMD) to Iran's nuclear program, had according to the IAEA been uncovered both by IAEA officials and by third-party states that had shared intelligence information with the IAEA. The IAEA refused to divulge, even to Iran itself, the documents and other primary evidence forming the basis for these allegations. However, it is known that much of this evidence was procured from a laptop computer stolen in Iran and provided to Western intelligence agencies, and from them communicated to the IAEA, popularly nicknamed the "laptop of death."[15]

Iran provided a formal response to the November 8, 2011, report and its allegations of past nuclear weaponization work in Iran on December 12, 2011. Iran's response can be found in IAEA document

pronounced a fatwa forbidding the production, stockpiling and use of weapons of mass destruction, and specifically nuclear arms. He first issued the fatwa in October 2003 but has reiterated it several times ever since in an effort to underline the high significance of the issue.").

15. Julian Borger, *U.S. Iran Intelligence "Is Incorrect,"* THE GUARDIAN, Feb. 22, 2007.

INFCIRC/833. In it, Iran criticizes the IAEA for having acted outside its remit in officially reproducing these allegations and for having withheld from Iran the evidence on which the allegations were based. In this and other communications, Iran has consistently questioned the authenticity of evidence that has been alluded to by the IAEA and others and has denied the allegations of weaponization research and development contained in the November 2011 report.[16]

There has been lengthy debate among technical and scientific experts concerning the authenticity of the evidence relied upon by the IAEA and the overall validity of the PMD allegations made against Iran by the IAEA and the West.[17] It is well beyond my professional qualifications to wade into this debate. However, I do think that there are potential legal implications to the making of formal allegations by an international organization, such as the IAEA, of potentially legally wrongful behavior of a state, based upon intelligence information provided to the international organization by third-party states, the primary sources of which the international organization will not share even with the accused state. A number of other observers have also commented on the increasing use by the IAEA of intelligence information provided to it by third-party states that are in many cases known to be politically antithetical to the state against which they are providing evidence.[18] There is a general concern that as a technical nuclear materials accounting and monitoring body, the professional staff of the IAEA is ill-equipped, in terms of technical and resource competence, to independently authenticate intelligence information provided to it by national intelligence agencies. And that if independent authentication by the IAEA is impossible or impractical, its use by the Agency as

16. *See also* INFCIR/853; Mark Hibbs, *Handling Iran's Weaponization File, Arms Control Wonk*, Jan. 20, 2014.

17. *See, e.g.*, Scott Peterson, *Iran Nuclear Report: Why It Might Not Be a Game-Changer After All*, Christian Science Monitor, Nov. 9, 2011; Robert Kelley, *Nuclear Arms Charge Against Iran Is No Slam Dunk*, Bloomberg, Jan. 10, 2012; Julian Borger, *U.S. Iran Intelligence "Is Incorrect,"* The Guardian, Feb. 22, 2007.

18. *See, e.g.*, Mark Hibbs, *Intel Inside: Has the IAEA's Information Become Politicized?*, Foreign Pol'y, Dec. 10, 2012.

a basis for determinations of member-state compliance, and refusal to disclose such evidence even to the accused state, would appear improper and not in keeping with general principles of law regarding due process at best, and highly politicizing of the Agency's work at worst.[19]

While, again, I do not intend to present an independent analysis or conclusions concerning the question of whether and to what extent nuclear weaponization research and development activities have been carried on in Iran, I will say that I am personally persuaded by Robert Kelley's assessment on this question, which I think presents a fair, balanced, and reasonable assessment of the available evidence. Kelley, a former nuclear weapons analyst at Los Alamos National Laboratory in the United States and a former IAEA nuclear weapons inspector, has concluded that after its devastating war with Iraq, during which both conventional and chemical weapons were used against it, Iran, or at least elements within Iran's military, considered it prudent to develop the know-how to build a nuclear weapon in case Iran ever needed to do so in order to defend itself in any similar future conflict.[20] In pursuance of this aim, throughout the 1990s Iranian scientists and engineers conducted research and performed experimental trials on discrete components of a nuclear warhead, including work on warhead design. However, according to Kelley, there is no evidence that Iran ever constructed a complete nuclear explosive device or any of its primary components. Further, he concludes that there is no evidence that warhead component experiments were ever conducted using nuclear material. Rather, the research and development activities in Iran during this time, and ending around 2003, appear to have been capacity-building efforts

19. *See id.* ("Beginning two decades ago, the IAEA started relying less on information it gathers during its own field inspections alone and more on information that others provide, most of which is open-source, but some of which is not. This third-party data has become central to the IAEA's work, and it is about to become even more so. The leak of the graph to the AP underscores that if this data isn't rigorously vetted and handled carefully, the IAEA's technical and political credibility will be seriously compromised.").

20. *See* Francois Nicoullaud, *Rouhani and the Iranian Bomb*, N.Y. TIMES, July 26, 2013.

only—i.e., an acquisition of knowledge and capabilities, and not a program aimed at the actual construction of a nuclear explosive device. According to Kelley, the U.S.-led war in Iraq, initiated on the basis of allegations of Iraqi possession of weapons of mass destruction, created concern among Iranian officials that Iran's own research into nuclear weapons would be discovered and that this concern likely led to the cessation of Iran's efforts in 2003.[21] This factual narrative is also essentially consistent with the U.S. intelligence community's own formal conclusions about Iran's past weaponization activities, laid out in its 2007 National Intelligence Estimate. Indeed, Akbar Hashemi Rafsanjani, who was president of Iran from 1989 to 1997, seemed to confirm the essence of this assessment in an October 2015 interview:

> When we first began, we were at war and we sought to have that possibility for the day that the enemy might use a nuclear weapon. That was the thinking. But it never became real . . . Our basic doctrine was always a peaceful nuclear application, but it never left our mind that if one day we should be threatened and it was imperative, we should be able to go down the other path . . .[22]

21. Robert Kelley, *The Nuclear Agreement with Iran*, Norwegian Institute of International Affairs publication, Feb. 21, 2014. Kelley's assessment is essentially in harmony with the ultimate findings of the IAEA Director General, who on December 2, 2015, submitted a final report on the Iran PMD issue to the IAEA Board of Governors. The conclusion of the report stated: "The Agency assesses that a range of activities relevant to the development of a nuclear explosive device were conducted in Iran prior to the end of 2003 as a coordinated effort, and some activities took place after 2003. The Agency also assesses that these activities did not advance beyond feasibility and scientific studies, and the acquisition of certain relevant technical competences and capabilities. The Agency has no credible indications of activities in Iran relevant to the development of a nuclear explosive device after 2009.

The Agency has found no credible indications of the diversion of nuclear material in connection with the possible military dimensions to Iran's nuclear programme." GOV/2015/68.

22. Sam Wilkin, *Iran Considered Nuclear Weapons during the 1980's Iraq War, ex-President Says*, Reuters, Oct. 29, 2015.

Assuming that this is an essentially accurate portrayal of the facts, and applying the legal standard of Article II, and in particular the prohibition on the manufacture of nuclear weapons as interpreted above, it can be concluded that Iran has not violated NPT Article II. This is a conclusion shared by the two directors general of the IAEA immediately preceding the current director general, Yukiya Amano. Hans Blix, IAEA director general from 1981 to 1997, is on record as stating in 2013 that "[s]o far Iran has not violated the NPT," and adding, "and there is no evidence right now that suggests that Iran is producing nuclear weapons."[23] Similarly, Mohamed ElBaradei, the Nobel Peace Prize laureate and Director General of the IAEA from 1997 to 2009, is on record in 2011 as stating that "[d]uring my time at the agency . . . we haven't seen a shred of evidence that Iran is weaponizing, in terms of building nuclear-weapons facilities and using enriched materials . . . All I see is the hype about the threat posed by Iran."[24]

Before leaving the issue of Iran's past nuclear weaponization research and development efforts, I think it is important to bear in mind, for the sake of contextual understanding and appreciation, that what historical interest Iran has had in nuclear weapons, and the research and development efforts that Iran has undertaken in furtherance of that interest, is by no means unique or even particularly remarkable when viewed in the context of the efforts which many states, outside of the recognized NPT NWS parties, have at some point since 1945 expended in exploration of the possibility of developing nuclear weapons.

In the decades following World War II, and in particular during the decades of the 1960s and 1970s, many states in addition to the five NPT NWS considered, at one time or another, pursuing nuclear weapons. And many made substantial progress in their pursuit. We know that India, Pakistan, Israel, and North Korea ultimately

23. *See* Shafaat Shahbandari, *Iran's Nuke Threat Is Overhyped: U.N. Official*, Gulf News, Mar. 6, 2013.

24. Seymour Hersh, *Iran and the Bomb: How Real Is the Nuclear Threat?*, The New Yorker, June 6, 2011.

succeeded in those efforts, and currently have stockpiles of nuclear weapons.[25] South Africa successfully produced a number of nuclear weapons, though it has since disarmed.[26] But many other states chose at some point in their efforts, for a variety of reasons both political and economic, to stop short of actually manufacturing a nuclear weapon.

While more is known about some of their nuclear weapons research and development programs than about others, nevertheless Sweden, Switzerland, Australia, Canada, Egypt, South Korea, Brazil, Libya, Iraq, Taiwan, and Argentina are all known to have at one time or another over the past sixty years, seriously and secretly pursued nuclear weaponization studies.[27] Those, therefore, who perhaps rightly fault Iran for having historically maintained a "clandestine nuclear weapons program" must acknowledge that by application of the same standard, similar measures of fault lie with all of these other states, as well of course as with India, Pakistan, Israel, and North Korea, all of whose nuclear weapons programs also began secretly.

There are yet other states which, while not having pursued a nuclear weaponization program as far as is publicly known, are either known to have the capability to manufacture a nuclear weapon in relatively short order should they choose to do so or, alternatively, have other options for acquiring nuclear weapons from allies if needed. The best example of a state in the former category is Japan. While experts disagree on how long it would take for Japan to manufacture a nuclear weapon should they choose to do so—estimates vary from six months to more than a year—it is well known that Japan has all of the necessary knowledge and technical capabilities, as well as more than enough nuclear material, to successfully manufacture an

25. *See* JOSEPH CIRINCIONE ET AL., DEADLY ARSENALS, NUCLEAR, BIOLOGICAL AND CHEMICAL THREATS 333 (2d ed. Carnegie Endowment 2005).

26. NTI Country Profiles: South Africa, http://www.nti.org.

27. *See* JOSEPH CIRINCIONE ET AL., DEADLY ARSENALS, NUCLEAR, BIOLOGICAL AND CHEMICAL THREATS 333 (2d ed. Carnegie Endowment 2005); Ariel Levite, *Never Say Never Again: Nuclear Reversal Revisited*, 27.3 INT'L SECURITY 59–88 (2002–2003); Carey Sublette, Nuclear Weapons Archive, http://nuclearweaponarchive.org/.

arsenal of nuclear weapons.[28] In the latter category, Saudi Arabia is known to have helped finance Pakistan's nuclear weapons program, and, according to Philip Bleek, "[i]t appears likely that at least an implicit *quid pro quo* exists under which Saudi Arabia could procure some sort of nuclear weapons capability from Pakistan *in extremis*."[29]

Again, in mentioning these various other cases, I am simply attempting to contextualize Iran's interest in nuclear weapons and its research and development on weaponization particularly during the 1990s, within the broader phenomenon of similar interests, and similar research and development efforts, of other countries at varying times over the past sixty years. Iran is evidently in that category of states, along with Sweden, Switzerland, Australia, Canada, Egypt, South Korea, Brazil, Libya, Iraq, Taiwan, and Argentina, which have at some point seriously considered and secretly pursued the idea of developing a nuclear weaponization capability, but which for different reasons at some point stopped those efforts and are not now pursuing them. It is thus difficult to see how Iran's past weaponization studies can be characterized, as they often are by Iran's detractors, as being more inherently morally or normatively wrong than those of any of these other countries mentioned.

It may be that, again like a number of these other states, Iran's current position is best characterized as that of maintaining a latent nuclear weapons production capability, without an active weaponization studies program. This position has been defined by Ariel Levite as a "nuclear hedging" posture which, according to Levite, best explains the current position of many states that at one time or other in the past pursued nuclear weaponization but that no longer have active programs.[30] This conclusion would be in harmony with the latest

28. *See* Joseph Cirincione et al., Deadly Arsenals, Nuclear, Biological and Chemical Threats 333 (2d ed. Carnegie Endowment 2005); Douglas Birch, *Plutonium Fever Blossoms in Japan*, Center for Public Integrity, May 19, 2014.

29. Phillip Bleek, *Atomic Kingdom? Not So Fast . . .*, WMD Junction, Nov. 15, 2013.

30. Ariel Levite, *Never Say Never Again: Nuclear Reversal Revisited*, 27.3 Int'l Security 59–88 (2002–2003).

assessments of the U.S. intelligence community. In Congressional testimony given on February 3, 2015, the director of the U.S. Defense Intelligence Agency summed up this assessment as follows:

> We continue to assess Iran's goal is to develop capabilities that will allow it to build missile-deliverable nuclear weapons, should a decision be made to do so. The regime faces no insurmountable technical barriers to producing a nuclear weapon, making Iran's political will the central issue.[31]

In summary, then, I conclude that Iran has not at any time violated its obligations under the 1968 Nuclear Nonproliferation Treaty. This is an important conclusion, inasmuch as there is interest in the question of whether Iran has violated this cornerstone treaty and its provisions prohibiting the proliferation of nuclear weapons. Indeed, I think that this is one of the most misunderstood aspects of public debate about the Iran nuclear case. To restate this conclusion, Iran has not violated the rules of international law focused on the proliferation of nuclear weapons.

There are more controversial questions about whether Iran has violated rules of international law focused on keeping nuclear materials properly accounted for. But in a meaningful way, these latter rules, contained in IAEA safeguards agreements, are more procedural than substantive when it comes to any direct connection with the proliferation of nuclear weapons. They are several steps removed in their subject matter from the question of whether a state has nuclear weapons ambitions, or whether a state has an active nuclear weapons program. I think that this is an important distinction to bear in mind as we proceed to consider these safeguards questions.

31. Testimony of Vincent R. Stewart, Director, Defense Intelligence Agency, to the House Armed Services Committee, Feb. 3, 2015.

Chapter 4

Was Iran in Violation of Its Safeguards Obligations in 2003? What about Its Failures to Timely Declare Nuclear Facilities?

I will now move on to consider Western and International Atomic Energy Agency (IAEA) allegations that Iran has violated its obligations under its safeguards agreement with the IAEA. To do so, it is first necessary to provide an explication of IAEA safeguards law and its relationship to the NPT. Here again I wish to avoid unnecessary redundancy. I have written about this subject at length in my previous books, and particularly in *Interpreting the Nuclear Nonproliferation Treaty*. So I will provide here only a summary, along with a consideration of the concept of safeguards obligation compliance, before proceeding to an analysis of the application of that body of law to two specific questions posed in this chapter. These questions are, first, whether Iran was in violation of its safeguards obligations in 2003, when it was declared to be in noncompliance with its safeguards agreement by the IAEA; and second, whether Iran's alleged failures to timely declare design and other information concerning nuclear facilities to the IAEA constitute separate instances of safeguards obligation violations.

I. IAEA SAFEGUARDS LAW OVERVIEW

As previously noted, pursuant to Nuclear Nonproliferation Treaty (NPT) Article III(4) every Non-Nuclear Weapon States (NNWS) party to the NPT must conclude a safeguards agreement with the IAEA "for the exclusive purpose of verification of the fulfillment of its obligations assumed under this Treaty with a view to preventing diversion of nuclear energy from peaceful uses to nuclear weapons or other nuclear explosive devices."

In 1972, two years after the entry into force of the NPT, the comprehensive IAEA safeguards system was adopted in template form by the IAEA Board of Governors, and published as document INFCIRC/153, entitled "The Structure and Content of Agreements Between the Agency and States Required in Connection With the Treaty on the Non-proliferation of Nuclear Weapons." INFCIRC/153 is a recitation of the provisions which should be included in a comprehensive safeguards agreement (CSA) between the IAEA and each NNWS party to the NPT. Iran's comprehensive safeguards agreement with the IAEA, published by the IAEA as INFCIRC/214, entered into force in 1974, and is typical of an agreement following the INFCIRC/153 template.

Before proceeding, it is important to note that Iran's CSA with the IAEA is, as are all other CSAs entered into by the IAEA, a bilateral treaty between an individual state on the one side, and the IAEA acting in its legal personality as an international organization on the other side. Each IAEA CSA is bilaterally negotiated and agreed between the IAEA and the individual state entering into the agreement. Each CSA is a freestanding bilateral treaty, which only comes into force in accordance with its negotiated provisions, which typically include compliance with the individual state's constitutional and statutory requirements for ratification.

Iran's CSA provides in its Article I the basic undertaking of the treaty, and in Article II addresses the application of safeguards generally:

> **Article 1**
>
> The Government of Iran undertakes, pursuant to paragraph 1 of Article III of the Treaty, to accept safeguards, in accordance

with the terms of this Agreement, on all source or special fissionable material in all peaceful nuclear activities within its territory, under its jurisdiction or carried out under its control anywhere, for the exclusive purpose of verifying that such material is not diverted to nuclear weapons or other nuclear explosive devices.

Article 2

The Agency shall have the right and the obligation to ensure that safeguards will be applied, in accordance with the terms of this Agreement, on all source or special fissionable material in all peaceful nuclear activities within the territory of Iran, under its jurisdiction or carried out under its control anywhere, for the exclusive purpose of verifying that such material is not diverted to nuclear weapons or other nuclear explosive devices.

Iran's CSA comprises ninety-eight articles and is both lengthy and complex. But the safeguards regime agreed between Iran and the IAEA, and enshrined in the CSA's terms, can be fairly simply summarized. The CSA requires Iran to make reports to the IAEA, declaring the amounts, types, and locations of all nuclear material within its borders, with only a few delineated exceptions. The underlying idea of the CSA is that the IAEA will then act as an independent monitor and accountant of all of this nuclear material inside Iran. The theory being that, by keeping track of this material—from its sourcing through mining, import, or other production, all the way through the steps of the nuclear fuel cycle—the IAEA will be able to verify that none of the nuclear material inside Iran is used for military purposes, i.e., to build a nuclear weapon. This is the overall purpose of IAEA safeguards.

Part II of the CSA begins with Article 27, which provides that "the purpose of this part of the Agreement is to specify the procedures to be applied in the implementation of the safeguards provisions of Part I." Part II then proceeds to spell out the details of Iran's specific obligations to submit reports to the IAEA regarding the amounts and locations of all safeguardable nuclear materials within its territory, as well as detailed design information on any facilities related to that material. The IAEA's role is then to engage in inspections and other material accountancy efforts, in order to verify that these reports submitted by the government of Iran are correct and that all of the safeguardable nuclear material in Iran is accounted for and being used for exclusively peaceful purposes.

In an additional subsidiary arrangements agreement between Iran and the IAEA, the operating specifics of these activities are spelled out. Strategic points within declared nuclear facilities are agreed upon between Iran and the IAEA as places for the IAEA to conduct routine inspections. Frequency and the other details concerning routine inspections are also agreed upon in the subsidiary arrangements, as well as the form of reports that are to be exchanged between Iran and the IAEA. The subsidiary arrangements also specify when reports are to be made to the IAEA by Iran, including on the subject of new nuclear facilities or modifications to existing facilities.

There is provision made in the CSA for requests by the IAEA to inspect locations that have not been previously specified in the subsidiary arrangements. This is the special inspection process laid out in Articles 73 and 77. Thus, if the IAEA wishes to inspect a site that has not previously been agreed upon for inspections by Iran, it must make a formal request to the government of Iran, which then considers the request. If there is any disagreement or dispute about access under the special inspection procedure, the parties can submit the dispute to arbitration, pursuant to Article 22.

If the IAEA, through its inspections and other material accountancy efforts, is unable to verify that there has been no diversion of declared nuclear material from peaceful to military uses, it may, pursuant to its statute, report the matter to the U.N. Security Council.

The CSA safeguards regime is thus a system in which the government of Iran is responsible for submitting detailed and timely reports to the IAEA identifying the nuclear materials and related facilities within its borders. The IAEA is then responsible for accounting for this declared nuclear material, through agreed facility inspections and other material accountancy practices, as the material makes its way through the nuclear fuel cycle process.

In the aftermath of the 1990–1991 Gulf War in Iraq, IAEA inspectors returning to Iraq discovered that the Hussein regime had pursued a nuclear weapons program to an advanced stage, involving activities in facilities located all over the country. This program, according to IAEA Deputy Director of Inspections David Kay, had progressed to being within twelve to eighteen months of acquiring sufficient nuclear material to construct a nuclear explosive device.[1] This revelation of a large-scale clandestine nuclear weapons program in a state which had signed an INFCIRC/153 agreement with the IAEA, and which was under active IAEA safeguards, was troubling. Even more disturbing was the fact that one of the undeclared nuclear installations, the Tuwaitha Nuclear Research Center, was virtually next door to a declared, safeguarded research reactor. Iraq's ability to conceal such an advanced program, literally under the noses of IAEA inspectors, shook international confidence in the INFCIRC/153 safeguards system.[2]

Again, the CSA system relies almost entirely upon the declarations of facilities and materials made by the safeguarded state. The IAEA's role under that system is essentially to verify that these reports are accurate and to confirm that all declared nuclear material within the safeguarded state is accounted for and in peaceful uses. Under the INFCIRC/153 system, the IAEA has neither the legal authority nor the procedural framework necessary to determine the completeness of such reports or to detect undeclared nuclear activities.

Speaking at the 46th Session of the IAEA General Conference in 1991, IAEA Director General Hans Blix called for the construction of an IAEA safeguards system with "more teeth." Soon afterward, a

1. U.S. Senate, Committee on Foreign Relations, *Nuclear Proliferation: Learning from the Iraq Experience*, Hearing before the Committee on Foreign Relations, 102 Cong., 1st Sess., Oct. 17, 1991, 20.

2. Theodore Hirsch, *The IAEA Additional Protocol: What It Is and Why It Matters*, NON-PROLIFERATION REV. (Fall–Winter 2004).

committee of IAEA member states began negotiations on a protocol to strengthen and supplement the INFCIRC/153 system by granting the IAEA additional legal authorities and privileges of access. This process led to the adoption by the IAEA Board of Governors in 1997 of the Model Additional Protocol Agreement (INFCIRC/540).

The Additional Protocol has been characterized as "an effort to transform IAEA inspectors from accountants to detectives."[3] It attempts to do this by supplementing the INFCIRC/153 safeguards system in two primary areas. First, the Additional Protocol requires states to produce a more expansive declaration regarding nuclear fuel cycle activity being carried out within its territory as compared to that required by the INFCIRC/153 system. This expanded declaration is to include details on nuclear materials and the facilities involved in producing, processing, and utilizing them, as required under INFCIRC/153, but in addition must also include information on all nuclear-fuel-cycle-related research and development activities that do not themselves involve nuclear materials, but which may be used in the production of nuclear materials, including activities being carried out in privately owned facilities. This expansion of information required from the states significantly widens the Agency's understanding of the full range of nuclear-related activities being carried on within a state. This more complete understanding allows the IAEA to better assess the purpose and direction of nuclear programs within a safeguarded state.[4]

Second, the Additional Protocol provides for the IAEA to have "complementary access" to that it is granted under the INFCIRC/153 system. INFCIRC/540 gives the IAEA the right of access "on a selective basis in order to assure the absence of undeclared nuclear material" to "any place" on the site of a declared facility, and not only to agreed strategic points, as under the INFCIRC/153 system. It further provides for IAEA access to all sites on which information has been provided by the state regarding research and development activities on nuclear-fuel-cycle-related technologies, in order "to resolve

3. *See id.* at 143.
4. *See id.* at 143–144.

a question relating to the correctness and completeness of the information provided."[5]

Additionally, INFCIRC/540 provides for IAEA access to "any location specified by the Agency" in order to carry out "location-specific environmental monitoring." This provision enables IAEA inspectors to nominate undeclared locations at which they would like to take soil, water, and air samples in order to detect the presence of nuclear materials and thus potentially produce evidence of undeclared nuclear activities.

The notice requirements for the carrying out of inspections under the Additional Protocol are also significantly shortened from their length under the INFCIRC/153 system, and are typically set at twenty-four hours, down from the normal one-week notice period under INFCIRC/153. The Additional Protocol further requires the state to grant multi-entry visas to inspectors, which facilitates easier access by IAEA inspectors to safeguarded facilities.

These supplements to the information-gathering ability of the IAEA, as well as its ability to conduct inspections in a more efficient and effective manner, are significant improvements to the Agency's ability to verify not only the correctness but also the completeness of state declarations. They allow for increased confidence in the determinations of the IAEA that no undeclared nuclear-related activity is being carried out on a safeguarded state's territory.

Accession to the INFCIRC/540 Additional Protocol agreement is voluntary for NPT member states, in that the conclusion of an INFCIRC/540 agreement with the IAEA is not a part of the fundamental NNWS safeguards obligation contained in Article III(4) of the NPT.[6] NPT NNWS may, if they choose, maintain only the standard INFCIRC/153 agreement with the IAEA. According to the IAEA's most recent assessment, 117 states have both an INFCIRC/153 CSA

5. *See id.*

6. *See* Masahiko Asada, *The Treaty on the Non Proliferation of Nuclear Weapons and the Universalization of the Additional Protocol*, 16 J. CONFLICT & SECURITY L. 3–34 (2011); Pierre-Emmanuel Dupont, *Is the Conclusion of an Additional Protocol Mandatory under the NPT?*, ARMS CONTROL LAW, Aug. 1, 2012.

and an INFCIRC/540 Additional Protocol agreement in force with the IAEA. However 55 states have only an INFCIRC/153 CSA in force. This latter number includes Iran.

As noted above, Iran has had an INFCIRC/153 CSA in force with the IAEA since 1974. As noted in Chapter 1, in 2003 Iran signed an INFCIRC/540 Additional Protocol agreement with the IAEA and submitted the agreement to the Majlis (the Iranian parliament) for ratification. Pending ratification, Iran agreed to voluntarily implement the terms of the Additional Protocol, which it in fact did between 2003 and 2006. However, when Iran's case was referred by the IAEA to the U.N. Security Council in 2006, Iran ceased its voluntary implementation of the Additional Protocol. The Majlis had never approved ratification of Iran's Additional Protocol agreement, and therefore no instrument of ratification was ever deposited by Iran. Thus, Iran's Additional Protocol agreement never legally came into force, and this situation persisted throughout the period of confrontation regarding Iran's nuclear program (i.e., from August 2002 through to July 2015). The totality of Iran's safeguards legal obligations during this period, therefore, are to be found in its CSA.[7]

Since 1997, the IAEA's approach to administering safeguards has evolved through policy changes adopted by the IAEA's Secretariat and Board of Governors. In keeping with the concepts of the Additional Protocol, the IAEA has attempted to enhance its understanding of the nuclear programs of safeguarded states through the collection of an increased amount of information from a number of different sources and careful analysis of that information in order to arrive at a more holistic understanding of each safeguarded state's nuclear program. This is the so called "integrated safeguards" approach, adopted by the IAEA Board of Governors in 2002.[8] The integrated safeguards

7. Iran did agree, pursuant to the Joint Comprehensive Plan of Action, to provisionally apply the Additional Protocol as of JCPOA Implementation Day, January 16, 2016.

8. *See* Mark Hibbs, *The Plan for IAEA Safeguards*, Carnegie Endowment for International Peace, Nov. 20, 2012; *IAEA Has Made Progress in Implementing*

approach has evolved yet further over the past decade and is now expressed as the "state level safeguards approach." The state level safeguards approach is intended by the IAEA to continue in the vein of reaching a holistic understanding of a safeguarded state's nuclear program, but adds to it an element of discretion on the part of the IAEA to choose to allocate its resources to focus greater attention on some states' nuclear programs rather than others. In effect, the Agency can under its most recent policy focus its scrutiny on states whose nuclear programs are a source of concern to the Agency. Iran's nuclear program has been firmly situated in this category since the IAEA first declared Iran in noncompliance with its safeguards obligations in 2003.

The move by the IAEA to a state level safeguards approach has not been without controversy. A number of IAEA member states, most notably including Russia, have objected to the state level approach as being discriminatory and susceptible to politicization and as a policy device calculated to increase safeguards scrutiny upon some states without their consent.[9]

II. COMPLIANCE WITH SAFEGUARDS TREATIES

Having reviewed the essentials of the safeguards legal framework, I think it is now important to consider the concept of compliance with safeguards law. This may seem like a straightforward question, but it is one on which there have been significant disagreements and misunderstanding.

Critical Programs but Continues to Face Challenges, Report of the U.S. Government Accountability Office, GAO-13–139, May 2013.

9. *See* Mark Hibbs, *The Plan for IAEA Safeguards*, Carnegie Endowment for International Peace, Nov. 20, 2012; Daniel H. Joyner, *The IAEA State Level Safeguards Approach Report*, Arms Control Law, Aug. 29, 2013; Daniel H. Joyner, *Statement by Russian Representative to the IAEA Grigory Berdinnekov*, Arms Control Law, Oct. 21, 2014.

It is important to understand how the various sources of law in this area are related to each other in order to then understand the distinctions that should be drawn when considering the question of safeguards compliance. As I explained above, the cornerstone legal instrument in the nuclear energy and nuclear nonproliferation area is the 1968 NPT. For NNWS parties, the NPT contains a provision in Article II obligating NNWS not to acquire nuclear weapons by any means. Article III of the NPT contains the obligation for each of the NNWS to conclude a safeguards agreement with the IAEA "for the exclusive purpose of verification of the fulfillment of its obligations assumed under this Treaty with a view to preventing diversion of nuclear energy from peaceful uses to nuclear weapons or other nuclear explosive devices."

Article III of the NPT recognizes in this requirement to conclude a safeguards agreement the reality that is even more clearly spelled out in Article IV of the NPT, which is that nuclear materials are inherently dual use. I discussed the dual use nature of nuclear materials at length in Chapter 1 of *Interpreting the Nuclear Nonproliferation Treaty*. The essence of this realization is that nuclear materials can be used for both peaceful purposes (e.g., electricity production, medical diagnostic applications), as well as military purposes (i.e., a nuclear weapon). Thus, the requirement for each NNWS to conclude a safeguards agreement with the IAEA includes this acknowledgment that nuclear materials, and indeed the entire nuclear fuel cycle, are not presumptively suspect or evil things. Rather, nuclear materials can, and most typically are, put to exclusively peaceful uses. It is only their potential, and exceptional, diversion from those peaceful uses to military uses that a safeguards agreement is concerned with. Indeed, Article IV of Iran's CSA provides:

> The safeguards provided for in this Agreement shall be implemented in a manner designed:
>
> (a) To avoid hampering the economic and technological development of Iran or international co-operation in the

field of peaceful nuclear activities, including international exchange of nuclear material;

(b) To avoid undue interference in Iran's peaceful nuclear activities, and in particular in the operation of facilities . . .

I think that this recognition of the dual use nature of nuclear materials, which is written into both the NPT and the CSA, is vitally important to remember when considering the concept of safeguards law compliance. Unlike Article II of the NPT, which focuses exclusively on the acquisition of nuclear weapons, an INFCIRC/153 safeguards agreement with the IAEA must treat the subject of nuclear materials, and their actual and potential uses within a state, in a more holistic way, taking into full account the fact that there are perfectly legitimate peaceful uses to which nuclear materials may be, and indeed are typically, put within a state. The importance and function of a CSA is, then, to monitor that peaceful nuclear program in order to verify that no nuclear materials have been diverted from it to a military program.

This is an important understanding for the concept of compliance with safeguards law, because it puts into proper context instances of safeguards noncompliance by safeguarded states. In most cases, safeguards noncompliance results from the failure of a state to accurately report the locations, amounts, or types of nuclear material within its territory, or to fail to timely and accurately report the existence of facilities related to those materials. This failure to accurately report may, and typically does, have absolutely nothing to do with the existence of a clandestine nuclear weapons program. It may simply be a bookkeeping error or a misunderstanding between the IAEA and the safeguarded state as to the proper classification of material. An example of the latter situation occurred in June 2014, when reports surfaced that Japan had failed to report 645 kilograms of plutonium to the IAEA under its INFCIRC/549 agreement with the IAEA. The INFCIRC/549 agreement is an additional, voluntary regime adopted among the five declared nuclear weapons states plus Belgium, Japan, Switzerland, and Germany, and communicated to the IAEA, for the purpose of increasing the level of detail with which self-reports are made regarding stocks of non-military-use plutonium. In the end, it was determined that Japan had correctly declared its plutonium stocks in accordance with the procedures of one safeguards agreement with the IAEA, but had mistakenly, though innocently, underreported them in the context of yet another safeguards agreement with the IAEA. Ultimately the matter was quickly remedied by Japan through an amended declaration.[10] Incidents like this one involving Japan, in which there are accounting and reporting inaccuracies that are relatively minor, and are eventually concluded not to have involved any mishandling or diversion of nuclear material to military uses, occur fairly frequently.

In other cases, the reporting failures have been much more significant, as in the cases of Egypt (2005) and South Korea (2004). In both of these cases, the IAEA determined that the safeguarded state failed to report to the IAEA the existence and location of significant amounts of nuclear material and also failed to report design details of facilities related to them.[11] In the case of South Korea, it was revealed that uranium had been enriched to weapons grade, in experiments undeclared to the IAEA.[12] In both cases, however, the IAEA Board of Governors declined to report these instances of noncompliance with safeguards law to the U.N. Security Council, and the consensus among analysts is that in both cases the safeguarded state was not concealing a nuclear weapons program.

Of course, sometimes noncompliance with a safeguards agreement does evidence that something is seriously wrong in the safeguarded state and that there has been diversion of nuclear material from peaceful to military uses. The IAEA's determinations that North

10. Daniel H. Joyner, *Did Japan Violate Its Safeguards Obligations through Failure to Report Plutonium?*, Arms Control Law, June 18, 2014.

11. *See* Pierre Goldschmidt, *Exposing Nuclear Non-compliance*, 51 Survival 143–164 (2009).

12. Jungmin Kang et al., *South Korea's Nuclear Surprise*, 61 Bulletin of the Atomic Scientists 40–49 (2005).

Korea (1993) and Libya (2004) were respectively in noncompliance with their safeguards agreements turned out in both cases to constitute important findings that each state was in fact hiding a nuclear weapons program. And this finding by the IAEA was an important step in formally placing the issue of these programs onto the agenda of the U.N. Security Council.

So again, these various cases illustrate the fact that safeguards agreement noncompliance does not per se evidence the existence within a safeguarded state of a clandestine nuclear weapons program.[13] This is not to minimize the important role of the IAEA in monitoring and verifying safeguards agreement compliance. It is only to clarify that the entire safeguards regime—and *a fortiori* that regime when only an INFCIRC/153 agreement is in force between the IAEA and the safeguarded state—and the IAEA's role in it, is designed only to account for all of the nuclear material within a safeguarded state. The question of the implications of any particular circumstance of noncompliance with the terms of a state's safeguards agreement is not one that can be answered on an IAEA inspector's spreadsheet.

So how is safeguards noncompliance ultimately decided? And what does such a determination of safeguards noncompliance mean in a legal sense? The answer to the first question is found in the IAEA Statue, Article XII(C):

> The inspectors shall report any non-compliance to the Director General who shall thereupon transmit the report to the Board of Governors. The Board shall call upon the recipient State or States to remedy forthwith any non-compliance which it finds to have

13. *See* John Carlson, *Defining Noncompliance: NPT Safeguards Agreements*, Arms Control Today, May 2009 ("The language of Article XII.C ('compliance with . . . all . . . conditions of the . . . agreement') seems to indicate that noncompliance is a failure to observe any condition in a safeguards agreement. Nevertheless, clearly not every safeguards breach constitutes noncompliance. Otherwise, the agendas of the board and the Security Council would be taken up with safeguards cases. There is a need to distinguish serious from less serious breaches.").

> occurred. The Board shall report the non-compliance to all members and to the Security Council and General Assembly of the United Nations. In the event of failure of the recipient State or States to take fully corrective action within a reasonable time, the Board may take one or both of the following measures: direct curtailment or suspension of assistance being provided by the Agency or by a member, and call for the return of materials and equipment made available to the recipient member or group of members. The Agency may also, in accordance with article XIX, suspend any non-complying member from the exercise of the privileges and rights of membership.

Article XII(C) lays out a process for the determination of safeguards noncompliance which begins with a determination by IAEA inspectors that noncompliance has occurred. The inspectors are then to transmit this finding to the IAEA's thirty-five-state Board of Governors, which will then make its own finding regarding noncompliance. If it does find that noncompliance has occurred, the Board of Governors then communicates this finding to the U.N. General Assembly and Security Council and calls upon the safeguarded state in question to remedy the noncompliance. So, within the IAEA there are actually two decision makers regarding noncompliance—the inspectors themselves in the first instance, and ultimately the IAEA Board of Governors. It should be noted that Article XII(C) of the IAEA Statute is the only provision in that treaty addressing safeguards noncompliance. It does not provide any criteria on which either the inspectors, or the Board of Governors, are to base their determination of safeguards noncompliance.

The INFCIRC/153 CSA template, mirrored in most CSAs in force, adds a bit of flesh to this consideration by providing:

> If the Board, upon examination of relevant information reported to it by the Director General, finds that the Agency is not able to verify that there has been no diversion of nuclear material required to be safeguarded under this Agreement, to nuclear

weapons or other nuclear explosive devices, it may make the reports provided for in paragraph C of Article XII of the Statute of the Agency . . .

CSA Article 19 thus describes one situation in which the IAEA Board of Governors may find safeguards noncompliance and report the same to the U.N. Security Council. However, since all states who have concluded CSAs with the IAEA are also parties to the IAEA Statute, it would seem to make sense to read CSA Article 19 and IAEA Statute Article XII(C) together. In doing so, CSA Article 19 would appear to be essentially a lesser included basis for finding noncompliance, within the more broadly termed "any non-compliance" standard of IAEA Statute Article XII(C). So again, there are no clear, comprehensive criteria in either the IAEA Statute or the CSA to guide IAEA inspectors or the Board of Governors in making a determination of safeguards noncompliance by a safeguarded state.

Over the years, the IAEA Board of Governors has adopted its own, quite complicated taxonomy concerning how a compliance standard should be applied to each individual IAEA member state. This standard varies according to the type(s) of safeguards agreements in force between the IAEA and each safeguarded state. The IAEA's 2013 annual Safeguards Implementation Report illustrates these different standards in its summary findings:

1. One hundred and seventeen States had both comprehensive safeguards agreements and additional protocols in force:
   (a) For 63 of these States, the Secretariat found no indication of the diversion of declared nuclear material from peaceful nuclear activities and no indication of undeclared nuclear material or activities. On this basis, the Secretariat concluded that, for these States, all nuclear material remained in peaceful activities.
   (b) For 54 of these States, the Secretariat found no indication of the diversion of declared nuclear material from peaceful nuclear activities. Evaluations regarding the

absence of undeclared nuclear material and activities for each of these States remained ongoing. On this basis, the Secretariat concluded that, for these States, declared nuclear material remained in peaceful activities.

2. Safeguards activities were implemented for 55 States with comprehensive safeguards agreements in force, but without additional protocols in force. For these States, the Secretariat found no indication of the diversion of declared nuclear material from peaceful nuclear activities. On this basis, the Secretariat concluded that, for these States, declared nuclear material remained in peaceful activities.

While the Secretariat concluded that, for 2013, declared nuclear material in Iran remained in peaceful activities, it was unable to conclude that all nuclear material in Iran was in peaceful activities.

As illustrated in these findings, for states that have concluded both an INFCIRC/153 CSA and an INFCIRC/540 Additional Protocol with the IAEA, the IAEA applies two separate compliance standards: (1) Diversion of declared nuclear material from peaceful to military uses; and (2) Indication of undeclared material or activities. For those states with both a CSA and an Additional Protocol in force that have been determined to pass the test of both of these standards in a given year, the IAEA gives what it refers to as a "broader conclusion" that all nuclear material in these states remains in peaceful activities. Thus, in the excerpt above, in 2013 there were 63 states, out of the 180 total safeguarded states, which merited this "broader conclusion." However, 54 states that had both a CSA and an Additional Protocol in force with the IAEA passed only one of the two standards in this category, and thus the IAEA finds in its report only that *declared* nuclear material in those states remained in peaceful activities.

For states that only have an INFCIRC/153 CSA in force with the IAEA, the IAEA considers that it does not have the procedural tools necessary to collect sufficient information to make a "broader determination," so it has to limit itself to determining only whether declared nuclear material remains in peaceful activities. This standard is clearly stated elsewhere in the 2013 Safeguards Implementation Report, which in paragraph 17 states: "[T]he conclusion in the *Safeguards Statement* for a State with a comprehensive safeguards agreement alone relates only to the non-diversion of declared nuclear material from peaceful activities." It proceeds in paragraph 19 to explain, concerning states with only an INFCIRC/153 in force:

> In the course of its evaluation, the Agency also seeks to determine whether there is any indication of undeclared nuclear material or activities in the State which would need to be reflected in the *Safeguards Statement*. However, without the measures provided for in the *Model Additional Protocol* being implemented, the Agency is not able to provide credible assurance of the absence of undeclared nuclear material and activities for the State as a whole.

This then explains why, for states like Iran that only have an INFCIRC/153 CSA in force with the IAEA, the proper standard for determining safeguards compliance, pursuant to IAEA policy, is whether the IAEA is able to verify that declared nuclear material within the safeguarded state remains in peaceful activities.

Looking again, however, at the compliance determinations for 2013 made in the Safeguards Implementation Report, it is worth noting the following paragraph, already quoted above, specifically regarding Iran:

> While the Secretariat concluded that, for 2013, declared nuclear material in Iran remained in peaceful activities, it was unable to conclude that all nuclear material in Iran was in peaceful activities.

I will return to this matter in Chapter 5, but I wanted to note it while discussing the IAEA's application of compliance standards. Note that it is only Iran, out of the fifty-five states that had only an

INFCIRC/153 CSA in force with the IAEA during 2013, to which the IAEA applied not only the proper standard regarding declared nuclear material but also the improper—*by the IAEA's own policy, expressed in the same document*—standard regarding undeclared nuclear material. Again, I will return to that subject of improper standards in the next chapter.

For purposes of the present discussion, the important observation to take away from this review of the compliance standards created by IAEA policy, expressed in the 2013 Safeguards Implementation Report, and the compliance determinations based upon them therein, is that while there are few if any criteria in the relevant treaty sources to guide IAEA inspectors and the Board of Governors in their safeguards noncompliance determinations, the IAEA has nevertheless constructed a policy framework pursuant to which it makes such determinations. This policy framework is complex and multifaceted, applying different standards depending upon the type(s) of safeguards agreements in force between the IAEA and a safeguarded state, and at times applying different standards to states with the same profile of safeguards agreements in force.

Pierre Goldschmidt, former Deputy Director General of the IAEA and Head of the Department of Safeguards, has been quite critical of the IAEA Board of Governors' track record of inconsistency in applying its constructed noncompliance standards. In a 2009 article in the journal *Survival*, Goldschmidt is particularly critical of the IAEA's failure to formally determine that Egypt's and South Korea's actions, respectively, constituted noncompliance with their safeguards obligations, notwithstanding the significant failures of both states to accurately report concerning nuclear materials and related facilities within their territory. He writes, "It is therefore necessary for the agency to formally acknowledge that in the past some of its decisions have created potentially damaging precedents that need to be corrected to avoid any impression that the implementation of the IAEA Statute is selective."[14]

14. Pierre Goldschmidt, *Exposing Nuclear Non-compliance*, 51 Survival 143–164, at 158–159 (2009).

This perhaps begs the question, mentioned earlier, of the legal significance and implication of a finding of safeguards noncompliance by the IAEA Board of Governors. I considered this question in *Interpreting the Nuclear Nonproliferation Treaty* on pages 89–93. In summary, I concluded there that a determination by the IAEA Board of Governors that a safeguarded state is in noncompliance with its safeguards agreement should be understood to constitute a preliminary technical determination of treaty noncompliance and not *per se* as a finding of treaty breach under the law of state responsibility. As Article XII of the IAEA Statute stipulates, such a finding of noncompliance by the Board of Governors triggers reporting requirements for the IAEA, but it also marks the beginning of a diplomatic process through which the IAEA is to work with the state in question to bring its actions—which again may consist of no more than reporting or accounting errors or omissions—into full compliance with the obligations of its safeguards agreement(s). It is only if the noncompliant state fails to take corrective action within a reasonable time that the IAEA may proceed to suspend the state's assistance from the organization, or ultimately to suspend its IAEA membership and privileges, pursuant to the process detailed in Article XIX of the IAEA Statute. Pursuant to this interpretation, a determination by the IAEA Board of Governors that a state is in noncompliance with its safeguards agreement(s) is not *per se* equivalent to or constitutive of a determination of an internationally wrongful act entailing the international legal responsibility of the safeguarded state.

This is not to say that the actions of a safeguarded state that are found by the Board of Governors to be in noncompliance with that state's safeguards obligation cannot additionally constitute actions that do breach the relevant treaty(ies), and therefore do constitute an internationally wrongful act entailing that state's responsibility under general international law. Rather, the discrete point I am making here is that IAEA Board of Governors' findings of noncompliance pursuant to Article XII(C) of the IAEA Statute do not *per se* or necessarily imply that the safeguarded state in question is in formal breach of its treaty obligations, entailing its state responsibility.

In this context, the IAEA regime for noncompliance determination is in many ways analogous to treaty implementation supervisory procedures established under other treaty frameworks.[15] It most closely resembles the noncompliance procedure developed under the 1987 Montreal Protocol on Substances that Deplete the Ozone Layer.[16] The Montreal Protocol's noncompliance procedure grew out of Article 8 of the Montreal Protocol, which states simply that the parties "shall consider and approve procedures and institutional mechanisms for determining non-compliance with the provisions of this Protocol and for treatment of Parties found to be in non-compliance." Eventually, a noncompliance procedure was adopted which allows for situations of alleged noncompliance with the provisions of the Montreal Protocol to be investigated by an Implementation Committee of experts, which then provides a report and recommendations to the plenary Meeting of the Parties.

Concerning the legal implications of the findings of the various treaty-based organs involved in the Montreal Protocol's noncompliance procedure (NCP), Martti Koskenniemi has observed:

> The *travaux preparatoires* of the NCP as well as the composition and functions of the Implementation Committee and, *a fortiori*, the Meeting of the Parties, make it clear that neither can, or is expected to, work as a judicial body, assessing the performance of the parties' obligations with a view of determining whether or not there has been a wrongful act triggering state responsibility. A dispute about whether some particular type of non-performance is a wrongful act is, by its very nature, a dispute about the interpretation or application of the treaty and

15. *See, e.g.*, the Trade Policy Review Mechanism established by the World Trade Organization Treaty, and the Human Rights Committee, which monitors the implementation of the International Covenant on Civil and Political Rights.

16. *See generally* Tim Stephens, International Courts and Environmental Protection 82–83 (2009).

> capable of being resolved only within the procedures of Article 11 of the Vienna Ozone Convention. Moreover, the question of wrongfulness is one of general international law, and not a question that can be solved, or indeed even approached, from within the special regime of the Vienna Ozone Convention and the Protocol at all.[17]

Koskenniemi's analysis here can be applied equally to the context of the IAEA, in that there is certainly no evidence, either in the provisions of the IAEA Statute or in its *travaux preparatoires*, that the thirty-five-state-member IAEA Board of Governors was intended to be endowed by the parties to the IAEA Statute with judicial functions or authorities. And just as Koskenniemi points to Article 11 of the Vienna Ozone Convention as providing the proper procedural forum for disputes concerning the interpretation or application of the treaty and its protocols, so Article XVII of the IAEA Statute similarly provides that "[a]ny question or dispute concerning the interpretation or application of this Statute which is not settled by negotiation shall be referred to the International Court of Justice in conformity with the Statute of the Court, unless the parties concerned agree on another mode of settlement." Thus, analogous to the context of the Montreal Protocol noncompliance procedure, a determination by the IAEA Board of Governors that a safeguarded state is in noncompliance with its safeguards agreement obligations does not *per se* constitute a determination of treaty breach, but is rather better interpreted as constituting a preliminary technical finding of treaty noncompliance, which results

17. Martti Koskenniemi, *Breach of Treaty or Non-Compliance? Reflections on the Enforcement of the Montreal Protocol*, 3 YEARBOOK OF INTERNATIONAL ENVIRONMENTAL LAW 123–162, at 144 (1992). For similar scholarly arguments in the context of the International Monetary Fund, *see* F. A. Mann, *The "Interpretation" of the Constitutions of International Financial Organizations*, 1968–1969 BRITISH YEARBOOK OF INTERNATIONAL LAW.

in explicitly detailed rights and responsibilities for the IAEA under Article XII of its Statute.

This conclusion is important for a number of reasons. First, it allows us to properly take into account the wide range of acts and omissions by a safeguarded state, of varying degrees of seriousness and significance to the object and purpose of the relevant safeguards agreement(s), that may be determined by the IAEA Board of Governors to constitute noncompliance. And further to understand that not all noncompliance determinations are of equal significance and should not be considered of equal import. This is particularly important as, again, the standards against which the IAEA Board of Governors measures safeguards compliance are not essentially based in either the IAEA Statute or in safeguards agreements, but have rather been constructed by the Board of Governors and the Secretariat as a matter of institutional policy, with little formal legal foundation.

It is also an important conclusion in light of the claims made by some observers that a finding of noncompliance by the IAEA Board of Governors serves to shift the burden of proof to the safeguarded state in question, to prove to the IAEA's satisfaction that all nuclear material within its borders is in exclusively peaceful use.[18] Such an assertion is reminiscent of a claim that a state's international responsibility has been triggered by its commission of an internationally wrongful act and that this responsibility entails the legal consequences outlined in Part II of the International Law Commission's Draft Articles on State Responsibility. The conclusion that IAEA Board of Governors' determinations of noncompliance do not constitute a *per se* determination of an internationally wrongful act serves to discredit this notion.

18. *See* John Carlson, *Defining Noncompliance: NPT Safeguards Agreements*, Arms Control Today, May 2009 ("In these circumstances, the onus is then on the state to show that nonpeaceful purposes are not intended. It can attempt to do this through full cooperation with and transparency to the IAEA.").

III. COMPLIANCE WITH SUBSIDIARY ARRANGEMENTS

I noted above that the INFCIRC/153 comprehensive safeguards agreement is to be supplemented by the separate conclusion of subsidiary arrangements between the IAEA and the safeguarded state. It is in this separate set of subsidiary arrangements that the operating modalities of the IAEA's various material accountancy activities, to be conducted within the territory of the safeguarded state, are detailed through agreement between the parties. The conclusion of subsidiary arrangements is provided for in Articles 39 and 40 of Iran's CSA with the IAEA:

> **Article 39**
> The Government of Iran and the Agency shall make Subsidiary Arrangements which shall specify in detail, to the extent necessary to permit the Agency to fulfil its responsibilities under this Agreement in an effective and efficient manner, how the procedures laid down in this Agreement are to be applied. The Subsidiary Arrangements may be extended or changed by agreement between the Government of Iran and the Agency without amendment of this Agreement.
>
> **Article 40**
> The Subsidiary Arrangements shall enter into force at the same time as, or as soon as possible after, the entry into force of this Agreement. The Government of Iran and the Agency shall make every effort to achieve their entry into force within ninety days of the entry into force of this Agreement; an extension of that period shall require agreement between the Government of Iran and the Agency. The Government of Iran shall provide the Agency promptly with the information required for completing the Subsidiary Arrangements.

Provisions regarding the content of the subsidiary arrangements are then scattered throughout the CSA. They stipulate that in the subsidiary arrangements are to be agreed, *inter alia*, strategic points within declared nuclear facilities for the IAEA to conduct routine inspections, frequency and other details concerning those routine inspections, and the form of reports that are to be exchanged between Iran and the IAEA. The subsidiary arrangements also specify when reports are to be made to the IAEA by Iran, including on the subject of new nuclear facilities or modifications to existing facilities.

Exactly what the legal character of these subsidiary arrangements is, is an interesting question. In Articles 39 and 40 of Iran's CSA, quoted above, the CSA provides that Iran and the IAEA shall "make subsidiary arrangements." It's not clear from this phrase, or from the rest of the text of Articles 39 and 40, whether this separate agreement on subsidiary arrangements is intended or conceived by the parties to the CSA to comprise yet an additional treaty relationship between the parties, or rather to comprise simply a nonbinding agreement on modalities, best understood from a legal perspective as a legally nonbinding memorandum of understanding.

While descriptive terminology is not *per se* dispositive of legal character, the term "arrangements" is not one commonly employed to denote a treaty relationship. It is more reminiscent of terms associated with legally nonbinding international accords, such as the Nuclear Suppliers Group "guidelines," the Basel I and II "standards" issued by the Basel Committee on Banking Supervision, or the 1975 Helsinki Final "Act" of the Conference on Security and Cooperation in Europe.

The dispositive test for determining whether an international agreement is a legally binding treaty is of course found in Articles 11–17 of the 1969 Vienna Convention on the Law of Treaties. Essentially, this test boils down to the intent of the parties. If the parties to an agreement intend that agreement to constitute a legally binding treaty, and if that intention is manifest in the terms of the agreement and through the forms and procedures for concluding the agreement, then the agreement is legally binding. However, if that intent cannot be found to be manifest in the agreement's terms, or in the forms of concluding the agreement, the agreement is not legally binding and is simply a political commitment, accord, or understanding between the parties.

Looking to the forms for concluding subsidiary arrangements, no provision is made in the CSA for ratification or approval of subsidiary arrangements by domestic political authorities. Only the agreement of the two parties is mentioned. This is in contrast to the provisions for entry into force of the CSA itself, which are provided in detail in Article 25, and which do reference satisfaction of national constitutional requirements. While it is of course possible for a legally binding treaty to come into being through agreement of the parties alone, without resort to domestic constitutional approval, this is a relative rarity in international practice. Particularly on a subject as sensitive as nuclear energy. More significantly, the absence in the CSA text of any provision regarding procedures for the manner of entry into force of subsidiary arrangements does not appear consistent with common international practice regarding the conclusion of legally binding treaties.

Article 39 of the CSA further provides: "The Subsidiary Arrangements may be extended or changed by agreement between the Government of Iran and the Agency without amendment of this Agreement." The fact that the parties are able to change the content of the subsidiary arrangements without resort to a formal amendment procedure, again in contrast to the CSA itself, which specifies such a formal amendment procedure in Article 24, also appears to belie the idea that the subsidiary arrangements themselves are intended to be legally binding as a separate treaty.

Of course, the primary source of information necessary to answer the question of whether subsidiary arrangements are intended by the parties to constitute a legally binding treaty relationship is the text of the subsidiary arrangements themselves. Unfortunately, however, the text of subsidiary arrangements, and the communications between states and the IAEA concerning their conclusion, are not typically publicly available documents but are kept closely confidential by both state parties and the IAEA. Thus, it is not possible to examine the text of Iran's subsidiary arrangements or the correspondence between Iran and the IAEA concerning their conclusion.

Fortunately, however, template subsidiary arrangements are accessible and by reference to these one can observe the form that subsidiary arrangements typically take. These templates similarly make no reference to procedures for formal entry into force. They simply state:

> These Subsidiary Arrangements give effect to Article ___ of the Agreement between ________ and the International Atomic Energy Agency (hereinafter "the Agency") for the application of safeguards in connection with the Treaty on the Non-Proliferation of Nuclear Weapons.

The subsidiary arrangements template describes the contents of the subsidiary arrangements (again with spaces left for the name of the state party) as follows:

> These Subsidiary Arrangements consist of:
>
> (a) A general Part applicable to all peaceful nuclear activities in ________ which also contains the substance of various communications to be made between ________ and the Agency, of other relevant documents, the procedures to be followed and the time limits for various actions; and
> (b) A separate Attachment for each facility and each material balance area outside facilities in ________.

The subsidiary arrangements template does provide some additional insight on amendment procedures:

> These Subsidiary Arrangements may be amended or supplemented by exchange of notes between ________ and the Agency.

The balance of the subsidiary arrangements template contains pages of agreed procedures for communication between the IAEA and the safeguarded state, presented in a tabular format, as well as examples of templates for forms to be used by the state party in making reports to the IAEA and by the IAEA in connection with inspections and inspectors (e.g., a form for requesting an inspector's visa for entry).

On balance, having reviewed the provisions in the CSA relating to the conclusion of subsidiary arrangements, and having reviewed the content requirements for subsidiary arrangements both in the CSA text and in the text of a subsidiary arrangements template, I think that the most persuasive conclusion is that subsidiary arrangements agreed between the IAEA and a safeguarded state, pursuant to an INFCIRC/153 CSA, are intended by the parties to constitute legally nonbinding memoranda of understanding stipulating the modalities for implementation of the provisions of the CSA, and not to constitute a separate treaty relationship between the parties.

This conclusion is supported by Mohammed Shaker, whose 1980 two-volume treatise on the negotiating history of the NPT is widely considered to be the most authoritative record of the NPT's *travaux preparatoires*. In Volume II of his treatise he makes the following observation specifically regarding safeguards agreement subsidiary arrangements:

> A final word has to be said here on the "Subsidiary Arrangements" as an attached document to the safeguards agreement, containing the detailed procedures and technicalities left open in the agreement itself. Contrary to previous practice, the Subsidiary Arrangements do not contain any rights or obligations additional to those in the safeguards agreement, but consist of a series of tables, information sheets, report forms, etc., and indicate the mechanism for keeping them up to date.[19]

19. Mohamed Shaker, The Nuclear Non-proliferation Treaty: Origin and Implementation 1959–1979, Vol. 2, at 759 (1980).

Shaker's description of the subsidiary arrangements template is exactly accurate, and his opinion concerning the lack of formal legal bindingness of these subsidiary arrangements is in harmony with my conclusion herein.

This conclusion also makes sense from a system perspective. Legally nonbinding international agreements are of course commonplace in international diplomatic practice. And there is a well-developed scholarly literature explaining why such politically binding, yet legally nonbinding, agreements are often preferable to states over formal treaties, depending largely upon the issue area being addressed.[20] According to this literature, in issue areas where concerns regarding political sensitivity and confidentiality of information are high, where high levels of specificity and detail are required, and where frequent need for amendment due to technological change or other circumstantial dynamics is anticipated, legally nonbinding forms of agreement are likely to be preferable in order to avoid the difficulties of having to secure approval by national political bodies for both original and amended texts. These concerns are all present in the context of the detailed modalities of implementation of safeguards on nuclear facilities and nuclear material within the territory of a safeguarded state.

A separate example taken from the nuclear nonproliferation issue area of such a legally nonbinding, yet important, politically binding international agreement, established for the purpose of implementing treaty obligations, may be found in the Nuclear Suppliers Group, mentioned earlier. The NSG is founded upon a set of guidelines and a trigger list of items of proliferation concern.[21] The NSG was conceived

20. *See* Charles Lipson, *Why Are Some International Agreements Informal?*, 45 INT'L ORG. 495, 507 (1991); George W. Downs et al., *Is the Good News About Compliance Good News About Cooperation?*, 50 INT'L ORG. (1996); Judith Goldstein & Lisa L. Martin, *Legalization, Trade Liberalization and Domestic Politics: A Cautionary Note*, 54 INT'L ORG. 603 (2000); Joel Trachtman, *Bananas, Direct Effect and Compliance*, 10 EUROPEAN J. INT'L L. 655 (1999); Kenneth Abbot et al., *The Concept of Legalization*, 54 INT'L ORG. 401 (2000); Kenneth Abbot & Duncan Snidal, *Hard and Soft Law in International Governance*, 54 INT'L ORG. 421 (2000).

21. *See* Daniel H. Joyner, *Restructuring the Multilateral Export Control Regime System*, 9 J. CONFLICT & SECURITY L. (Oxford University Press 2004); Daniel H.

of originally as a forum through which the export control provisions of NPT Article III could be given more specificity and implemented among supplier states of proliferation-sensitive materials.[22] Similar concerns to those present in the safeguards subsidiary arrangements context, regarding a need for specificity and detail, technological change, and the requirement of regular amendment of normative sources, were at the root of the NSG framers' choice to create and maintain the NSG's guidelines as legally nonbinding rules, nevertheless expressing important political commitments. Thus, NSG participating states simply declare their adherence to the guidelines of the regime in an express yet legally nonbinding manner. Admittance of new participant states and amendments to the guidelines must be approved by consensus among NSG participating states, through similarly legally nonbinding diplomatic accord. Actions of participating states that are not compliant with NSG guidelines are typically expressed to be of significant concern to other participants, but are never characterized as violations of law.[23]

Joyner, *The Nuclear Suppliers Group: History and Functioning*, INT'L TRADE L. & REG. 11(2), 33–42 (Sweet & Maxwell 2005).

22. *See* Daniel H. Joyner, *The Nuclear Suppliers Group: History and Functioning*, INT'L TRADE L. & REG. 11(2), 33–42 (Sweet & Maxwell 2005).

23. It was the full-scope safeguards commitment in the NSG guidelines that was the basis for harsh criticism by the United States of Russia's 2001 transfer of low-enriched uranium to the Terapur reactor in India. At a special meeting in December 2000, upon news of the proposed transfer, thirty-two of thirty-four NSG members declared that the shipment would be inconsistent with Russia's commitments under the NSG guidelines. On February 16, 2001, the U.S. State Department issued the following condemnation of the Russian shipments: "We deeply regret that the Russian Federation has shipped nuclear fuel to the Terapur power reactors in India in violation of Russia's nonproliferation commitments. As a member of the 39-nation Nuclear Suppliers Group, Russia is committed not to engage in nuclear cooperation with any country that does not have comprehensive International Atomic Energy Agency safeguards on all its nuclear facilities . . . At a December 2000 meeting of the Nuclear Suppliers Group, the overwhelming majority of the members expressed their strong concerns about Russia's planned shipment of nuclear fuel to India, which they regarded as inconsistent with Russia's commitments. We join other nuclear suppliers in calling on Russia to cancel this supply arrangement and live up to its nonproliferation commitments. Russia's disregard of its Nuclear Supplier Group commitments, together with its sensitive nuclear assistance to Iran, raises serious questions about Russia's support for the goal of preventing nuclear proliferation." (Philip T. Reeker, U.S. Department of State, Office of the Spokesman, Feb. 16, 2001).

Notwithstanding its legal informality, the NSG is generally considered to play an important role in the nuclear nonproliferation normative architecture, by providing a forum for harmonizing national laws and policies of participating states regarding export controls of nuclear proliferation-sensitive items and technologies. The example of the NSG evidences the fact that very important issues of high international security sensitivity, including issues of nuclear nonproliferation, are sometimes addressed by legally nonbinding international agreement, counter to the arguments of some observers.[24]

Thus, from a system perspective it makes perfect sense for the general obligations of a safeguards agreement, which is itself a legally binding treaty, to be implemented by the parties to the treaty through a separate set of legally nonbinding subsidiary arrangements, which contain the detailed procedures and forms which are to order the working relationship of the parties in carrying out their various obligations under the treaty. I think that this is exactly how IAEA safeguards subsidiary arrangements should be understood.

So why is this question of the legal character of subsidiary arrangements important? It is important in its implications for the concept of compliance. Though there is no hierarchy in the sources of international law (i.e., as between treaties, custom, and general principles of law), the entire framework of state responsibility in international law applies only to formally binding legal obligations and not to commitments of an exclusively political nature. These latter commitments, sometimes referred to in scholarly literature as "soft law," play an important role in international relations, as the example of the NSG above demonstrates. But it is necessary to keep separate the concept of compliance with formal legal obligations from the concept of compliance with legally nonbinding political commitments. The former belongs to the well-developed frameworks of state responsibility in international law. The latter does not.

24. *For example*, Christopher Ford's assertions in his paper, *Iran, Nonproliferation, and the IAEA: A Legal History*, Hudson Institute, Nov., 2012.

IV. APPLICATION TO THE IRAN CASE

Having established an understanding of the relevant legal sources, their nature and substance, and an understanding of the complex nature of the concept of compliance in the context of IAEA safeguards agreements and related subsidiary arrangements, I will now proceed to apply these sources of law to the facts of the Iran case, in order to examine two discrete questions of disputed legal compliance. The first is whether Iran was in violation of its safeguards obligations in 2003, when it was declared to be in noncompliance with its safeguards agreement by the IAEA Director General. The second question concerns Iran's alleged failures to timely declare design and other information concerning nuclear facilities to the IAEA, which have been argued by some to constitute separate and additional instances of safeguards obligation violations.

A. Was Iran in Violation of Its Safeguards Obligations in 2003?

As detailed in Chapter 1, on November 10, 2003, IAEA Director General Mohamed ElBaradei submitted a report (GOV/2003/75) to the IAEA Board of Governors, detailing recent discoveries IAEA inspectors had made concerning Iran's nuclear program. In paragraph 47 the report stated:

> Based on all information currently available to the Agency, it is clear that Iran has failed in a number of instances over an extended period of time to meet its obligations under its Safeguards Agreement with respect to the reporting of nuclear material and its processing and use, as well as the declaration of facilities where such material has been processed and stored.

Shortly thereafter, on November 26, 2003, the IAEA Board of Governors issued a resolution (GOV/2003/81) in which it responded to the Director General's report, stating that it "[s]trongly deplores Iran's past failures and breaches of its obligation to comply with the provisions of its Safeguards Agreement."

The "failures and breaches" of Iran's safeguard obligations to which the Director General and the Board of Governors referred in these documents, which together comprised the IAEA's determination that Iran was indeed in noncompliance with its safeguards agreement with the Agency, related to Iran's failure to declare to the IAEA the existence, transfer, and facility-specific location of nuclear materials in a number of instances over the preceding decade, its failure to declare experiments conducted using those nuclear materials, and its failure to declare design details of certain facilities related to nuclear materials.[25] As noted in Chapter 1, these instances included *inter alia* the following:

- Iran's failure in 1991 to declare the importation from China of 1.8 tons (0.13 effective kg) of natural uranium compounds (UF4, UF6, and UO2), their transfer for further processing, their use in experiments to test its conversion processes, as well as the facilities in which these materials were kept;
- Iran's additional undeclared use in 1999 and 2002 of a small amount of its imported UF6 in the P1 centrifuges at the Kalaye Electric Company centrifuge workshop;
- Undeclared experiments carried out between 1989 and 1993 that produced Polonium-210, a highly radioactive but unstable material with a short half-life;
- Iran's failure in 1994 to declare the importation of 50 kg of natural uranium metal; 8 kg of which were used at the Tehran Nuclear Research Center in experiments involving atomic vapor laser isotope separation;
- Undeclared experiments carried out by Iran between 1988 and 1993 involving plutonium separation using UO2.

25. As a formal matter, Resolution GOV/2003/81 is probably best understood only as the Board of Governors' recognition of the Director General's report of Iran's safeguard agreement noncompliance in GOV/2003/75, and not as the Board of

There is no question that the IAEA Director General and the IAEA Board of Governors were correct in their respective determinations that the delineated failures by Iran to report nuclear material and related experiments to the IAEA constituted instances of noncompliance with Iran's safeguards agreement. These and other acts and omissions by Iran documented by the IAEA in 2003, and others that came to light in subsequent years prior to 2008, were clearly in disharmony with the provisions of Iran's comprehensive safeguards agreement, requiring it to declare to the IAEA the amounts and types of nuclear materials on its territory, transfers of nuclear material into its territory, facilities in which nuclear materials are present, and experiments conducted involving nuclear material on its territory.

I spent a considerable amount of time above distinguishing between IAEA findings of safeguards agreement noncompliance, on the one hand, and the determination that an internationally wrongful act has occurred entailing the responsibility of the safeguarded state—i.e., safeguards treaty breach—on the other. So it remains to be considered whether these documented instances of safeguards agreement noncompliance amount to a formal breach by Iran of its comprehensive safeguards agreement with the IAEA. This is a separate and considerably more complicated question.

Treaty breach is a subject addressed in international law in both the law of state responsibility and the law of treaties. The law of state responsibility addresses the legal implications of the violation of a primary international legal obligation by the international legal person subject to the obligation. The question of what specific acts or omissions constitute treaty breach is, quite intentionally, not comprehensively addressed in the law of state responsibility but is largely left to a case specific analysis of the primary rules of the treaty concerned.[26]

Governors' own explicit finding of Iran's noncompliance. A number of states in the Board of Governors desired not to involve the U.N. Security Council at this point in 2003 and so waited to explicitly determine Iran's safeguards noncompliance until September 24, 2005 in Resolution GOV/2005/77.

26. *See* James Crawford, State Responsibility: The General Part 216–217 (2013).

The law of treaties, on the other hand, addresses treaty breach only in the specific context of Article 60 of the Vienna Convention on the Law of Treaties, which provides that a treaty may be terminated or suspended in the event of a "material breach" of the treaty.

There is a rich scholarly literature, and some case law, examining questions on this topic, such as: What is the distinction between a breach of a treaty and a material breach of a treaty? Is the gravity or significance of the breach a relevant factor in determining the materiality of the breach?[27] While some conclusions can be drawn from treaty interpretation, case law, and scholarly writing, in the end the question of whether state conduct in a particular case constitutes treaty breach, either material or nonmaterial, is one that will be made by a court or other dispute settlement mechanism, based upon a fact-specific analysis.

In that context, I think it is appropriate, as a normative matter, to employ the general principle of *de minimis non curat lex* in some specific treaty contexts, and in specific cases, in order to establish a threshold of gravity of noncompliance below which treaty noncompliance will not be considered formal treaty breach. The *de minimis* principle itself is of course of long pedigree, originating in Roman law, and is present in both or either of its procedural and substantive forms in most developed domestic legal systems.[28] It should, in my opinion, be considered a "general principle of law recognized by civilized nations," in the words of Article 38(1) of the Statute of the International Court of Justice.[29]

27. *See, e.g.*, Christine Chinkin, *Nonperformance of International Agreements*, 17 Texas Int'l L.J. 387–432 (1982).

28. *See* Janja Hojnik, *De Minimis Rule within the EU Internal Market Freedoms: Towards a More Mature and Legitimate Market?*, 6 European J. Legal Studies 26–28 (Spring/Summer 2013).

29. The principle was mentioned by Judge Ad Hoc Van Den Wyngaert in her dissenting opinion in the *Arrest Warrant* case before the International Court of Justice: "I also believe, assuming again that there has been an infringement of an international obligation by Belgium, that the declaratory part of the Judgment should have sufficed as reparation for the moral injury suffered by Congo. If there was an act constituting an infringement, which I do not believe exists (a Belgian arrest warrant that was not

Such a *de minimis* threshold for compliance analysis would appear particularly appropriate in contexts such as that of IAEA safeguards agreements, in which the obligations of the safeguarded state are highly detailed, technical, and comprehensive, requiring frequent reporting of exacting accuracy regarding a range of materials and facilities, and where as previously observed minor instances of noncompliance through acts or omissions by states is common.

This *de minimis* principle and the other principles of international law established in the law of state responsibility and in the law of treaties concerning treaty breach serve to distinguish the concept of formal safeguards treaty breach from the concept of safeguards treaty noncompliance as determined by IAEA inspectors and the IAEA Board of Governors.

However, in the specific case of Iran's nuclear program, the various failures by Iran to declare the existence and location of nuclear materials, and Iran's several failures to declare experiments conducted using those nuclear materials, documented by the IAEA in 2003 and found by the IAEA to constitute safeguards agreement noncompliance, almost certainly did additionally constitute a formal breach by Iran of its comprehensive safeguards agreement with the IAEA. This conclusion is supported by the principle reflected in Article 15 of the International Law Commission's Draft Articles on State Responsibility, which provides:

> The breach of an international obligation by a State through a series of actions or omissions defined in aggregate as wrongful occurs when the action or omission occurs which, taken with the other actions or omissions, is sufficient to constitute the wrongful act.

contrary to customary international law and that was moreover never enforced), it was trivial in comparison with the Congo's failure to comply with its obligation under Article 146 of the IV Geneva Convention (investigating and prosecuting charges of war crimes and crimes against humanity committed on its territory). The Congo did not come to the International Court with clean hands, and its Application should have been rejected. De minimis non curat lex." 2002 ICJ 3, 185. *See also, e.g.*, YORAM DINSTEIN, WAR AGGRESSION AND SELF-DEFENCE 174 (3rd ed., 2001).

One application of this principle, which I think is appropriate in this context, is that it is possible for an internationally wrongful act to comprise a series of individual actions which, while not wrongful in themselves, when taken together as a practice cumulatively produce a wrongful act. I think that, while each individual noncompliant act or omission by Iran with the provisions of its safeguards agreement pre-2003 may be arguable with regard to its character as a breach of Iran's safeguards agreement—i.e., each instance would need to be evaluated individually to determine whether or not it rose above a *de minimis* threshold of noncompliance—nevertheless, taken together cumulatively, as an interconnected practice, they almost certainly did comprise a treaty breach as a composite internationally wrongful act.

Accordingly, pursuant to the law of state responsibility, Iran was obligated to cease the violative conduct and to remedy the breach through reparation. Iran's cooperation with the IAEA—its bilateral treaty partner—between 2003, when the breach was identified, and 2008 should be seen as Iran's undertaking to do just that. As described in Chapter 1, between 2003 and 2008 Iran did cooperate with the IAEA's inspectors in fully declaring and submitting to inspection and safeguards accounting the various materials and facilities which were the subject of the "failures and breaches" the IAEA had identified in 2003. This process culminated in IAEA Director General ElBaradei's February 22, 2008, report to the Board of Governors in which he concluded that all declared nuclear material in Iran was in peaceful use and that all prior concerns the IAEA had registered involving nuclear materials and related facilities in Iran had been resolved through dialogue with Iranian authorities.

With regard to Iran's breach of its safeguards agreement, therefore, the IAEA's November 10, 2003, report and its February 22, 2008, report can essentially be seen as bookends, marking respectively the identification of the violative conduct and beginning of the period of Iran's duty of reparation and then the eventual end of the period of Iran's duty of reparation, brought about through the intervening process of cooperation between Iran and the IAEA, resulting in Iran's full declaration of subject nuclear materials and facilities and their submission to Agency safeguards. As of the IAEA's February 22, 2008, report, therefore, Iran's international legal responsibility for the internationally wrongful act it had committed prior to 2003 ceased.

It is important to be clear on this point. After the IAEA's February 22, 2008, report there have been no continuing violations committed by Iran regarding nuclear materials within Iran, and ever since that time the IAEA has consistently found that all declared nuclear materials and related facilities in Iran are properly under IAEA safeguards and are in exclusively peaceful use.

Since 2008, the only continuing, unresolved concerns identified by the IAEA have not been issues involving nuclear materials, but rather relate to the question of possible past military dimensions to Iran's nuclear program—i.e., allegations that Iran has engaged in research and development of a nuclear explosive device. These concerns were considered previously in Chapter 2 and will be further considered in Chapter 5.

B. Did Iran Violate Its Safeguards Obligations through Failure to Make Timely Declarations Regarding Nuclear Facilities?

Among the reporting obligations for a safeguarded state pursuant to an INFCIRC/153 safeguards agreement with the IAEA is the obligation to report design and other details regarding facilities in which nuclear materials are stored or used. This applies to both facilities existing at the time the safeguards agreement enters into force and to any facilities constructed after that date, i.e., new facilities. Article 42 of Iran's CSA with the IAEA provides the following:

> Pursuant to Article 8, design information in respect of existing facilities shall be provided to the Agency during the discussion of the Subsidiary Arrangements. The time limits for the provision of design information in respect of the new facilities shall be specified in the Subsidiary Arrangements and such information

> shall be provided as early as possible before nuclear material is introduced into a new facility.

Article 42 thus provides that the IAEA and Iran will separately agree in subsidiary arrangements on the modalities of declarations concerning new facilities, including on the timing of those declarations. However, it does stipulate that such information shall be provided to the IAEA "as early as possible before nuclear material is introduced into the new facility." This stipulation is the only provision in the actual text of the CSA itself regarding a time or point by which design information on, and thereby the existence of, a new facility must be declared to the IAEA.

The IAEA and Iran did subsequently agree in subsidiary arrangements on an even more specific standard concerning when design details on new facilities should be reported. On February 12, 1976, the IAEA and Iran agreed on subsidiary arrangements which in its most relevant provision, Section 3.1 of the tabulated stipulations, provided that preliminary design information on a new nuclear facility should be reported by Iran to the IAEA "not later than 180 days before the introduction of nuclear material" into the facility. This is sometimes referred to as the "Code 3.1" standard for provision of design information on new facilities.

On February 26, 2003, some twenty-seven years later, Iran sent a letter to the IAEA in which it agreed to modify the Code 3.1 provision of its subsidiary arrangements, in harmony with a decision of the IAEA Board of Governors regarding early provision of design information, which had been taken by the Board on April 1, 1992.[30] This "modified Code 3.1" standard, which had been approved by the Board of Governors and to which Iran agreed in its letter of February 26, 2003, stipulated that preliminary design information on new nuclear facilities must be reported to the IAEA "[a]s soon as the decision to construct or to authorize construction has been taken, whichever is earlier."

30. Document GOV/2554/Att.2/Rev.2.

However, following the IAEA Board of Governors' referral of Iran to the U.N. Security Council in 2006, and immediately after the Security Council adopted Resolution 1747 on March 14, 2007, Iran sent another letter to the IAEA on March 29, 2007, in which it stated that it was suspending its application of the modified Code 3.1 standard on provision of preliminary design information and reverting to the original Code 3.1 standard found in its February 12, 1976, subsidiary arrangements agreement with the IAEA. In a letter dated March 30, 2007, the IAEA responded to Iran's letter of the previous day, stating that Iran's decision to revert to the original Code 3.1 standard was contrary to the Board of Governors' decision of 1992 and urging Iran to continue adherence to the modified Code 3.1 standard.

This is the normative context in which allegations have been made by both the IAEA and Western governments that Iran violated its safeguards obligations by its failure to timely provide design information, i.e., report the existence of, several nuclear-purposed facilities constructed over the past two decades. Specifically, these are the uranium enrichment facility at Natanz and the heavy water reactor at Arak, the existence of both of which was revealed in 2002, and also the uranium enrichment facility at Fordow, which was reported by Iran to the IAEA in 2009.

At this point in the analysis, I want to return to an observation I made above, which is that the only provision in the actual text of Iran's comprehensive safeguards treaty with the IAEA regarding a time or point by which design information on a new facility must be declared to the IAEA, is contained in Article 42 and stipulates that such information shall be provided by Iran to the IAEA "as early as possible before nuclear material is introduced into the new facility." Article 42 further provides that a more specific agreement on this subject will be included in the subsidiary arrangements to be separately negotiated between the parties, and as noted above these subsidiary arrangements were indeed subsequently agreed.

However, it will be recalled that I concluded above that subsidiary arrangements agreed between the IAEA and a safeguarded state pursuant to an INFCIRC/153 CSA, as in the case of Iran, are intended by the parties to constitute legally nonbinding memoranda of understanding stipulating the modalities for implementation of the provisions of the CSA and not to constitute a separate treaty relationship between the parties. Thus, I concluded that while subsidiary arrangements between the IAEA and a safeguarded state are important political commitments between the parties, they do not comprise legally binding obligations.

The issue of provision of design information on new nuclear facilities brings this distinction into sharp relief. According to this distinction, the standard stipulated in the text of Article 42 of Iran's CSA itself is the only legally binding standard applicable between Iran and the IAEA on this issue. The more specific stipulations of agreement subsequently made between Iran and the IAEA in subsidiary arrangements, i.e., the various Code 3.1 formulas reviewed above, while representing important political commitments between the parties on the modalities of implementing Article 42 of the CSA, do not comprise legally binding obligations.

This conclusion has a direct bearing on the correct legal analysis of the question posed in this section, i.e., whether Iran violated its safeguards obligations through its failure to timely declare design and other information regarding new nuclear facilities, with specific reference to the Natanz, Arak, and Fordow facilities.

Applying the Article 42 standard as the only legally binding standard to the facts of these incidents of construction of new nuclear facilities, it will be observed that there is no disagreement between the parties regarding the fact that Iran did provide design and all other requisite information to the IAEA on these facilities prior to the introduction of nuclear materials into them. No allegation has been made that nuclear materials were introduced into any of these facilities prior to their declaration to the IAEA. Therefore, as a formal legal matter, the answer to the question posed in this section must be in the negative, i.e., that Iran did not violate its safeguards obligations through any failure to timely declare these facilities to the IAEA.

If this question were to be amended to include within its inquiry the issue of whether either Iran or the IAEA failed to comply with their respective political commitments undertaken in the context of the subsidiary arrangements agreed, and arguably subsequently amended, between the two parties, such an analysis could of course be undertaken. But again I would stress that this would not be a formal legal analysis, but rather simply an analysis of compliance with political commitments made between the parties, which would not carry with it implications for the legal responsibility of either party.

With that understanding in place, I will at this point, then, engage in this separate analysis briefly, for the sake of thoroughness and because it has been widely debated.[31] As noted above, there is no disagreement that the subsidiary arrangements applicable between Iran and the IAEA from February 12, 1976, until February 26, 2003, contained the original Code 3.1 standard, which stipulated that preliminary design information be provided to the IAEA on a new nuclear facility "not later than 180 days before the introduction of nuclear material" into the facility. As described in Chapter 1, the Natanz and Arak facilities were discovered by the IAEA in 2002, first through reports from an Iranian dissident political group, and then confirmed through satellite photos taken of the facilities, both of which were still under construction at the time. Neither facility was functional at that time, and no evidence has ever been produced that Iran had introduced nuclear material into either facility before their discovery and Iran's subsequent declaration of design and other information on the facilities to the IAEA.

Looked at through a holistic lens, the IAEA's shock and sense of outrage that these facilities had been planned and partially constructed by Iran without having been declared to the IAEA is certainly understandable. And it is unclear to this day precisely when Iran planned to divulge the existence of these facilities to the IAEA. So again, the reaction of the IAEA and of Western governments criticizing what could reasonably be perceived as the unjustifiably

31. *See, e.g.*, James Acton, *Iran Violated International Obligations on Qom Facility*, Carnegie Endowment Proliferation Analysis (Sept. 25, 2009), http://carnegieendowment.org/2009/09/25/iran-violated-international-obligations-on-qom-facility.

clandestine nature of Iran's actions regarding these facilities is understandable.

This being said, however, Iranian officials have pointed to the long history of distrust between Iran and the IAEA, and between Iran and Western governments, as a factor distinguishing Iran from other non-nuclear-weapon states parties to the NPT and as comprising Iran's motivation for keeping details of its nuclear program confidential until required by legal obligation to disclose them. These sources of distrust, of course, go all the way back to the CIA-led overthrow of Iranian Prime Minister Mohammed Mossadegh in 1953, and further include U.S. support for Iraq during its war with Iran in the 1980s, as well as the failings of U.N. arms inspectors in Iraq after the first Gulf War—failings that include subsequently substantiated allegations of inspection agencies being infiltrated by Western intelligence agencies.

In a piece published in 2007 in the *Columbia University Journal of International Affairs*, Mohammad Javad Zarif, who is at the time of this writing the Foreign Minister of Iran and its chief nuclear negotiator, wrote that the long history of discrimination and prejudice against Iran by Western suppliers of nuclear materials and technology since the 1979 Revolution, left Iran "with no option but to be discreet in its peaceful activities."[32] As he continues:

> In doing so, Iran remained within the confines of the NPT and did not divert its peaceful program to military activities. Meanwhile, in order to avoid the U.S.-led restrictions and impediments, Iran refrained from disclosing the details of its programs, which in nearly all cases—including the most publicized cases of the Natanz enrichment facility and the Arak heavy water plant—it was not obliged to disclose under the terms of its existing safeguards agreement with the IAEA.[33]

32. Mohammad Javad Zarif, *Tackling the Iran - U.S. Crisis*, COLUMBIA J. INT'L AFF. Pg. 81, Spring-Summer (2007).

33. *Id.*

I think that, again when viewed holistically, while the IAEA's perspective on and reaction regarding these new facility revelations in Iran is as I noted above reasonable and understandable, Iranian officials' perspective and approach to the declaration of new nuclear facilities to the IAEA is no less reasonable and understandable, in light of Iran's tumultuous history of dealings with the IAEA and the West. And since, as noted above, the Code 3.1 standard applicable between the IAEA and Iran in their agreed subsidiary measures was complied with by Iran (i.e., both facilities were ultimately declared by Iran at least 180 days prior to nuclear material being introduced into them), in the context of both the Natanz and Arak facilities there would appear to be no basis for concluding that Iran failed to keep its political commitment to the IAEA in these instances.

The Fordow facility case is more complicated. This is because Iran declared the existence of the Fordow facility to the IAEA in a letter on September 21, 2009, after the facility had been under construction for at least two years. As noted above, Iran agreed to revise its subsidiary arrangements with the IAEA to include the "modified Code 3.1" standard on February 26, 2003. Again, the modified Code 3.1 standard stipulates that preliminary design information on new nuclear facilities must be reported to the IAEA "[a]s soon as the decision to construct or to authorize construction has been taken, whichever is earlier." However, in a letter three years later, on March 29, 2007, Iran stated that it was suspending its application of the modified Code 3.1 standard and would be reverting to the original Code 3.1 standard found in its February 12, 1976, subsidiary arrangements agreement.

Essentially, the subsidiary arrangement analysis of the Fordow facility declaration boils down to two questions: (1) whether the purported amendment to Iran's subsidiary arrangements in 2003 was effective in making applicable the modified Code 3.1 standard; and (2) whether Iran's purported 2007 reversion back to the original Code 3.1 standard was effective.

Regarding the 2003 amendment, as noted above the subsidiary arrangements template provides that subsidiary arrangements between the IAEA and the safeguarded state may be amended or supplemented by a simple exchange of notes between the parties. This is contrary to some Iranian officials' claims that the 2003 amendment of Iran's subsidiary arrangements with the IAEA required the approval of the Majlis before becoming effective.[34] There appears to be no reason to question the conclusion that the 2003 amendment of Iran's subsidiary arrangements, to include the modified Code 3.1 standard, was effective in producing an updated legally nonbinding, yet politically important, commitment between the IAEA and Iran.

The next question, then, concerns Iran's purported 2007 reversion back to the application of the original Code 3.1 standard. Again, since the subsidiary arrangements between Iran and the IAEA are legally nonbinding, I cannot invoke the normal tools of treaty interpretation or treaty law generally. But just as a logical matter, it would appear that the agreement between the parties in the subsidiary arrangements themselves, that amendments to the subsidiary arrangements may be made by exchange of notes between the parties, would be the most persuasive operative paradigm through which to view Iran's action. Since Iran's purported reversion was not agreed to by the IAEA, but was quite the contrary explicitly opposed by return letter from the IAEA, it would appear that Iran's attempted 2007 reversion to the original Code 3.1 standard should not be viewed as effectively amending the political commitments made by the IAEA and Iran in their subsidiary arrangements.[35]

Pursuant to this analysis, it would appear that the most reasonable understanding of the political commitments applicable between Iran and the IAEA in 2009, when the Fordow facility was declared by Iran to the IAEA, includes the understanding that the modified Code 3.1 standard on provision of preliminary design details on new nuclear facilities was the applicable subsidiary arrangements standard. Pursuant to this understanding, the fact that the Fordow facility had by that time been under construction for at least two years leads to the conclusion that Iran's declaration in 2009 was not consonant with the modified Code 3.1 standard, which stipulates that design

34. *See, e.g.*, GOV/INF/2007/8 (Mar. 30, 2007).
35. *Id.*

information must be declared "[a]s soon as the decision to construct or to authorize construction has been taken, whichever is earlier."

So that there can be no confusion, let me restate and clarify my conclusion regarding the Fordow facility case. Since the CSA Article 42 standard is the only formal legal obligation to which Iran is subject on the issue of declaration of new nuclear facilities, just as in the Natanz and Arak cases Iran did not violate its safeguards obligations through failure to timely declare to the IAEA the existence of the Fordow facility. Iran did, however, act contrary to its political commitment to the IAEA, contained in its subsidiary arrangements with the IAEA, to declare the existence of the Fordow facility prior to the beginning of construction of the facility.

The fact that Iran acted contrary to this political commitment is significant and makes the critical IAEA and Western state responses to the Fordow incident even more understandable and justified. However, it is also important to note the statement by the IAEA Legal Adviser Johan Rautenbach, the IAEA's chief lawyer, to the Board of Governors in March 2009, which referenced Iran's 2007 letter purporting to revert to the original Code 3.1 standard. In this statement Rautenbach observed:

> While Iran's actions are inconsistent with its obligations under the Subsidiary Arrangements to its Safeguards Agreement, this should be seen in proper context. Given the fact that Article 42 is broadly phrased and that the old version of Code 3.1 has been accepted as complying with the requirements of this Article for some 22 years prior to the Board's decision in 1992 to modify it as indicated above, it is difficult to conclude that providing information in accordance with the earlier formulation in itself constitutes non-compliance with, or a breach of, the Safeguards Agreement as such. It should also be noted that currently more than 60 States with operative SQPs [Small Quantities Protocols] based on the old standard text for SQPs, and 27 States party to the NPT but without a CSA in force, are not yet bound by provisions similar to that in the modified Code 3.1.

Chapter 5

Was Iran in Violation of Its Safeguards Obligations in July 2015? And Did the IAEA Use Proper Standards in Its Assessments of Iran's Compliance?

In Chapter 4, I concluded that Iran was in noncompliance with its safeguards agreement and was in fact in formal violation of its safeguards legal obligations in 2003, but that this violation and its implications for Iran's state responsibility were resolved by 2008. I further concluded that Iran did not violate its safeguards obligations through failure to timely declare new nuclear facilities.

Thus, by 2008, Iran had rectified its safeguards agreement noncompliance and had remedied its violations of its safeguards obligations. At the time of the International Atomic Energy Agency (IAEA) Director General's report on February 22, 2008, therefore, Iran was in full compliance with its safeguards obligations.

In this chapter, I will proceed to consider whether there were any further instances of noncompliance by Iran with its safeguards agreement since 2008 through the remainder of the period of confrontation ending in July 2015, including importantly whether Iran was in continuing noncompliance at the time of the Joint Comprehensive Plan of Action's (JCPOA) conclusion, as the IAEA and some states have maintained. I will also be asking a corollary question, which is whether the IAEA has used proper standards in its evaluations and assessment of Iran's nuclear program, particularly when it has made determinations concerning Iran's compliance with its safeguards agreement.

I think it will be best to consider the questions presented in this chapter by looking in turn at the discrete matters that have been argued, in some cases by the IAEA and in some cases by other states, to present continuing violations by Iran of its safeguards obligations since 2008. The first such matter regards the question of whether there are undeclared nuclear materials in Iran. The second is the possible military dimensions issue, previously discussed in Chapter 3 in the context of Nuclear Nonproliferation Treaty (NPT) Article II.

I. UNDECLARED NUCLEAR MATERIALS

In the IAEA Director General's report to the Board of Governors on February 22, 2008—the same report in which the Director General found that all declared nuclear materials in Iran were in exclusively peaceful uses—the following provision was included on the subject of possible undeclared nuclear materials in Iran:

> With regard to its current programme, Iran needs to continue to build confidence about its scope and nature. Confidence in the exclusively peaceful nature of Iran's nuclear programme requires that the Agency be able to provide assurances not only regarding declared nuclear material, but, equally importantly, regarding the absence of undeclared nuclear material and activities in Iran. With the exception of the issue of the alleged studies, which remains outstanding, the Agency has no concrete information about possible current undeclared nuclear material and activities in Iran. Although Iran has provided some additional detailed information about its current activities on an ad hoc basis, the Agency will not be in a position to make progress towards providing credible assurances about the absence of undeclared nuclear

> material and activities in Iran before reaching some clarity about the nature of the alleged studies, and without implementation of the Additional Protocol.

With this language, Director General Mohamed ElBaradei signaled that, while the IAEA was satisfied by that point that all known nuclear material in Iran was in peaceful uses, an even higher level of international confidence in the peaceful nature of Iran's nuclear program could only be achieved if Iran became a party to an Additional Protocol agreement with the IAEA. Only with an Additional Protocol in place, the Director General stressed, would the IAEA have the legal authority to conduct investigations and assessments purposed in providing increased assurance that there were no undeclared nuclear materials in Iran.

Note, however, that at no point in this statement, or in the rest of the report, did the Director General assert that Iran was under a legal obligation to adopt an Additional Protocol and grant the IAEA this additional authority. It has long been settled that the adoption of an Additional Protocol agreement by IAEA member states is purely voluntary and is not required either by the IAEA Statute or by the NPT.[1] Nor did the Director General claim that, even without an Additional Protocol in place, the IAEA had the legal authority or mandate to assess the question of whether undeclared nuclear materials existed in Iran. The Director General's exhortation to Iran was, rather, that it continue to increase confidence regarding the peaceful nature of its nuclear program through adoption of an Additional Protocol, which would give the IAEA the legal authority to undertake investigations and assessments that could increase international confidence in the peaceful nature of all nuclear materials on Iran's territory. This exhortation was, in brief, hortatory, not mandatory.

1. *See* Masahiko Asada, *The Treaty on the Non Proliferation of Nuclear Weapons and the Universalization of the Additional Protocol*, 16 J. CONFLICT & SECURITY L. 3–34 (2011).

In subsequent years, the IAEA Director General's reports continued without exception to conclude that all declared safeguardable nuclear material in Iran was in exclusively peaceful use. The reports also continued to include in their conclusion paragraphs text which stressed that further confidence in the peaceful nature of Iran's nuclear program could only be achieved through Iran's adoption of an Additional Protocol agreement with the Agency and to note that both the IAEA Board of Governors and the U.N. Security Council had requested that Iran do so.[2]

However, the tone and construction of these concluding paragraphs changed markedly over the succeeding years, becoming more consolidated, terse, and conclusory; such that by the November 16, 2012, report, the relevant text had been updated to state:

> While the Agency continues to verify the non-diversion of declared nuclear material at the nuclear facilities and LOFs declared by Iran under its Safeguards Agreement, as Iran is not providing the necessary cooperation, including by not implementing its Additional Protocol, the Agency is unable to provide credible assurance about the absence of undeclared nuclear material and activities in Iran, and therefore to conclude that all nuclear material in Iran is in peaceful activities.

In this and in subsequent reports, this paragraph was accompanied by the following footnote:

> The Board has confirmed on numerous occasions, since as early as 1992, that paragraph 2 of INFCIRC/153 (Corr.), which corresponds to Article 2 of Iran's Safeguards Agreement, authorizes and requires the Agency to seek to verify both the non-diversion of nuclear material from declared activities (i.e. correctness) and

2. *See, e.g.*, GOV/2009/35 (June 5, 2009).

the absence of undeclared nuclear activities in the State (i.e. completeness) (see, for example, GOV/OR.864, para. 49).

This evolved statement of conclusions reads much less like a hortatory exhortation and much more like an expression of several different yet cumulative standards, by reference to which Iran's compliance with its safeguards agreement is being determined by the IAEA. This reading is supported by the attached footnote, which asserts that the IAEA is both authorized and required pursuant to an INFCIRC/153 comprehensive safeguards agreement (CSA) in force, such as that to which Iran is a party, to not only assess whether declared nuclear material is in peaceful uses within a safeguarded state (i.e., the correctness of a state's declaration) but also to assess whether there are any undeclared nuclear materials within the safeguarded state (i.e., the completeness of the state's declaration). By November 2012, therefore, the IAEA's assessment of Iran's compliance with its *existing* safeguards agreement had been expanded in scope to include three separate criteria:

1. Whether declared nuclear material in Iran is in exclusively peaceful use;
2. Whether there are undeclared nuclear materials in Iran; and
3. Whether all nuclear material in Iran is in exclusively peaceful use.

Thus, between 2008 and 2012 the question of whether undeclared nuclear material existed in Iran had been reconceptualized from an original understanding, expressed by Director General ElBaradei, that this question was not a required part of the IAEA's assessment of Iran's compliance with its safeguards agreement, and could only be confidently assessed if Iran acceded to the Additional Protocol (which it had not done, and was not legally required to do, but could voluntarily do); to an understanding, expressed by Director General Yukiya Amano, that the IAEA already had all of the legal authority it needed to assess this question, on the basis of Iran's existing CSA, and indeed that Iran's existing CSA *required* the IAEA to assess this question.

IAEA Director General reports on Iran continued to express their conclusions regarding Iran's compliance in essentially this same pattern through the remainder of the period of confrontation ending in July 2015. And while neither the IAEA Director General nor the IAEA Board of Governors has explicitly found Iran to be in noncompliance with its safeguards agreement since 2008, the fact that reports to the Board of Governors during this period included all three standards identified above and consistently stated that the IAEA was unable to determine that Iran's nuclear program meets two of these standards (standards 2 and 3), Director General reports on Iran's nuclear program since at least the February 18, 2010, report and continuing through to July 2015 appeared to communicate that the IAEA was withholding its determination that Iran was in full compliance with its safeguards agreement.

It will be recalled that in Chapter 4, I referenced the 2013 Safeguards Implementation Report and explained the different categories of assessment standards employed therein, which were linked to the type(s) of safeguards agreement(s) in force for individual safeguarded states. I noted there that, for a state like Iran with only an INFCIRC/153 CSA in force, the assessment standard used in the report for all states *with the sole exception of Iran* was the standard of whether all declared nuclear materials were in peaceful use within the state. For such states with only a CSA in force, this was the end of the IAEA's inquiry into their compliance with their safeguards agreement. I further noted that in Iran's case, the report very clearly deviated from this normal standard of assessment and instead applied to Iran the standard which the report, by its own terms, explained should only be applied to states that have both a CSA and an Additional Protocol in force. As Iran did not throughout the period of confrontation have an Additional Protocol in force, I explained that this was an erroneous application of assessment standard by the IAEA to Iran and therefore an erroneous conclusion regarding Iran's compliance with its safeguards agreement.

Just to reinforce the validity of my conclusion on this matter, I want to note that it is not only in the 2013 Safeguards

Implementation Report that this categorization of states by safeguards agreement type, and corresponding application of different compliance standards to different states, has been maintained by the IAEA. This understanding of applicable standards for determining compliance has been explained by the IAEA in other documents as well, including in this fact sheet published on the IAEA's website:

> Basically, two sets of measures are carried out in accordance with the type of safeguards agreements in force with a State.
>
> One set relates to verifying State reports of declared nuclear material and activities. These measures—authorized under NPT-type comprehensive safeguards agreements—largely are based on nuclear material accountancy, complemented by containment and surveillance techniques, such as tamper-proof seals and cameras that the IAEA installs at facilities.
>
> Another set adds measures to strengthen the IAEA's inspection capabilities. They include those incorporated in what is known as an "Additional Protocol"—this is a legal document complementing comprehensive safeguards agreements. The measures enable the IAEA not only to verify the non-diversion of declared nuclear material but also to provide assurances as to the absence of undeclared nuclear material and activities in a State.[3]

Again, these sources demonstrate that since at least February 18, 2010, through to the conclusion of the JCPOA in July 2015, the IAEA applied incorrect standards to its compliance assessment of Iran's nuclear program *according to the IAEA's own consistent recitation of those standards*. And that the IAEA thereby reached erroneous conclusions regarding Iran's compliance with its safeguards agreement.

So what are we to make of this? What explains this enigmatically exceptional and erroneous treatment of Iran's case by the IAEA? And is there any legally valid reason why the IAEA would not simply

3. Http://www.iaea.org/Publications/Factsheets/English/sg_overview.html.

determine, as it did for all other states with only a CSA in force, that Iran's nuclear program was definitively in compliance with the terms of its safeguards agreement because, as in these other cases, the IAEA consistently determined that all declared nuclear material in Iran was in peaceful use?

I think that there are both legal and political dimensions to the answers to these questions. Let us first explore the legal dimension. In brief, within the past few years there has been a debate going on in nuclear nonproliferation circles regarding the question of the proper standards of IAEA investigation and assessment, particularly of a state that only has a CSA and not an Additional Protocol in force with the IAEA. One group of commentators—among whom the most prominent is former longtime IAEA official Laura Rockwood—have supported the IAEA's position that the Agency has the legal authority and responsibility to investigate and assess such states' nuclear programs on the basis of standards including both the correctness and completeness of their declaration to the IAEA. I and others, on the other hand, have argued that these commentators make improperly revisionist arguments in support of the IAEA's position and that these revisionist arguments are both legally erroneous and harmful to the IAEA, in that they damage the IAEA's credibility as an independent, objective, technical monitoring, and verification body.[4]

In order to understand and evaluate this debate, we will have to return to the text of the INFCIRC/153 comprehensive safeguards agreement, and in particular to Iran's CSA with the IAEA. It is in the terms of this treaty that we must find both Iran's obligations under the CSA, as well as the IAEA's lawful authority to investigate and assess Iran's compliance with its obligations during the period of confrontation.

4. *See* Pierre Emmanuel Dupont, *Compliance with Treaties in the Context of Nuclear Non-Proliferation: Assessing Claims in the Case of Iran*, 9 J. CONFLICT & SECURITY L. (2014); *Interpretation of Nuclear Safeguards Commitments: The Role of Subsequent Agreements and Practice*, in Jonathan Black-Branch and Dieter Fleck eds., NUCLEAR NONPROLIFERATION IN INTERNATIONAL LAW, VOL. II, at 36 (2015).

Before commencing that evaluation, I think it is important to remember that the structure of the IAEA's safeguards treaty system is unique and that it poses particular challenges for treaty interpretation. As I have explained previously, the IAEA existed as an international organization prior to the conclusion of the NPT in 1968. The NPT in Article III referenced the IAEA and gave it a prominent role in the safeguards system envisioned under the treaty, but the IAEA and its Statute had already been in existence for more than a decade by the time the NPT was concluded and were in fact not originally constructed with this role primarily in mind. Nevertheless, since the signing of the NPT, the IAEA has fulfilled its role given to it by the NPT and has concluded bilateral treaties with all of the Non-Nuclear Weapon States (NNWS) parties to the NPT willing to do so. There is in fact a complex web of these treaties, ranging from facility- specific safeguards treaties (INFCIRC/66), to voluntary offer agreements, to INFCIRC/153 comprehensive safeguards agreements, to INFCIRC/540 Additional Protocols. Different safeguarded states have different combinations of these treaties in force at any given time. This makes the task of identifying the legal obligations of safeguarded states, and the investigative authority of the IAEA, a very state-specific exercise.

The INFCIRC/153 CSA has been established as the standard, full-scope safeguards framework. Again, however, it is important to understand that while the INFRCIRC/153 template itself was negotiated by all IAEA member states and adopted by the IAEA Board of Governors, the actual treaties concluded between the IAEA and individual safeguarded states are in every case bilateral treaties that are individually negotiated and brought into force in accordance with each respective state's national constitutional processes. The same is true of all Additional Protocol agreements. This gives both a multilateral and a bilateral aspect to the provisions included in any particular CSA.

All of this means that it can be a challenge to apply the rules on treaty interpretation correctly when examining a particular bilateral CSA between a state and the IAEA. It is important, therefore, to be careful, methodical, and rigorous in conducting interpretive analysis and to hew closely to the rules on treaty interpretation contained in the 1969 Vienna Convention on Law of Treaties (VCLT) Articles 31 and 32.

Let us now turn to an examination of Iran's CSA with the IAEA, which came into force on May 15, 1974, and which is identified as INFCIRC/214. Articles I and II of the treaty provide as follows:

> **Article 1**
> The Government of Iran undertakes, pursuant to paragraph 1 of Article III of the Treaty, to accept safeguards, in accordance with the terms of this Agreement, on all source or special fissionable material in all peaceful nuclear activities within its territory, under its jurisdiction or carried out under its control anywhere, for the exclusive purpose of verifying that such material is not diverted to nuclear weapons or other nuclear explosive devices.
>
> **Article 2**
> The Agency shall have the right and the obligation to ensure that safeguards will be applied, in accordance with the terms of this Agreement, on all source or special fissionable material in all peaceful nuclear activities within the territory of Iran, under its jurisdiction or carried out under its control anywhere, for the exclusive purpose of verifying that such material is not diverted to nuclear weapons or other nuclear explosive devices.

Thus, in Article 1 we find Iran's basic undertakings in the treaty, which include accepting safeguards on all nuclear material within its territory in accordance with the terms of the treaty, which as explained in Chapter 4 includes a range of required declarations to the IAEA concerning the location and amounts of nuclear materials and the facilities related to those materials.

In Article 2 we find provisions regarding the application of safeguards by the IAEA. Article 2 provides that the IAEA is to ensure that safeguards will be applied in accordance with the terms of the treaty, for the exclusive purpose of verifying that nuclear material is not diverted from peaceful to military uses.

I'd like to make a couple of initial textual observations regarding these two paragraphs. First, I think it is important to see these provisions as addressing different, though of course related, subjects. Article 1 describes the safeguarded state's—here Iran's—obligations under the treaty. Article 2 describes the IAEA's authority and obligations under the treaty. These are separate subjects, and the obligations stipulated are addressed to different parties, and there is no reason to assume, or to find implicit, that the rights and obligations of the two parties are coextensive. Rather, both articles stipulate that the rights and obligations of the parties identified within them are to be defined "in accordance with the terms of this Agreement." This means that the scope and meaning of the obligations and rights identified in Articles 1 and 2 of the treaty can only be understood and interpreted in accordance with the specific provisions contained in the balance of the agreement. This is an important observation and is often misunderstood by those who would take Articles 1 and 2 out of their context within the treaty and interpret them standing alone.[5]

In essence, all that these clauses do is make explicit within the treaty text what is already a general principle of treaty interpretation stated in VCLT Article 31, which is that provisions of a treaty must be interpreted in their context within the treaty as a whole, and not in isolation.

The provisions of the treaty that spell out how safeguards are actually to be applied by Iran and by the IAEA begin in Part II of the treaty, the first provision of which is Article 27, which provides: "The purpose of this part of the Agreement is to specify the procedures to be applied in the implementation of the safeguards provisions of Part I." The articles of Part II of the treaty proceed to specify in detail the kinds of nuclear materials and the types of facilities that are subject to safeguards. It then delineates Iran's obligations to provide the IAEA with regular, comprehensive reports concerning all such

5. *See, e.g.*, the contributions of both Andreas Persbo and Christopher Ford to the online roundtable debate entitled "Iran and the Bomb: The Legal Standards of the IAEA," at the *Bulletin of the Atomic Scientists* website, published in November 2012.

material and facilities, including locations, types and amounts of materials, and design information concerning facilities.

Next, Part II specifies the procedures by which IAEA inspections and other material accountancy efforts regarding safeguarded materials and facilities are to be carried out. As I noted in Chapter 4, all of these matters are further subject to additional operational agreement between the parties in subsidiary arrangements.

The provisions in Part II of the CSA are highly technical and complex, but can be accurately and parsimoniously described as follows. Iran is responsible for providing detailed and comprehensive regular reports concerning all safeguardable nuclear materials, and related facilities, within its territory. The IAEA is responsible for examining these reports and undertaking inspections and material accountancy efforts, including due diligence on the sources of these reports, to verify that these reports are accurate. Nowhere in Part II of the treaty is there any mention of the IAEA's authority or responsibility to search for undeclared nuclear materials, or undeclared nuclear facilities, in Iran.

There is a special inspections procedure laid out in Articles 73 and 77 of the CSA. This procedure can be invoked:

> If the Agency considers that information made available by the State, including explanations from the State and information obtained from routine inspections, is not adequate for the Agency to fulfill its responsibilities under the Agreement.

If the IAEA invokes the special inspection procedure, the next step is for the Agency to request that it be granted access by the state to inspect information or locations which have not been previously reported to the IAEA. This is the only procedure in the CSA that even potentially includes inspections by the IAEA of locations not identified in the reports submitted to the IAEA by Iran. It is worth noting that the IAEA has never once invoked the special inspections process in its dealings with Iran.

Having reviewed the rest of the CSA, let us return now to Articles 1 and 2, which, as I noted earlier, explicitly state that the obligations and rights identified within them are subject in their scope and meaning to definition according to the terms of the treaty, in their entirety. Reading Articles 1 and 2, according to their plain meaning and in their context within the treaty, the following interpretation becomes clear.

Iran is to follow all of its specified obligations of reporting and cooperating with IAEA inspectors delineated in Part II of the treaty. It is through this process, and according to these terms, that Iran "accept[s] safeguards" on all nuclear material within its territory. For its part, the IAEA is to follow the specified procedures for carrying out inspections and accounting for nuclear material, as delineated in Part II of the treaty. It is through this process, and according to these terms, that the IAEA has "the right and the obligation to ensure that safeguards will be applied" to all nuclear material on the territory of Iran.

In other words, the IAEA's right and obligation to apply safeguards within Iran are limited to the terms and the procedures delineated in Part II of the treaty. As observed above, these terms and procedures provide the IAEA with the authority only to verify the correctness of the reports and declarations submitted to it by Iran, with the notable exception of the special inspection process, which the IAEA has not invoked in Iran's case. Thus, the IAEA's rights and obligations under the CSA, as provided in Article 2, are limited to verifying the correctness of Iran's declaration to the IAEA, subject only to the potential exception of the special inspection process.

According to a plain meaning, context-inclusive interpretive analysis, therefore, the IAEA's lawful authority to investigate and to assess Iran's nuclear program pursuant to the only safeguards treaty in effect between the two parties is limited to declared material and facilities and does not extend to undeclared material or facilities, except through the IAEA's potential invocation of the special inspection process laid out in the CSA.[6] And again, the IAEA has not invoked this special inspection process.

6. In support of this conclusion, *see* Pierre-Emmanuel Dupont, *Interpretation of Nuclear Safeguards Commitments: The Role of Subsequent Agreements and Practice*, in Jonathan Black-Branch & Dieter Fleck eds., NUCLEAR NONPROLIFERATION IN INTERNATIONAL LAW, VOL. II (2015).

Having rendered this textual interpretation, according to VCLT Article 32 reference may additionally be had to the *travaux preparatoires* of the treaty in order to confirm this interpretation. But again, as noted above, this is where things get complicated in the context of bilateral safeguards agreements between the IAEA and a safeguarded state. The actual *travaux preparatoires* documents for each bilateral treaty, inclusive of Iran's bilateral CSA with the IAEA, are sketchy at best. While some negotiations between the IAEA and the safeguarded state in each individual case will have been had, records of these negotiations are difficult to find if they exist at all. And most of these negotiations will have been on fairly discrete points, because the templates for the CSA and the Additional Protocol, respectively, are generally followed quite closely for each actual bilateral treaty.

The *travaux preparatoires* for the CSA and Additional Protocol templates, on the other hand, comprise a much richer collection of documents. Although again, the general discussion and negotiation history of the templates themselves, consisting of views expressed by all IAEA states parties, is a bit problematic to take in formal supplantation of the more focused *travaux preparatoires* of the two parties that actually, eventually, signed a CSA or Additional Protocol treaty.

With that word of caution, I do think that there is at least some probative value to be found in the general negotiating history of both the INFCIRC/153 CSA template and the INFCIRC/540 Additional Protocol template for purposes of confirming the textual interpretation I have given of Iran's CSA.

Among the best sources for an accurate and balanced account of the negotiating history of the INFCIRC/153 CSA template is the official history of the first forty years of the IAEA, published by the IAEA itself in 1997 and written by longtime IAEA official David Fischer. Writing specifically concerning the 1970–1971 negotiations leading up to the adoption of the INFCIRC/153 template agreement, Fischer writes in this history:

> The EURATOM delegations succeeded in sustaining the principle, implicit in the NPT, that safeguards should be applied

> only to nuclear material . . . and in limiting the access of inspectors, during routine inspections, to previously agreed "strategic points". In simple language, this meant that IAEA inspectors would normally—i.e. during routine inspections—verify only nuclear material at locations that had been declared by the State and would do so by access that would be limited to pre-defined strategic points in the plant concerned . . .
>
> The EURATOM delegations accepted, however, that there would be no limit on the IAEA's access rights if the Board considered that a "special inspection" was needed, and the State gave its agreement, or if the Board decided that a special inspection was urgent and essential to verify non-diversion.[7]

From another volume published by the IAEA itself in 1970, as the INFCIRC/153 template negotiations were ongoing, and entitled *The Law and Practices of the International Atomic Energy Agency*, we find the following passage written by IAEA legal adviser Paul Szasz expressing a legal understanding of the IAEA's safeguards remit:

> Even more broadly than the Tlatelolco Treaty, the safeguards Under the Non-Proliferation Treaty are to relate to all peaceful nuclear activities within the territory of each non-nuclear-weapon State, or otherwise "under its jurisdiction, or carried out under its control anywhere". Again the Agency under its present system will only be able to control those activities that are reported to it—and thus both unregistered items and those officially declared to be used for a non-weapon military purpose will escape its scrutiny; unlike the Latin American instrument, the Non-Proliferation Treaty does not provide for special inspections to be carried out on the basis of accusations.[8]

7. History of the International Atomic Energy Agency: The First Forty Years, 256 (1997).

8. *Id.* at 549.

Yet another publication by the IAEA, this one a 1998 monograph entitled "The Evolution of IAEA Safeguards," observes the following:

> Since most governments were unwilling to give the IAEA a free hand to scout for undeclared plants or stocks, the 1970–1971 safeguards focused almost exclusively on verifying that there was no diversion of nuclear material that the governments concerned had declared and placed under safeguards. The possibility that undeclared plants might exist was, of course, recognized by the architects of the 1970–1971 system, but it was tacitly assumed that if such plants were built they would be detected by means other than IAEA safeguards. In practice, accounting for nuclear material in declared nuclear operations thus became the main task of IAEA safeguards.[9]

From these and other excerpts from authoritative sources of the negotiating history of the INFCIRC/153 template, support can be drawn for the textual interpretation I have given above, which is that the IAEA's legal authority under a CSA is limited to investigation and assessment of declared nuclear materials and related facilities, with the sole exception of the special inspections process detailed in the CSA text.

I generally do not like to rely on statements by individual state officials from negotiating parties to a treaty when considering the treaty's *travaux preparatoires*. Such statements are simply too easy to cherry-pick in order to provide selective support for one's interpretive view. However, since the United States is one of the chief state supporters of the IAEA's recent view that it has the general legal authority to investigate and assess not only declared but also undeclared nuclear materials and facilities within a state with only a CSA in force, it does seem fair and perhaps probative to include here the following exchange between William Foster, head of the U.S. delegation to the negotiation of the NPT, and Senator Claiborne Pell, from

9. IAEA, The Evolution of IAEA Safeguards 14 (Vienna: International Atomic Energy Agency 1998).

Foster's 1968 testimony about the NPT and IAEA safeguards to the Senate Foreign Relations Committee:

SENATOR PELL: "Another question: Will the International Atomic Energy Agency inspection be restricted only to the declared peaceful nuclear facilities or will they also apply to the undeclared or clandestine facilities? How will they be sought out? . . ."

MR. FOSTER: "The IAEA inspection would only be as to declared. If there were undeclared, if they were found, this would be a breach of the treaty."

SENATOR PELL: "But under the treaty there is no provision for searching out the clandestine?"

MR. FOSTER: "No sir."

SENATOR PELL: "Just as there is no sanction?"

MR. FOSTER: "But there would be great alertness on the part of many, including ourselves, on that latter point, Senator."[10]

While these materials concerning the *travaux preparatoires* of the INFCIRC/153 template are useful in confirming the correctness of the textual interpretation I have given, in a sense the *travaux preparatoires* and other official statements concerning the negotiation of the INFCIRC/540 model Additional Protocol agreement, which occurred more than two decades following the adoption of the INFCIRC/153 CSA template, are actually even more useful for understanding the correct interpretation of agreements following the INFCIRC/153 template than are documents originating from the time of the negotiation of INFCIRC/153 itself. This sounds counterintuitive, I know. But recall that in Chapter 4 I explained that negotiations leading to the adoption of the model Additional Protocol agreement began shortly after the 1990–1991 Gulf War and were purposed explicitly

10. Testimony of William Foster, Hearings on Nonproliferation Treaty before the Committee on Foreign Relations of the Senate, 90th Cong., 2nd Sess., 52 (1968); S. Exec. Rep. No. 9, 90th Cong., 2nd Sess., 5 (1968).

in supplementing the authority that IAEA inspectors were given under the original INFCIRC/153 CSA template—authority which had been seen to be inadequate through the Agency's experience in Iraq. Negotiations on a new Additional Protocol at this time were thus directly related to the understanding existing at the time concerning the proper legal scope of the INFCIRC/153, and particularly its limits—limits that the new Additional Protocol was to expand. In a formal treaty interpretation methodology sense, therefore, I think it is useful and accurate to view the model Additional Protocol and its *travaux preparatoires*, as representing interpretive aids separately satisfying all three subcategories described in VCLT Article 31(3), which states:

> There shall be taken into account, together with the context:
>
> (a) any subsequent agreement between the parties regarding the interpretation of the treaty or the application of its provisions;
> (b) any subsequent practice in the application of the treaty which establishes the agreement of the parties regarding its interpretation;
> (c) any relevant rules of international law applicable in the relations between the parties.

The question of how the new Additional Protocol would relate, in a legal sense, to the INFCIRC/153 CSA framework, and what additional powers the Additional Protocol would give to IAEA inspectors, were subjects that were debated thoroughly during the mid-1990s negotiations leading up to the adoption of the Additional Protocol template in 1997. Regarding the INFCIRC/153 system generally and the eventual recognition during this time of the necessity of an Additional Protocol to increase the investigative authority of the IAEA, David Fischer writes the following in his official history of the IAEA:

> It will be recalled that in verifying compliance with comprehensive safeguards agreements IAEA inspectors had essentially

> confined their focus, during routine inspections, to the nuclear material at locations that had been declared by the State ... The IAEA's inspectors would verify the State's reports on its stocks of nuclear material and changes in those stocks ... chiefly by access limited to a number of pre-defined strategic points in the plant concerned. The 1971 system was thus largely one of auditing the State's nuclear material accounts, and it had worked well in regard to locations and nuclear material that had been reported to the IAEA. The IAEA's experience in Iraq and the DPRK had shown, however, that it was essential that the Agency should go beyond auditing the State's nuclear accounts. The Agency must be able to assure itself that the State's declarations were also complete—that the State had reported all its nuclear material ... In 1995, the Board authorized the Secretariat to put into effect those elements of the "Programme 93+2" that did not require additional legal authority. In May 1997, the Board approved a protocol, to be added to existing comprehensive safeguards agreements, which will provide the legal authority for several safeguards measures that go beyond the existing system, for instance, access by the IAEA to more information about a State's nuclear activities, more intensive inspections, including access beyond previously agreed "strategic points" in a safeguarded plant, access to any installation within the perimeter of a nuclear site, and access to plants engaged in nuclear related activities such as those manufacturing components of enrichment plants ... [t]he Board approved the protocol on 15 May 1997.[11]

Similarly, a three-volume review of the negotiating history of the model Additional Protocol, published in 2010 by Brookhaven National Laboratory, makes the following observation concerning debates held during the negotiations on whether the model Additional Protocol in fact provided additional legal authority to

11. History of the International Atomic Energy Agency: The First Forty Years 296–299 (1997).

IAEA inspectors, as compared to that which was provided for in the INFCIRC/153 CSA template:

> Although the issue of whether additional legal authority was needed for many of the proposed measures for strengthening safeguards was fundamental to many of the decisions of the Board and Committee 24, it received relatively little debate in either forum. Both the Secretariat and the member states either wanted new explicit authority or seemed prepared to proceed on the basis of an assumption of the need for additional legal authority. This would, thereby, avoid a lengthy and possibly contentious and inconclusive debate as to which measures did and which did not require additional legal authority. Although suggestions arose that would have permitted States to use different mechanisms for providing the IAEA with the necessary authorities, a consensus emerged, and is reflected in the Model Additional Protocol, that a single instrument was best. This would achieve uniformity and avoid any risk of different interpretations arising.
>
> Although some Board actions during the period from 1991–1997 suggest that the Agency might have the legal authority to apply protocol measures in states with comprehensive safeguards agreements that have not concluded a protocol, the fact of the Additional Protocol, itself, suggests otherwise politically, if not also legally. As a result, obtaining universal adherence to Additional Protocols is the best, perhaps, the only way, to provide the Agency everywhere with the authorities contained in the Model Additional Protocol.[12]

Hans Blix, who was the Director General of the IAEA from 1981 to 1997, throughout the entirety of the period of negotiations leading to the adoption of the model Additional Protocol, has written the

12. Michael Rosenthal et al., *Review of the Negotiation of the Model Protocol Additional to the Agreement(s) between State(s) and the International Atomic Energy Agency for the Application of Safeguards*, Brookhaven National Laboratory, Volume II, pg. 11(BNL-90962-2010).

following, contrasting the CSA system with that of the Additional Protocol system:

> Agency inspection was in principle confined to declared nuclear material in declared installations. The correctness and consistency of declarations could and should be verified by the Agency—but not their completeness. The Agency had no access to satellite imagery and inspectors could not roam the territory of states at random in search of possible clandestine installations. Through the Security Council mandated inspections in Iraq in 1991 these deficiencies were glaringly demonstrated . . . The discovery prompted the agency to embark on a program to upgrade and strengthen the safeguards system. It took some time. In 1997 the General Conference of the IAEA adopted a model Additional Protocol to the existing—insufficient—model safeguards agreement. The growing—but slow—acceptance of the Additional Protocol is now considerably sharpening the eyes and ears of the watchdog.[13]

13. Hans Blix, Introduction, in Olav Njølstad ed., NUCLEAR PROLIFERATION AND INTERNATIONAL ORDER. CHALLENGES TO THE NON-PROLIFERATION TREATY, at 5 (Abingdon: Routledge 2011). A 2013 study by the U.S. Government Accountability Office explains the matter clearly: "The safeguards program has evolved over the past two decades as IAEA has made several efforts to strengthen its effectiveness and efficiency. Starting in the early 1990s, in response to the 1991 discovery of a clandestine nuclear weapons program in Iraq, IAEA made a radical departure from its past practice of generally verifying only the peaceful use of a country's declared nuclear material at declared facilities; at that time, IAEA expanded its safeguards efforts to detect potentially undeclared nuclear activities as well. Specifically, through its Department of Safeguards, the agency began exercising its existing authority under safeguards agreements with individual countries to obtain additional information about their nuclear and nuclear-related activities. However, IAEA recognized that these additional measures were not adequate. As a result, in 1997 the Board of Governors approved what it called the 'Model Additional Protocol' (Additional Protocol)—which, when ratified or otherwise brought into force by a country, requires that country to provide the agency with a broader range of information on its nuclear and nuclear-related activities. It also gives the agency's inspectors access to an expanded range of declared activities and locations, including buildings at nuclear sites, and locations where undeclared activities may be suspected." *Nuclear Nonproliferation: The IAEA Has*

Similarly, Mohamed ElBaradei, who was the head of the IAEA's Office of Legal Affairs from 1984 to 1993, during the period leading up to and immediately following the first Gulf War, before becoming the Director General of the IAEA from 1997 to 2009, has written the following of the period immediately following the first Gulf War and the revelations concerning Iraq's secret nuclear weapons program:

> Back in Vienna, at the IAEA Secretariat, we had begun work on the concept of a Model Additional Protocol to make the Agency's in-country verification authority more robust and explicit . . . Finally, on May 13, 1997, the Model Additional Protocol was adopted by the IAEA Board of Governors. It was a breakthrough legal instrument that would strengthen the effectiveness of the NPT safeguards system. So what had changed? In countries that accepted the Additional Protocol, IAEA inspectors had more freedom on the ground, with more access to information and sites, and could now search more effectively for undeclared nuclear material and facilities. In the past, the IAEA could theoretically invoke the right to look for undeclared material and facilities through a "special inspection" mechanism. But special inspections were arduous to invoke and had almost never been used. The Additional Protocol enabled greater access as a routine matter . . . For countries that had only a safeguards agreement in place, the IAEA was expected to provide assurance that declared nuclear material and facilities had not been diverted for non-peaceful purposes. But for those that brought an Additional Protocol into force, the IAEA could provide, in addition, the equally important assurance about the absence of *undeclared* nuclear material and facilities.[14]

Made Progress in Implementing Critical Programs but Continues to Face Challenges, May 2013, 9 (GAO-13-139).

14. Mohamed ElBaradei, The Age of Deception: Nuclear Diplomacy in Treacherous Times 27, 29–30 (2011).

Again, the point of looking at these reviews of the *travaux preparatoires* of the model Additional Protocol and other high-level IAEA officials' statements of understanding concerning the differences between the model Additional Protocol and the INFCIRC/153 CSA is to shed light upon the proper legal interpretation of the INFCIRC/153 CSA itself, and by extension upon the proper legal interpretation of Iran's CSA with the IAEA.

As these materials make clear, from the inception of the INFCIRC/153 template in 1972, and continuing through the negotiation of the INFCIRC/540 model Additional Protocol in the mid-1990s, it was generally understood both by states parties and by the IAEA itself that the INFCIRC/153 CSA system was properly understood as granting the IAEA the legal authority to investigate and assess nuclear materials and related facilities that were declared to the IAEA by a safeguarded state, with the sole exception of the special inspections process laid out in the CSA, through which the IAEA could request access to undeclared locations. It is further clear from these materials that the primary *raison d'être* of the model Additional Protocol was precisely to grant additional legal authority to IAEA inspectors, so that they could with increased ability and confidence investigate and assess the possibility of the existence of undeclared nuclear materials and related facilities within a safeguarded state that had entered into an Additional Protocol with the IAEA.

All of these materials, then, related to both the INFCIRC/153 and INFCIRC/540 templates and their negotiating histories, support my textual interpretation of Iran's CSA above. The implications of this interpretation of Iran's CSA with the IAEA are, as stated previously, that since at least 2010 the IAEA has been applying incorrect standards to its compliance assessment of Iran's nuclear program and that the IAEA has thereby reached erroneous conclusions regarding Iran's compliance with its safeguards agreement and has improperly withheld its determination that Iran in fact has been and continues to be in compliance with its safeguards agreement obligations.

Before proceeding I want to briefly address the concept of evolutive treaty interpretation. This is a term that I think is often misunderstood. It can be briefly stated as the idea that the meaning of treaty terms should be understood to be capable of evolution or change over time, in order to continually reflect the intent of the parties to the treaty.[15] The concept of evolutive treaty interpretation is sometimes misunderstood to constitute a theory or method of treaty interpretation separate from, or at least parallel to, the normal rules of treaty interpretation contained in the VCLT. It has been suggested to me on multiple occasions, as I have given talks on the subjects of this book in different fora, that the theory of evolutive treaty interpretation should be taken into account as a theory by which a changed meaning—i.e., one which justifies the IAEA's approach to undeclared materials in Iran—may be attached to the terms of Iran's CSA, as compared to that originally intended by its parties, or that which can be divined through application of the normal VCLT rules. The problem with this argument is that it seeks for a distinction in treaty interpretation methodology where there is none.

Evolutive treaty interpretation is best understood not as a separate methodology to that contained in VCLT Articles 31 and 32, but rather as a description of the end result of the disciplined application of those very methods. As Eirik Bjorge has explained:

> [I]t could legitimately be interjected, except for the oblique mention in [VCLT] Article 31(4), the general rule of interpretation does not mention "intention" at all!
>
> This is true. But the general rule of interpretation fails to mention, amongst the means of interpretation, "the intention of the parties" for the same reason that a cake recipe would normally fail to mention, amongst the ingredients, "cake". Like the various ingredients that go into a cake, "all the elements of the general rule of interpretation", as the Tribunal in *Rhine Chlorides*

15. *See, e.g.*, Sondre Torp Helmersen, *Evolutive Treaty Interpretation: Legality, Semantics and Distinctions*, 6 EUROPEAN J. LEGAL STUDIES 127–148 (Spring/Summer 2013).

> put it, "provide the basis for establishing the common will and intention of the parties" . . .
>
> On the correct reading of the approach set out in Articles 31–33 of the Vienna Convention, the treaty interpreter reconstructs the meaning of an intention of the parties; the means of interpretation are the objective means which guide the treaty interpreter to the establishment of what the law of treaties calls the intention of the parties.[16]

As anyone who has ever read VCLT Articles 31 and 32 knows, Article 31(3) (a) and (b) are explicitly designed to instruct the interpreter to identify and take into account in interpretation the objective indicia of changing intention on the part of the parties to the treaty, i.e., through either their subsequent practice or subsequent agreement. The VCLT rules, then, provide a methodology which, when applied correctly, give proper place in the treaty interpretation exercise to the evolving intentions of the parties. And it is therefore improper to consider as a separate exercise, pursuant to a misguided understanding of the theory of evolutive treaty interpretation, indicia of the changing intent of parties to a treaty derived from less sound sources—for example, evidence of the action of unrepresentative organs of international organizations.

So, having employed the rules on treaty interpretation found in the VCLT to interpret Iran's CSA, and having applied this interpretation to the question of the IAEA's authority to investigate and assess undeclared nuclear facilities and materials in Iran, I will now proceed to consider and to critique the legal arguments of those commentators that have attempted to provide legal support for the IAEA's more expansive claims relative to its investigative and assessment authority under a CSA, which it has made in the context of its assessments of Iran's nuclear program. I referred to these arguments previously as

16. *Introducing the Evolutionary Interpretation of Treaties*, EJIL:TALK!, Dec. 15, 2014. The author here introduces his 2014 monograph on the subject.

being improperly revisionist in character and as having for their chief public apologist former longtime IAEA legal adviser Laura Rockwood.

Rockwood retired from her position as head safeguards legal adviser in the IAEA's Office of Legal Affairs in 2013, having worked in that office since 1985. In that position, she was responsible for all legal aspects of the negotiation, interpretation, and implementation of IAEA safeguards. In August 2014, Rockwood published an article in *Arms Control Today* in which she reiterated points she had made in previous publications and in verbal addresses while still in the employ of the IAEA, but with a focus and thorough explication of her views on the question of the legal authority of IAEA inspectors under the INFCIRC/153 CSA framework.[17] It seems fair to infer that these were also her views when she acted as the head safeguards lawyer for the IAEA—the post from which she had retired less than a year earlier—and that these views would have been reflected in her legal advice to the various organs within the IAEA, including the Director General's office, during her time in that position.

Rockwood's article provides a robust defense of the idea that IAEA inspectors have the legal authority, pursuant to an INFCIRC/153 CSA alone, to fully investigate and assess the question of whether there are undeclared nuclear materials or facilities within a safeguarded state. Her argument in the article is explicitly revisionist, in that she recognizes explicitly that the view of the law she is expounding runs counter to the conventional understanding of the correct interpretation of the INFCIRC/153 CSA held at least up until 1991—almost two decades after the INFCIRC/153 template was adopted. As she writes:

> The state-level concept has its roots in efforts by the IAEA and its member states to strengthen safeguards in the aftermath of the discovery in 1991 of a clandestine nuclear weapons program

17. *The IAEA's State Level Concept and the Law of Unintended Consequences*, 44 Arms Control Today (Sept. 2014). *See also* George Bunn, *Inspection for Clandestine Nuclear Activities: Does the Nuclear Nonproliferation Treaty Provide Legal Authority for the International Atomic Energy Agency's Proposals for Reform?*, 57 Nuclear Law Bulletin (June 1996).

> in Iraq. This discovery triggered a reassessment of the then-conventional, ill-founded belief that the IAEA's legal authority under comprehensive safeguards agreements pursuant to the nuclear Nonproliferation Treaty (NPT) was limited to verifying nuclear material and facilities declared by the state

She proceeds to argue that this conventional interpretation, which had subsisted for nineteen years among both states and IAEA officials, was in fact mistaken all along and that:

> Between 1991 and 1993, the IAEA Board and General Conference made a number of decisions reaffirming the agency's right and obligation to ensure that, in a state with a comprehensive safeguards agreement, no nuclear material, whether declared or undeclared, is diverted to nuclear weapons or other nuclear explosive devices. In other words, the objective of IAEA inspections under such agreements is verification of not just the nondiversion of declared nuclear material (the correctness of state declarations), but also the absence of undeclared nuclear material and activities (the completeness of state declarations).

In response to the fairly obvious rebuttal that, if the IAEA in fact has the authority to investigate for correctness and completeness under a CSA alone, then the adoption by the IAEA of the Additional Protocol was purposeless, Rockwood offers the following analysis:

> Some states question the need for an additional protocol if the IAEA already has the right to verify completeness of a state's declarations under a comprehensive safeguards agreement. The answer is straightforward: the IAEA's right and obligation to verify correctness and completeness derive from the comprehensive safeguards agreement, but in such an agreement, there are limited tools for doing so, such as special inspections. An additional protocol secures for the IAEA broader access to information and locations on a more routine, predictable, and reliable

basis. This permits the IAEA to detect indications of undeclared nuclear material and activities earlier and more effectively than it otherwise would.

I have already provided above my own legal analysis of the question of the scope of IAEA legal authority under a CSA. Clearly, Rockwood and I disagree on this question. In addition to her argument being explicitly revisionist of the original understanding of the interpretation of the CSA, held by both states and the IAEA itself for the first almost two decades of CSA treatymaking on the basis of the INFCIRC/153 template, I would note that she never offers in her *Arms Control Today* article a detailed textual analysis of the CSA itself, inclusive of a holistic consideration of its terms, to support her interpretation. In my opinion this fact is fatally problematic for her analysis and conclusions for a number of reasons.

Firstly and most basically, this means that her method of interpretive analysis does not follow the rules on treaty interpretation provided for in VCLT Article 31 and 32. I have attempted above to provide an analysis which does closely follow the rules of treaty interpretation in reaching my conclusions and have done so on the primary basis of a textual analysis of the provisions of the CSA, taken in their entirety. I think that this textual analysis is the key to understanding the correct interpretation of the treaty.

Secondly, reading through her article, it's clear that instead of relying on the actual text of the CSA, Rockwood rather relies primarily on decisions of the IAEA Board of Governors as interpretive authority for understanding the terms of the CSA. Rockwood's implicit belief that the IAEA Board of Governors in particular has the legal authority to unilaterally interpret bilateral treaties to which the IAEA itself is only one party (e.g., Iran's CSA with the IAEA) is, however, itself erroneous as a matter of law. As with any international organization, the international legal personality and legal competences of the IAEA are a product of its constituting documents (the IAEA Statute), other authorities specifically given to it by states (e.g. CSAs and Additional Protocols), and its practice as accepted generally by states.[18] There is no provision in either the IAEA Statute or in the INFCIRC/153 or INFCIRC/540 templates that accords to the IAEA Board of Governors or to the IAEA General Conference the power to authoritatively interpret either the IAEA Statute or bilateral safeguards agreements concluded between states and the IAEA. Quite the contrary, Article XVII of the IAEA Statute and Article 22 of the INFCIRC/153 template explicitly provide for outside arbitration or adjudication in the event of a dispute concerning the interpretation or application of the respective treaties. There is further no general principle of international organizational law that would allow for a sub-organ of an international organization, like the IAEA Board of Governors, to authoritatively interpret either the organization's constitutive instrument, or treaties to which the organization is a party. This is particularly true if, as in the case of the IAEA Board of Governors, the sub-organ in question comprises only 35 states party to the organization, out of a total organizational membership of 162 states.

The International Court of Justice has, in fact, recently had the opportunity to consider this question in the *Australia v. Japan Whaling* case, handed down on March 31, 2014. In this case, Australia argued that the court should accord interpretive weight to resolutions of the International Whaling Commission, which had asserted a restrictive interpretive view of provisions of the 1946 International Convention for the Regulation of Whaling. The International Whaling Commission (IWC) had been created by the Convention as a supervisory body and had been given certain specific roles under the Convention's terms. However, nowhere in those terms was there a grant of power to the IWC to authoritatively interpret the Convention. And even though the IWC itself comprised one representative from every state party to the Convention, nevertheless the Court found no general authority in the IWC to interpret the Convention. In fact, the Court concluded

18. *See Reparation for injuries suffered in the service of the Nations*, Advisory Opinion, [1949] ICJ Rep 174, ICGJ 232 (ICJ 1949), 11th April 1949, International Court of Justice.

that even resolutions adopted by the IWC on a nonconsensual yet supermajority basis were not capable of standing as authoritative interpretations of the Convention. As the Court stated:

> [T]he Court is of the view that Australia and New Zealand overstate the legal significance of the recommendatory resolutions and Guidelines on which they rely. First, many IWC resolutions were adopted without the support of all States parties to the Convention and, in particular, without the concurrence of Japan. Thus, such instruments cannot be regarded as subsequent agreement to an interpretation of Article VIII, nor as subsequent practice establishing an agreement of the parties regarding the interpretation of the treaty within the meaning of [VCLT 31(3) (a) and (b)].[19]

If a sub-organ of an international organization which formally represents all of the member states of that organization cannot authoritatively interpret the organization's constitutive instrument without consensus, then certainly a sub-organ of an international organization representing only 35 out of the total 162 states party to the organization cannot authoritatively interpret the organization's constitutive instrument and *a fortiori* cannot authoritatively interpret bilateral treaties to which the organization is only one of the two contracting parties. Rockwood's reliance on the decisions of the IAEA Board of Governors as authoritative sources of treaty interpretation for the CSA between the IAEA and Iran appears to be a prime example of precisely the sort of misunderstood application of the theory of evolutive treaty interpretation that I discussed previously.

Thirdly, Rockwood's failure to provide a full textual analysis of the CSA, I think, gives rise to her argument distinguishing between the authority that the CSA gives to IAEA inspectors on the one hand and the "tools" that the CSA gives to IAEA inspectors on the other.

19. Judgement on the merits, Mar. 31, 2014, ¶83.

A proper textual analysis of the CSA demonstrates that this is a false dichotomy that finds no basis in the text of the treaty itself. As I have explained through my analysis above, the authority of the IAEA to investigate and assess under the CSA is explicitly defined by reference to the procedures outlined in Part II of the CSA. Hence, the procedural tools outlined in the CSA are coextensive and codefinitional with the IAEA's authority under the CSA. No distinction between the two is warranted according to the text of the treaty.[20]

Finally, Rockwood's failure to interpret the CSA on the primary basis of the treaty text itself obscures the manifestly absurd and unreasonable implications—to reference VCLT Article 32—to which her interpretation, if correct, would give rise. Arguing that under the CSA alone the IAEA has the authority to investigate and assess the question of undeclared material and facilities within a safeguarded state would have the following such implications.

First, it would mean that the IAEA would have the authority under the CSA alone to demand access to sites not covered in the safeguarded state's declaration, potentially anywhere within the territory of the state, inclusive of both civilian and military sites. And since the CSA's terms are silent as to the procedures that would need to be followed for these off-declaration inspections, the IAEA would assumedly have unlimited discretion in choosing sites, and specific areas within them, as well as unlimited discretion in determining how many times a site must be visited, and how many times and how persons connected with the sites must be interviewed, in order for the IAEA to satisfy its suspicions regarding the existence of undeclared nuclear material within the state.

Second, it would mean that until the IAEA was satisfied that no undeclared nuclear materials or facilities exist within the state—i.e., until the state proves the negative—the IAEA would have full

20. Pierre-Emmanuel Dupont agrees with my conclusion on this point in his chapter *Interpretation of Nuclear Safeguards Commitments: The Role of Subsequent Agreements and Practice*, in Jonathan Black-Branch & Dieter Fleck eds., NUCLEAR NONPROLIFERATION IN INTERNATIONAL LAW, VOL. II, at 36 (2015).

discretion to withhold its determination that the state is in compliance with its safeguards obligations. No state on earth would agree to this kind of *carte blanche* authority for an international organization to inspect both civilian and military sites on its territory at the organization's complete discretion, or for the organization to exercise its authority in such a subjective and unstandardized manner. This implication of Rockwood's interpretive argument can only be described as a manifestly absurd and unreasonable interpretive result.

Third, Rockwood herself notes another implication of her argument, i.e., that if indeed the IAEA has the legal authority to investigate and assess undeclared materials and facilities on the basis of a CSA alone, there would have been no need for the adoption of the Additional Protocol as a supplement to the CSA. Rockwood at this point tries to explain away this implication with her erroneous "authority vs. tools" distinction referenced above. Notwithstanding her attempts to demur, however, this is in fact yet another inescapable implication of Rockwood's argument. If all of the legal authority that the IAEA needed to investigate both the correctness and completeness of a state's declaration was already contained within the terms of the CSA, there would indeed have been no need or purpose for the post-1991 efforts to negotiate an Additional Protocol, the *raison d'être* of which as we have seen above, and has been explained in many *travaux preparatoires* sources, was to supplement the legal authority of IAEA inspectors to search for undeclared material and facilities.

In fact, taking Rockwood's argument to its logical extension, if the IAEA indeed had all of the legal authority it needed in the CSA alone, then it follows that when the IAEA does enter into an Additional Protocol treaty with a state, it is in fact taking an action *diminishing* its legal authority. This is because the Additional Protocol text *does* provide for procedural limitations on inspections purposed in verifying the absence of undeclared materials and facilities, whereas the CSA text does not. So if Rockwood's interpretation is correct, not only would the Additional Protocol be purposeless, it would also, if entered into by the IAEA, *decrease* the IAEA's authority to investigate and assess undeclared nuclear materials and facilities in a state that already has a CSA in force with the Agency. Surely this is yet a further manifestly absurd and unreasonable interpretive conclusion.[21]

Finally, returning to the explicitly revisionist nature of Rockwood's analysis, were she to be correct in her analysis, and in light of the quotes I have provided above from IAEA Directors General and other IAEA officials expressing the conventional understanding of the IAEA's authority under the CSA that Rockwood rejects, one would have to conclude that between 1972 and 2009 the IAEA possessed legal authorities under the INFCIRC/153 CSA that IAEA officials outside of the Safeguards Branch of the Office of Legal Affairs, up to and including all of the Directors General prior to Director General Amano, were unaware of. The manifest absurdity of this proposition seems self-evident.

To conclude this section's analysis, I return to the questions that began it, i.e., why did the IAEA apply incorrect standards to its

21. In a 2015 book chapter, co-authored with Larry Johnson, Rockwood supplements her arguments in her 2014 *Arms Control Today* article by *inter alia* arguing that passages in NPT Review Conference Final Documents provide evidence of subsequent agreement and subsequent practice in support of her interpretation of the INFCIRC/153 CSA. The problem with this line of argumentation is that while the *travaux preparatoires* of the INFCIRC/153 template may be relevant for purposes of interpretation of a particular state's CSA with the IAEA, as I have noted above, subsequent agreement or practice of all of the parties to the NPT—meaning agreement or practice subsequent to the point at which the particular CSA came into force between the state and the IAEA—is not relevant to the interpretation of that particular bilateral treaty, in this case Iran's CSA with the IAEA. Only subsequent practice or agreement of the parties to the bilateral CSA itself, establishing an agreed interpretation, are relevant under VCLT Article 31(3). Iran has on multiple occasions formally expressed its conflicting views with those of the IAEA on the interpretation of its CSA. Thus, the two parties to the specific bilateral treaty in question in this case (INFCIRC/214) have not manifest subsequent agreement, or practice demonstrating an agreement, on its interpretation. Pierre-Emmanuel Dupont agrees with my conclusion on this point in his chapter *Interpretation of Nuclear Safeguards Commitments: The Role of Subsequent Agreements and Practice*, in Jonathan Black-Branch & Dieter Fleck eds., NUCLEAR NONPROLIFERATION IN INTERNATIONAL LAW, VOL. II, at 32–33 (2015). *See* Rockwood & Johnson's chapter in the same volume: *Verification of Correctness and Completeness in the Implementation of IAEA Safeguards: The Law and Practice*, in Jonathan Black-Branch & Dieter Fleck eds., NUCLEAR NONPROLIFERATION IN INTERNATIONAL LAW, VOL. II (2015).

assessment of Iran's nuclear program during the period of confrontation ending in July 2015, particularly on the subject of undeclared nuclear materials and facilities? And why did the IAEA improperly withhold its determination that since 2008 has been in full compliance with its safeguards agreement with the IAEA? I noted that there are both legal and political aspects to the answers to these questions.

I have attempted to demonstrate in this section that, with regard to the legal dimension to these questions, the answer appears to be that, particularly since Director General Amano's assumption of office in 2009, IAEA officials have based their assessments and determinations concerning Iran's safeguard compliance on incorrect understandings of the scope of the IAEA's legal authority to investigate and assess pursuant to an INFCIRC/153 CSA.

II. PMD

In addition to concerns regarding undeclared nuclear material and facilities on the territory of Iran, the IAEA also consistently expressed concerns in its reports on Iran during the period of confrontation, regarding allegations that had been made, and evidences proffered in support of them, to the effect that Iran maintained at least some elements of a nuclear weapons research and development program on its territory in the past. I discussed these concerns, often referred to as the possible military dimensions (PMD) issue, in Chapter 1 and again in Chapter 3 in the context of my examination of NPT Article II. It will be recalled that I concluded that examination by finding that Iran had not violated NPT Article II through any nuclear weaponization activity, even taking these contested allegations *arguendo* as correct.

I'd like to turn attention now to the question of whether Iran violated its safeguards agreement obligations with regard to this issue and to the corollary question of on what legal basis the IAEA maintained its scrutiny, investigations, and assessments of PMD-related activity inside Iran during the period of confrontation ending with the adoption of the JCPOA in July 2015.[22]

This section is, frankly, going to be a lot shorter than the undeclared materials section. That's because there's really no serious controversy about whether issues of nuclear weaponization not including nuclear materials are covered by a safeguards agreement with the IAEA or whether the IAEA has the legal authority on the basis of its Statue and/or according to the terms of an INFCIRC/153 CSA, or even an INFCIRC/540 Additional Protocol, to investigate and assess nuclear weaponization issues not involving nuclear material within a safeguarded state. Weaponization-related activities not involving nuclear materials are absolutely not covered under safeguards agreements, and the IAEA absolutely does not have the legal authority to investigate or to assess this question.

One will look in vain for even the slightest hint that the drafters of the IAEA Statute, or the CSA and Additional Protocol templates, intended for the IAEA to be a nuclear weapons inspection Agency. The IAEA was created to be, and has always been maintained as, a nuclear materials accounting Agency. The question of whether the IAEA should be looking for and assessing declared or undeclared nuclear materials and facilities within a safeguarded state is therefore a serious legal question, with colorable legal arguments on both sides. But the idea that the IAEA should be in the business of investigating nuclear weapons programs not involving nuclear material, and assessing whether such programs have existed or do currently exist within a safeguarded state, has never been seriously argued on the basis of the IAEA's Statute or safeguards agreements. The IAEA has neither the legal authority nor, importantly, the independent technical resources necessary to conduct such investigations and assessments.

22. The IAEA's consideration of the PMD issue in fact formally came to a close with the Board of Governors' acceptance of the Director General's December 2, 2015 final report on the PMD issue (GOV/2015/68).

In 1991, the U.N. Security Council in Resolution 687 assigned the IAEA the task of uncovering and dismantling Iraq's clandestine nuclear weapons program. Pursuant to this assignment, the IAEA Director General created the IAEA Iraq Action Team, comprising nuclear weapons specialists, mostly seconded from member states, which carried out that task admirably over the next several years. Eventually, the Action Team was renamed as the Iraq Nuclear Verification Office within the IAEA, and it has assumed an ongoing monitoring role. But to be clear, the IAEA Iraq Action Team was not created on the basis of legal authority the IAEA itself possessed under its Statute or any safeguards agreement. It was created, rather, at the request of the U.N. Security Council and on the basis of the Security Council's legal authority under the U.N. Charter.

So again, the IAEA simply has no legal authority of its own to investigate or to assess nuclear weaponization activities within a safeguarded state. Mohamed Shaker, the author of the authoritative treaties on the *travaux preparatoires* of the NPT, has written the following regarding IAEA safeguards:

> The verification is restricted to the prevention of diversion of nuclear material from peaceful uses to nuclear weapons or other nuclear explosive devices. It follows that the NPT safeguards are not intended to verify noncompliance with the basic obligations in Articles I & II of the NPT relating to non-transfer and non-reception of nuclear weapons or other nuclear explosive devices. If a nuclear-weapon State were to transfer a nuclear weapon to any State Party to the NPT, it would obviously be a violation of the Treaty. However, no provisions are provided for in the NPT to guard against such a violation. Moreover, the NPT safeguards as in INFCIRC/153 are not intended to detect hidden nuclear weapons or clandestine production of such weapons.[23]

23. Mohamed Shaker, *The Evolving International Regime of Nuclear Non-Proliferation*, 321 Recueil des Cours 9–202, at 60 (2006).

As with the issue of undeclared nuclear material discussed above, in the early years of the crisis concerning Iran's nuclear program, IAEA Director General ElBaradei seemed to correctly understand the proper legal scope of the IAEA's investigative role and its limits when it came to investigating allegations of weaponization—as well he might, having served as the Head of the IAEA's Office of Legal Affairs prior to taking the position of Director General. In his February 27, 2006, report to the Board of Governors concerning Iran's nuclear program, he made this statement on the matter:

> The Agency continues to follow up on all information pertaining to Iran's nuclear programme and activities. Although absent some nexus to nuclear material the Agency's legal authority to pursue the verification of possible nuclear weapons related activity is limited, the Agency has continued to seek Iran's cooperation as a matter of transparency in following up on reports related to equipment, materials and activities which have applications both in the conventional military area and in the civilian sphere as well as in the nuclear military area.[24]

The IAEA's increased emphasis on the PMD issue, as one regarding which the IAEA's suspicions had to be resolved by Iran to the IAEA's satisfaction, can be dated to Director General Amano's November 8, 2011, report to the Board of Governors, which I discussed in Chapters 1 and 3.[25] In that report and in those following it, the IAEA has never formally claimed that Iran is in noncompliance with its safeguards agreement on the basis of the IAEA's unresolved PMD questions. Director General's reports since the November 2011

24. GOV/2006/15, para. 52.
25. GOV/2011/6.

report, rather, typically include a sentence such as the following from the February 24, 2012, report:

> The Agency continues to have serious concerns regarding possible military dimensions to Iran's nuclear programme, as explained in GOV/2011/6.[26]

Notwithstanding the fact that there has never been a formal determination by the IAEA that Iran was in noncompliance with its safeguards agreement due to the IAEA's concerns regarding the PMD issue, the IAEA nevertheless continued from 2011 throughout the remainder of the period of confrontation to place a high priority on Iran's cooperation with the Agency to resolve its concerns in this regard. I will return in Chapter 7 to discuss the means through which the PMD issue was eventually finally resolved in December 2015. For purposes of the present discussion, however, I would like to focus on the legal basis for the IAEA's investigations and assessments during the period of confrontation.

For Iran's part, the PMD issue was generally at least rhetorically dismissed as one that had been created on the basis of forged documents and false intelligence information given to the IAEA by hostile third-party states, as Iran explained in its June 5, 2013, explanatory note to the IAEA.[27]

> Taking into account the above-mentioned facts, and that no original document exists on the Alleged Studies, and there is no valid documentary evidence purporting to show any linkage between such fabricated allegations and Iran's activities . . . and the fact that the former DG has already indicated in his reports in June, September and November 2008 that the Agency has no information on the actual design or manufacture by Iran of nuclear material components for a nuclear weapon or of certain other

26. GOV/2012/9.
27. INFCIRC/853.

key components, such as initiators, or on related nuclear physics studies; therefore this subject must be closed.[28]

Since the publication of the November 2011 Director General's report on the PMD issue, one major obstacle to progressing the effort of resolving the IAEA's concerns was the very absence in the IAEA Statute, and in Iran's safeguards agreement, of any provisions or standards relating to weaponization activities. It is simply not a subject addressed in any IAEA-related legal source. The resultant problem for the IAEA in pursuing the route that it decided to take in investigating the PMD issue in Iran was that there is no guidance to be found in any relevant legal documents concerning the scope or subjects of such an investigation; what discretion the IAEA has in demanding access to sites or information; and what criteria or standards the IAEA should use to determine when it should consider its concerns resolved. There is therefore little save the IAEA's own subjective notions of "resolution of concerns" and "satisfactory cooperation," that it has mentioned in its resolutions concerning the matter, that is available to guide Iran or outside observers on the subject of what standards the IAEA could or should use in this case, on which to base their investigations and assessments.

It is frankly difficult to join a rigorous legal discussion on the PMD question because, unlike on the undeclared materials and facilities question, there are to my knowledge no serious defenders of the IAEA's legal authority to investigate and assess nuclear weaponization questions not involving nuclear material on the basis of IAEA legal documents. I could set up any number of straw-man arguments to this effect to attack, but I don't see any value in such an exercise. There simply are no serious arguments to be made to justify the IAEA's actions in this regard, by reference to IAEA legal documents.

I think that an understanding of why the IAEA pursued the course of prioritizing and formalizing the PMD issue in Iran's case since 2011 will have to be based not upon a legal argument or debate,

28. Para. 51.

but rather on a political assessment, which I will give briefly in the next section of this chapter.

It will suffice at this point to say that, from a legal perspective, the IAEA clearly overstepped the bounds of its legal authority in any of its organization-specific legal sources (i.e., the IAEA Statute and safeguards agreements) through its engagement in investigations and assessment of the PMD issue in the Iran case.[29]

III. THE POLITICAL DIMENSION

As a legal summary, then, according to an application of the correct legal standards, Iran was in compliance with its safeguards agreement with the IAEA and had not violated its safeguards law obligations, from 2008 up through the adoption of the JCPOA in July 2015. Furthermore, the IAEA during this time used incorrect legal standards for assessment in the Iran case, both on the question of undeclared nuclear materials in Iran and on the question of possible military dimensions to Iran's nuclear program. Due to the application of these incorrect legal standards, the IAEA during that time reached erroneous conclusions regarding Iran's compliance with its

29. It has also, in connection with its PMD investigation particularly, engaged in practices of intelligence sharing with third-party states, and reliance upon such intelligence in making its safeguards compliance determinations, that has concerned a number of states. As I discussed in Chapter 1, the IAEA's reliance upon information shared with it by national intelligence agencies of states, but not made publicly available for review and not even submitted to the accused state for its interrogation and response, has raised concerns about the propriety of the IAEA's accepting and basing safeguards compliance assessments on such information. The IAEA is certainly not itself an intelligence agency and does not have the physical capacity to independently review information submitted to it for veracity. And particularly following the intelligence-led debacle of the 2003 war in Iraq, the possibility of states sharing fraudulent or simply incomplete intelligence information with an international organization, which the organization cannot independently vet, in order to allow the organization to take prejudicial legal action against another state, strikes many, including myself, as a very real concern that argues strongly against allowing such organizational practice. *See, e.g.*, Mark Hibbs, *Intel Inside: Has the IAEA's Information Become Politicized?*, FOREIGN POL'Y, Dec. 10, 2012.

safeguards agreement and improperly withheld its determination that Iran was in fact in compliance with its safeguards obligations.

The Non-Aligned Movement (NAM), an informal group of 120 mostly developing states, has noted the IAEA's departures from normal safeguards standards application in its reports on Iran. In a 2010 statement to the IAEA Board of Governors, the Egyptian ambassador, speaking on behalf of the NAM, said the following:

> NAM noted with concern the possible implications of the continued departure from standard verification language in the summary in the Director General's report, which stated that "Iran has not provided the necessary cooperation to permit the Agency to confirm that all nuclear material in Iran is in peaceful activities", and it had sought further clarification from the Agency on that matter, given that the Safeguards Implementation Report for 2009 contained in document GOV/2010/25 stated that "while the Agency was able to conclude for Iran that all declared nuclear material remained in peaceful activities, verification of the correctness and completeness of Iran's declarations remained ongoing". NAM regretted that no further clarification had been received to date.[30]

This recognition by a majority of states that the IAEA has applied incorrect legal standards to Iran's case raises the inevitable question of why the IAEA has done this. I have given my opinion as to the legal dimension of this question previously. But as I have noted, there is a political dimension to the answer to this question as well. I will offer my thoughts on this point briefly, as it is not the primary focus of this book. But I do think it is important to identify relevant political dynamics in the context of which the law operates and which have an inescapable bearing upon how the law is used or misused by interested parties.

It has been widely reported that, just prior to Yukiya Amano's ascendance to the Director Generalship of the IAEA in December 2009,

30. GOV/OR.1280, at para. 44.

in private diplomatic cables subsequently revealed by WikiLeaks, U.S. diplomatic staff in Vienna noted the convergence of Amano's views with those of the United States, including with regard to Iran, and U.S. hopes to capitalize on this convergence to influence Amano during his tenure as Director General. Quoting from those cables:

> Amano reminded [the] ambassador on several occasions that he would need to make concessions to the G-77 [the developing countries group], which correctly required him to be fair-minded and independent, but that he was solidly in the U.S. court on every key strategic decision, from high-level personnel appointments to the handling of Iran's alleged nuclear weapons program. More candidly, Amano noted the importance of maintaining a certain "constructive ambiguity" about his plans, at least until he took over for DG ElBaradei in December . . .
>
> This meeting, Amano's first bilateral review since his election, illustrates the very high degree of convergence between his priorities and our own agenda at the IAEA. The coming transition period provides a further window for us to shape Amano's thinking before his agenda collides with the IAEA Secretariat bureaucracy.[31]

The apparent correspondence between, on the one hand, this identified convergence of views between Director General Amano and the United States and, on the other hand, the demonstrably harsher language of Director General's reports on Iran and more aggressive approach to the PMD issue since Amano took the reins of the IAEA Secretariat in 2009, is difficult to ignore. It has produced a deep suspicion, often voiced by Iranian officials, of political bias against Iran within the IAEA leadership.[32]

31. Julian Borger, *Nuclear WikiLeaks: Cables Show Cosy U.S. Relationship with IAEA Chief*, The Guardian, Nov. 30, 2010.

32. *Interview with IAEA Head Yukiya Amano*, Der Spiegel, Jan. 11, 2011.

More systemically, and of longer standing, experts have identified a significant gap between the expectations placed upon the IAEA by governments and the IAEA's ability, both with regard to its legal authority and physical resources, to meet those expectations, particularly since the first Gulf War of 1990–1991. Pierre Goldschmidt, the former Deputy Director General of the IAEA and head of its Department of Safeguards from 1999 to 2005 has described this gap:

> There are two main reasons the safeguards system has been "manifestly failing." First, the Department of Safeguards doesn't have the legal authority it needs to fulfill its mandate and to provide the assurances the international community is expecting. Second, the Department lacks the necessary cooperation and transparency from Member States of the IAEA . . .
>
> Under the IAEA Statute, safeguards are "designed to ensure that special fissionable and other materials, services, equipment, facilities, and information . . . under [Agency] supervision or control are not used in such a way as to further any military purpose" (Article III.5) To reach that objective, Article XII.A. provides that the Agency will have the right and responsibility "to send into the territory of the recipient State inspectors . . . who shall have access at all times to all places and data and to any person who by reason of his occupation deals with materials, equipment, or facilities which are required by this Statute to be safeguarded, as necessary . . . to determine whether there is compliance with the undertaking against use in furtherance of any military purpose."
>
> This excellent and forward looking mandate was agreed more than half a century ago. Unfortunately, in practice the commitments accepted by Non-Nuclear-Weapon States (NNWSs) under Comprehensive Safeguards agreements (CSA) and even the Additional Protocol (AP) are much more limited.[33]

33. "Looking Beyond Iran and North Korea from Safeguarding the Foundations of Nuclear Nonproliferation," address given to NPEC conference, Nov. 3, 2011.

Since the discovery of Iraq's clandestine nuclear weapons program in 1991, governments and international civil society have placed upon the IAEA an expectation that it play the role of "the United Nations nuclear watchdog"—a phrase that is today quite common in media references to the Agency. A mistaken impression of the IAEA as a general nuclear weapons supervision regime, or a sort of an international bureau of investigation for rooting out and dismantling secret nuclear weapons programs, has emerged. It is true, as I noted previously, that a small team of inspectors organized by the IAEA did in fact play such a role in Iraq in the aftermath of the first Gulf War, on the assignment of the U.N. Security Council. And perhaps this is where the confusion originates.

But as I stressed above, the IAEA Iraq Action Team was in actuality not an IAEA-authorized group at all, but rather simply an IAEA-organized group under the authority of the Security Council, acting according to the Council's power under the U.N. Charter. I think that this crucial distinction has been lost on many states and that since that time states and international civil society have come to expect the IAEA to continue on as the international community's law enforcement Agency for all nuclear-weapons-related issues.

The problem with this expectation is that it is completely divorced from the actual legal authority that the IAEA's member states have given to the organization in the IAEA Statute and in the various safeguards agreements which states have negotiated and concluded with the Agency. As I have explained in this chapter, the IAEA's authority under these legal sources is actually quite limited and is focused solely on nuclear materials accountancy. This limitation on the legal authority of the IAEA was quite deliberate, as states have always been understandably reluctant to grant authority and discretion to the IAEA, or to any international organization, to delve too deeply into their security infrastructure. The IAEA is simply not the international nuclear weapons watchdog that so many think it is, and that some states want it to be.

These heightened expectations create immense political pressure for the Agency to be active and aggressive in dealing with cases of suspected clandestine nuclear weapons programs, particularly, I think it must be said, when those cases concern states that are otherwise generally perceived by powerful states as being "bad actors."

For IAEA officials and for state members of the IAEA Board of Governors, there are a number of possible ways to respond to this gap between expectations and authority. One is to fastidiously stay within the Agency's actual legal authority when conducting safeguards inspections and assessments, even in cases in which this path might result in the disappointment of some states, including powerful states that contribute the lion's share of the Agency's budget.

Another option, which could be pursued alongside the first option, is to push for states to increase the authority of the IAEA yet further, through the conclusion of additional legal sources even beyond the 1997 Additional Protocol, in order to close the expectations/authority gap.

A third option is to bend to the desires of particularly influential states, recognizing that states are unlikely to give the IAEA significant additional legal authority to close the gap, and attempt rather to fulfill the broader expectations placed upon the Agency through internal policy evolution, justifying this path through less-than-satisfactory legal arguments grounded in the Agency's existing authority.

This is of course a simplistic assessment of the Agency's options, and to be fair I know from researching the history of deliberations within the IAEA on these issues that they have been considered seriously and thoroughly and generally in good faith by IAEA officials and IAEA member states on many occasions throughout the Agency's history, in order to determine the best course for the Agency to follow. I do think, however, that particularly during Amano's tenure as Director General, and as illustrated by the IAEA's treatment of the Iran case, the Agency has in a number of instances unfortunately chosen the third option outlined above and has overstepped its legal authority to a troubling extent in its safeguards policy and practice, in order to please powerful states seeking to use the Agency as a tool of their own foreign policy.

In addition to this long-standing mandate-authority gap, the IAEA has also suffered for some time from increasing systemic politicization in its governing organs, and particularly in the Secretariat and Board of Governors. This increased politicization can be traced to the lead-up to the second Gulf War in 2003 and to the IAEA's actions at the time—for which the IAEA and Director General ElBaradei jointly won the Nobel Prize, but which also seriously alienated powerful Western countries that led the charge for war in Iraq. As Mark Hibbs explained in a 2012 article:

> During the past decade, the world's global nuclear governance has come unhinged. Beginning in 1958 and until the mid-2000s, the members of the International Atomic Energy Agency (IAEA) resolved conflicts over nuclear issues on the basis of consensus reached at the IAEA's most important decision-making body, its board of governors. About eight years ago this arrangement broke down, and the IAEA has become subject to intense politicization, which has eroded its credibility and hindered its effectiveness. In parallel, the big powers on the IAEA board and in the UN Security Council cannot agree on a common approach to solve important nuclear security issues . . .
>
> Politicization of the IAEA, its limited authority, and the lack of cooperation of major powers deters effective global governance in areas of crisis that have a nuclear dimension: North Korea, Iran, and South Asia.[34]

Unfortunately, it appears that the IAEA is currently continuing to move its safeguards policy and practice in a direction that is likely only to increase the potential for discriminatory, subjective, and politicized administration of safeguards through the

34. *Nuclear Energy 2011: A Watershed Year*, 68 Bulletin of the Atomic Scientists 10–19 (2012).

adoption of its "state level concept" safeguards initiative, discussed in Chapter 4.[35]

In summary, the combined systemic phenomena of the gap between expectations and capacity for the IAEA and the deep politicization of the IAEA's governing bodies, added to the pro-Western views of the current IAEA Director General, have in my view created a political environment in the IAEA which is ripe for producing an overstepping of the bounds of the IAEA's legal authority, in order to please powerful Western governments by over-aggressively pursuing allegations of wrongdoing by Iran.

The implications of these excesses by the IAEA are not confined solely to the Iran case, however. The IAEA's influence in international affairs is based upon a perception that it is an independent, objective, technical body tasked with supervising states' compliance with their safeguards agreements, which are linked to the Nuclear Nonproliferation Treaty. It is for this reason that states and international organizations, including importantly the U.N. Security Council, rely on IAEA assessments of safeguarded states' nuclear programs. To the extent that the IAEA is perceived as having become politicized, acting as an agent for powerful states to achieve their national interests, and using incorrect legal standards in the Agency's safeguards compliance assessments, the IAEA's support among states, particularly in the developing world, will decrease.

35. *See* Mark Hibbs, *The Plan for IAEA Safeguards*, CARNEGIE ENDOWMENT FOR INTERNATIONAL PEACE, Nov. 20, 2012; Daniel H. Joyner, *The IAEA State Level Safeguards Approach Report*, ARMS CONTROL LAW, Aug. 29, 2013; Daniel H. Joyner, *Statement by Russian Representative to the IAEA Grigory Berdinnekov*, ARMS CONTROL LAW, Oct. 21, 2014.

Chapter 6

What Were the Implications of the Actions of the U.N. Security Council?

To this point I have concluded the following. First, that Iran has not violated the provisions of the 1968 Nuclear Nonproliferation Treaty (NPT) by its actions with regard to its nuclear program. Second, that Iran did violate its obligations contained in its safeguards agreement with the International Atomic Energy Agency (IAEA) and was correctly determined to be in noncompliance in 2003 by the IAEA. This violation, and its implications for Iran's state responsibility, were however resolved by 2008. Third, since 2008 Iran has been in full compliance with its safeguards agreement with the IAEA, and the IAEA has improperly withheld its determination of Iran's full compliance due to its application of erroneous standards of investigation and assessment. All of these conclusions have been based upon my legal analysis of the NPT and of IAEA-specific legal sources, i.e., the IAEA Statute and Iran's safeguards agreement with the IAEA.

There is however another source of law that has been argued by some, including the IAEA itself, to be a basis on which additional safeguards obligations have been imposed upon Iran and through which additional legal authorities have been given to the IAEA with regard to Iran's nuclear program. This source is the U.N. Charter, to which Iran has been a party since 1945, and specifically the authority that that instrument gives to the U.N. Security Council. In this chapter I will consider the question of the implications of the actions of the Security Council for Iran's legal obligations and the IAEA's legal authority, relative to Iran's nuclear program during the period of confrontation from August 2002 through to the adoption of the Joint Comprehensive Plan of Action (JCPOA) in July 2015.

In the IAEA Director General's report to the Board of Governors on May 29, 2015, the Director General made the following statement concerning the implications of decisions of the U.N. Security Council for the IAEA's authority regarding Iran:

> The Security Council has affirmed that the steps required by the Board of Governors in its resolutions are binding on Iran. The relevant provisions of the aforementioned Security Council resolutions were adopted under Chapter VII of the United Nations Charter and are mandatory, in accordance with the terms of those resolutions. The full implementation of Iran's obligations is needed in order to ensure international confidence in the exclusively peaceful nature of its nuclear programme.[1]

The Director General is making quite a bold claim in this paragraph, and one which, if correct, could potentially have a significant impact upon the legal analysis of Iran's obligations and the IAEA's legal authority in the context of the dispute over Iran's nuclear program during the period of confrontation. Basically what the Director General is claiming here is that the Security Council, under its power conferred by the U.N. Charter, made all of the IAEA Board of Governors' otherwise legally nonbinding decisions regarding Iran's nuclear program, taken during the period of confrontation, legally binding on Iran. This is a strong claim regarding both the scope of Iran's legal obligations and the derivative legal authority of the IAEA to impose legal obligations on Iran, including, for example, the imposition of obligations that go beyond what is required of Iran under its safeguards agreement with the IAEA. If the IAEA's decisions during

1. GOV/2015/34.

this period were indeed made legally binding on Iran through the authority of the Security Council, then this would potentially have a significant bearing on an analysis of the correctness of the IAEA's arguments regarding the standards of investigation and assessment the IAEA used in evaluating Iran's safeguards compliance, possibly even including the IAEA's efforts in the context of allegations of possible military dimensions to Iran's nuclear program.

And indeed, reading through Director Generals' reports over the past several years, one can see that this understanding by the Director General—i.e., that the IAEA's authority had been enhanced by the decisions of the Security Council beyond IAEA-specific legal sources—was thoroughly internalized by the IAEA and integrated into its reports concerning the legal basis on which it acted in its investigations and assessments of Iran's nuclear program. However, this understanding is ultimately erroneous, at least in the generalized sense in which the IAEA has propounded it.

I. SECURITY COUNCIL DECISIONS ON IRAN'S NUCLEAR PROGRAM

The paragraph I excerpted above from the May 29, 2015, IAEA Director General's report on Iran cites specifically in a footnote to Security Council Resolution 1929 as the basis for the claim that the Security Council made all of the IAEA Board of Governors' decisions regarding Iran during the period of confrontation legally binding. However, Resolution 1929 was not the Security Council's first resolution concerning Iran's nuclear program. Its first resolution was Resolution 1696, adopted on July 31, 2006.

Resolution 1696 was adopted after three years of discussions between Iran and the IAEA and after a number of diplomatic initiatives purposed in resolving the concerns of the IAEA and the West regarding Iran's nuclear program had failed. In February 2006, the thirty-five-member IAEA Board of Governors had referred Iran's case to the Security Council in a split vote, in which five developing nations abstained and three voted against. This split was a rare departure from the Board of Governors' practice, which traditionally was to act only by consensus.[2]

Writing about the adoption of Resolution 1696, Mohamed ElBaradei, who was the Director General of the IAEA at the time of its adoption, has made the following observations:

> It was hard for me to imagine a less sensible, more divisive action than Resolution 1696. First, the investigation of Iran's nuclear program had, at that point, been ongoing for nearly four years. Waiting three weeks for Iran's answer, using those weeks to find a solution to the suspension question—this would have been an eminently reasonable investment of time and energy . . . Second, the resolution was of dubious legality. There was still no proof that Iran's nuclear activity involved a weapons program. It was quite a stretch to say that a small laboratory-scale centrifuge cascade constituted "a threat to international trade and security" when peaceful uranium enrichment is legal for all states under the NPT . . . In my view, Security Council Resolution 1696 was not only counterproductive from a policy perspective, but also a misuse of the council's authority under Chapter VII of the UN Charter. It was staggering to compare the difference in treatment of North Korea and Iran. North Korea had walked out of the NPT and made explicit threats about developing nuclear weapons . . . yet the Americans were ready to join them in direct dialogue . . . By contrast, Iran, which remained under safeguards and party to the NPT, was penalized for possibly having future intentions to develop nuclear weapons, and the Americans refused to talk to them without preconditions.[3]

2. *See* MOHAMED ELBARADEI, THE AGE OF DECEPTION: NUCLEAR DIPLOMACY IN TREACHEROUS TIMES 193 (2011).

3. *Id.* at 199, 203.

Iran itself has consistently denied the legality of the IAEA's referral of its case to the Security Council and the legality of the Security Council's subsequent decisions regarding its nuclear program. As it stated in its July 23, 2013, communication to the IAEA:

> The Islamic Republic of Iran has already made it clear, that based on the legal provisions such as those of the Agency's Statute and the Safeguards Agreement, the BOG resolutions against Iran are illegal and unjustified. The issue of Iran's peaceful nuclear program has unlawfully been conveyed to the UNSC and the Council has taken a wrong approach by adopting the politically-motivated, illegal and unjust UNSC resolutions against Iran. Therefore any request by the Agency stemming from those resolutions is not legitimate and not acceptable.[4]

Notwithstanding, the Security Council adopted Resolution 1696 and in it called upon to Iran to take the steps which the IAEA Board of Governors had requested of it to that point, expressed its "determination to reinforce the authority of the IAEA process," and demanded that Iran suspend all enrichment-related and reprocessing activities. I will return to a consideration of this last element of the resolution—the demand for Iran to suspend its uranium enrichment program—a bit later in this chapter.

It is perhaps necessary at this point to talk about the subject of how to properly interpret resolutions of the Security Council. This has been a subject addressed in some academic literature, though I think it's fair to say that this is still a subject requiring further development in our understanding and practice.[5] It is tempting for the interpreter

4. INFCIRC/853, para. 95.

5. *See, e.g.*, Jochen Abr. Frowein, *Unilateral Interpretation of Security Council Resolutions—A Threat to Collective Security?*, in Volkmar Götz, Peter Selmer, & Rüdiger Wolfrum eds., LIBER AMICORUM GÜNTHER JAENICKE—ZUM 85. GEBURTSTAG (Berlin: Springer 1998); Michael Wood, *The Interpretation of Security Council Resolutions*, 2 MAX PLANCK YEARBOOK OF UNITED NATIONS LAW 73 (1998); Paul Szasz, *The Security Council Starts Legislating*, 96 AM. J. INT'L L. 901 (2002).

to simply apply the same rules of interpretation to Security Council resolutions that we apply to the interpretation of treaties, as found in the Vienna Convention on the Law of Treaties (VCLT), Articles 31 and 32. And indeed there is undoubtedly some overlap in the elements of good interpretive practice.

However, as a formal matter, VCLT Articles 31 and 32 cannot simply be applied *mutatis mutandis* to the interpretation of Security Council resolutions, which are not treaties but rather the unilateral pronouncements of an organ of an international organization. In his article on the subject, Michael Wood reaches this same conclusion and says that, rather, resolutions of the Security Council must be interpreted in light of an understanding of the legal character of the Security Council and its role under the U.N. Charter. He notes that the Security Council is "a political organ of limited competence," and one that should not be misunderstood to have the character either of a legislature or a judicial body.[6] In light of this understanding, he cautions:

> SCR's cannot be interpreted as though they were domestic legislation or even necessarily in the same way as treaties. Unlike treaties most provisions of SCR's are not intended to create rights and obligations binding on states. Many are operational or internal to the United Nations or of a political nature, and they often deal with short-term matters.[7]

Wood's caution here is important, I think. I have written on the subject of the Security Council's authority and its limits extensively elsewhere, and I agree with Wood that it is necessary not to allow oneself to fall into the too-easy trap of thinking of the Security Council as some sort of super legislative or judicial body within the international legal system, capable of making legal pronouncements

6. Michael Wood, *The Interpretation of Security Council Resolutions*, 2 Max Planck Yearbook of United Nations Law 73, 77–78 (1998).

7. *Id.* at 81.

and creating legal obligations with every word adopted under its Chapter VII powers.[8] This is simply not a correct understanding of the legal character of the Security Council and its powers under the U.N. Charter.

The Security Council does have broad powers to adopt legally binding decisions pursuant to its authority granted by the states parties to the U.N. Charter in Articles 25, 39, 40, 41, and 42 of the Charter. However, a number of principles should guide our understanding of how to interpret Security Council resolutions in order to determine *inter alia* when the Security Council is in fact invoking its authority to make binding decisions, creating legal obligations for states party to the U.N. Charter.

First, words matter. And the Security Council employs a variety of words and phrases in order to express different meanings and intended effects of the provisions of its resolutions. Even within the same resolution, the Council will choose leading words—typically verbs occurring at the beginning of each operative paragraph—which the members of the Council can agree upon to express the Council's will regarding the content of each respective paragraph, or sometimes of different sentences within the same paragraph. Some limited empirical work has been done in identifying these different leading words and the meaning that they convey concerning the Council's will regarding the content of the paragraphs or sentences they lead.[9] Some of these leading words include "decides," "recommends," "calls upon," "requests," "demands," "warns," and "urges." Each such leading word of course has a unique meaning in a semantic sense, and that meaning must be correctly understood and factored into the interpretive exercise in order to determine whether it is the Council's intention to

8. Daniel H. Joyner, International Law and the Proliferation of Weapons of Mass Destruction, ch. 4 (2009); *The Security Council as a Legal Hegemon*, 43 Geo. J. Int'l L. 225 (2012).

9. *See* Justin Gruenberg, *An Analysis of United Nations Security Council Resolutions: Are All Countries Treated Equally?*, 41 Case Western Reserve J. Int'l L. 469 (2009).

invoke its authority to make a legally binding decision and to create legal obligations in the relevant sentence or paragraph.[10]

It is important to note in this connection that the text of Article 25 of the Charter explicitly states that the member states of the United Nations agree to accept and carry out the "decisions" of the Security Council. This provision is the basis of member states' obligation to abide by the resolutions of the Security Council and to accept them as legally binding. When interpreting Security Council resolutions, therefore, the term "decision" should be understood to be the standard language of expression by the Security Council, signifying the Council's intent to create legally binding obligation.[11]

Second, in harmony with Michael Wood's caution not to consider Security Council resolutions to presumptively comprise sources of legal obligation for states, it is important in fact to maintain exactly the opposite presumption, i.e., that state sovereignty and independence from legal obligation should be presumed and that only clear, explicit, specific, and definitive expressions by the Security Council, signifying that it is imposing legal obligations upon a state, should

10. *See, e.g.*, Paul Szasz, *The Security Council Starts Legislating*, 96 AM. J. INT'L L. 901, 902 (2002) ("In recent years, however, the Security Council has increasingly adopted decisions that deal not with any particular conflict or situation but, rather, with conflicts in general. Thus, it has addressed the protection of children and civilians, the role of women with respect to peace and security, humanitarian questions, and even international terrorism. Nevertheless, the operative paragraphs of these resolutions that are addressed to states are not formulated in compulsory terms but, for the most part, merely 'call upon' states or parties to a conflict, or even more weakly just 'urge' them-terminology that is understood as not implying compulsion. Other provisions 'condemn' certain practices but, again, without requiring states to refrain from them. Consequently, these decisions of the Council also cannot be considered as establishing new rules of international law.") *See also* Michael Byers, *Policing the High Seas: The Proliferation Security Initiative*, 98 AM. J. INT'L L. 526, 532 (2004); SYDNEY D. BAILEY, THE PROCEDURE OF THE U.N. SECURITY COUNCIL 204–205 (1975); Stefan Talmon, *The Security Council as World Legislature*, 99 AM. J. INT'L L. 175, 186 (2005).

11. *See* the following piece by John Bellinger, who served as the Legal Adviser to the U.S. Department of State from 2005 to 2009 and who was intimately involved in the negotiation of the wording of Security Council resolutions during that time. *The New UNSCR on Iran: Does It Bind the United States (and Future Presidents)?*, LAWFARE, July 18, 2015.

be understood to have this effect. Jochen Frowein has explained this presumption previously:

> An old rule of interpretation of international treaties, frequently invoked before the Vienna Convention on the Law of Treaties, was the rule according to which treaties must be interpreted as respecting the sovereignty of States as far as possible. The idea behind that rule was that States may not be presumed to have given up their sovereign rights in a treaty. The Vienna Convention did not include such a rule. In fact, the International Law Commission was of the opinion that the starting point must always be the intention of the parties as expressed by the specific language of the treaty. This is in line with the nature of a treaty as an instrument in which the consensus among the parties has been expressed.
>
> It is quite different with Security Council resolutions, particularly from the point of view of the state against whom enforcement measures are being taken. Such a resolution is the legal basis for the most severe encroachment upon the sovereignty of a member of the United Nations. It is submitted, therefore, that for the interpretation of such a resolution the old rule according to which limitations of sovereignty may not be lightly assumed is fully justified.[12]

With these principles of interpretation of Security Council resolutions in mind, we can proceed to interpret the Security Council's resolutions regarding Iran's nuclear program, beginning with Resolution 1696. A careful review of the language employed by the Council in the text of Resolution 1696 reveals that by far most of the operative paragraphs within the resolution are led by words which should not be interpreted to create binding legal obligations for Iran. These leading words include "calls upon," "expresses," "endorses," "requests," and

12. Jochen Abr. Frowein, *Unilateral Interpretation of Security Council Resolutions—A Threat to Collective Security?*, in Volkmar Götz, Peter Selmer, & Rüdiger Wolfrum eds., *Liber Amicorum Günther Jaenicke—Zum 85. Geburtstag* 99 (Berlin: Springer, 1998) (as reprinted in Michael Byers, *Agreeing to Disagree: Security Council Resolution 1441 and Intentional Ambiguity*, 10 GLOBAL GOVERNANCE 165–186 (2004).

"confirms." None of these leading words carry with them the mandatory meaning necessary to infer an intent on the part of the Security Council to create a legal obligation, sufficient to overcome the presumption of sovereign independence of the state of Iran. However, operative paragraph 2 of Resolution 1696 states that the Security Council:

> *Demands,* in this context, that Iran shall suspend all enrichment-related and reprocessing activities, including research and development, to be verified by the IAEA;

A demand, unlike a request or an endorsement, is synonymous with a command or an authoritative injunction. The word "demand," therefore, like the word "decision," likely should be understood to express the will of the Security Council to invoke its binding authority under the Charter to impose a new legal obligation on the target state—here, of course, Iran—in a manner sufficiently clear to overcome the presumption of state sovereign independence. Again, I will return to the substance of this obligation later.

Having identified these principles of interpretation of Security Council resolutions and applied them to the text of Resolution 1696, let us now move to consider Security Council Resolution 1929, which is as previously noted the specific resolution of the Security Council which the IAEA Director General explicitly cited as the basis for the IAEA's understanding that the Security Council made all of the IAEA Board of Governors' decisions regarding Iran during the period of confrontation legally binding.

Resolution 1929, adopted on June 9, 2010, was in fact the sixth Security Council resolution adopted regarding Iran's nuclear program.[13] Its second operative paragraph provides as follows that the Council:

> *Affirms* that Iran shall without further delay take the steps required by the IAEA Board of Governors in its resolutions

13. Previous resolutions include Resolution 1696 (2006), Resolution 1737 (2006), Resolution 1747 (2007), Resolution 1803 (2008), and Resolution 1835 (2008).

> GOV/2006/14 and GOV/2009/82, which are essential to build confidence in the exclusively peaceful purpose of its nuclear programme, to resolve outstanding questions and to address the serious concerns raised by the construction of an enrichment facility at Qom in breach of its obligations to suspend all enrichment-related activities, and, in this context, further affirms its decision that Iran shall without delay take the steps required in paragraph 2 of resolution 1737 (2006);

The word "affirm" means to declare something as a fact or to assert or support a principle. It is synonymous with words such as "pronounce" and "proclaim." It is a statement announcing or supporting a fact or principle, but it is not a word that conveys the notion of the origination of a new legal obligation under the authority of the Security Council, in the same manner as the words "decide" or "demand" do. In fact, there are many examples of the Security Council's use of the word "affirm" in this proclaiming or supporting fashion. In Resolution 2106, adopted in 2013, the Security Council stated that it:

> *Affirms* that sexual violence, when used or commissioned as a method or tactic of war or as a part of a widespread or systematic attack against civilian populations, can significantly exacerbate and prolong situations of armed conflict and may impede the restoration of international peace and security;

In this paragraph, the Council is clearly not creating new legal obligations. Rather, it is signifying its support for already established facts and principles. In Resolution 2189, adopted in 2014, the Security Council stated that it:

> *Affirms* its readiness to revisit this resolution in the context of the Council's consideration of the situation in Afghanistan

Again, the Council here is not creating new legal obligations, but simply proclaiming its intent as a fact.

Significantly, the Security Council used similarly nonmandatory language in Resolution 1696 when addressing the same subject of IAEA decisions, stating that it:

> *Calls upon* Iran without further delay to take the steps required by the IAEA Board of Governors in its resolution GOV/2006/14, which are essential to build confidence in the exclusively peaceful purpose of its nuclear programme and to resolve outstanding questions;

This similarity of nonmandatory language from the beginning of its references to IAEA decisions in its resolutions on Iran's nuclear program appears to express the Security Council's intention to support the IAEA's decisions on Iran—or as the Security Council itself says in Resolution 1696, to express its "determination the reinforce the authority of the IAEA process." However, the leading words "affirms" and "calls upon" do not appear to indicate, in either Resolution 1696 or 1929, the Council's intent to create new legal obligations for Iran in a manner that is sufficiently clear, explicit, specific, and definitive to overcome the presumption of Iran's sovereign independence.

Returning to the text of Resolution 1929, in its operative paragraph 3 it states that the Council:

> *Reaffirms* that Iran shall cooperate fully with the IAEA on all outstanding issues, particularly those which give rise to concerns about the possible military dimensions of the Iranian nuclear programme, including by providing access without delay to all sites, equipment, persons and documents requested by the IAEA, and *stresses* the importance of ensuring that the IAEA have all necessary resources and authority for the fulfilment of its work in Iran.

Here again, by the use of the leading word "reaffirms," the Council appears to be expressing its support for the IAEA's work and decisions on Iran's nuclear program, specifically as they related to the possible military dimensions (PMD) issue. However, as explained above, "reaffirms" should be understood to have the same nonmandatory meaning as the words "affirms" and "calls upon" and therefore should not be understood to create new legal obligations for Iran.

It is worth noting that in Resolution 1737 in operative paragraph 8, the Security Council states that it:

> *Decides* that Iran shall provide such access and cooperation as the IAEA requests to be able to verify the suspension outlined in paragraph 2 and to resolve all outstanding issues, as identified in IAEA reports, and *calls upon* Iran to ratify promptly the Additional Protocol.

Here, the Security Council does use the leading word "decides," which clearly conveys the Council's intention to create binding legal obligations for Iran.[14] The Council decides that Iran must provide the IAEA the access and cooperation the IAEA has requested, in order to verify the suspension of its uranium enrichment program "and to resolve all outstanding issues, as identified in IAEA reports." This final clause is the only text in any Security Council resolution on Iran that should be read to impose a legally binding obligation on Iran to provide access and cooperation to the IAEA in order to resolve the IAEA's concerns regarding undeclared nuclear materials and PMD. However, it is a very brief, very broadly, and indeterminately written clause, which does not include any specification of a particular legal obligation on Iran. Indeed, this clause rather reads as something of an afterthought to the first clause of the sentence, which focuses on the much more clearly and specifically outlined legal obligation on Iran, imposed in operative paragraph 2, to suspend its uranium enrichment activities. For these reasons, the second clause

14. *See, for example*, the text of Security Council Resolution 687 (1991), which imposed far-reaching and invasive legal obligations on Iraq with regard to its WMD programs. In every operative paragraph creating these obligations, the Council used the leading word "decides" and never the word "affirms."

of operative paragraph 8 seems to be a rather weak basis on which to justify the idea that the Security Council made all of the IAEA Board of Governors' decisions regarding Iran during the period of confrontation legally binding.

Furthermore, in the final clause of operative paragraph 8 of Resolution 1737, the Council returns to nonmandatory language when it "calls upon" Iran to ratify the Additional Protocol. The Council uses the same language in operative paragraph 5 of Resolution 1929. This invitation further undermines the idea that the Council made all of the IAEA's decisions on Iran binding. This is because one of the IAEA's chief demands on Iran has been for it to ratify and bring into force its Additional Protocol.[15] If this demand by the IAEA for Iran to bring its Additional Protocol into force is already legally binding on Iran on the basis of the Security Council's authority, it wouldn't make any sense for the Security Council to additionally call upon or invite Iran to do so.

There are really no other provisions in Resolution 1929, or in any of the other resolutions adopted by the Security Council relative to Iran's nuclear program, that provide colorable support for the IAEA's claim that the Security Council made all of the IAEA's decisions on Iran legally binding. As I have explained, the provisions in these resolutions that do reference the IAEA's decisions and IAEA-specific legal sources such as safeguards agreements are all either marked by leading language that does not manifest the Security Council's intent to create new legal obligations or are too indeterminate to overcome the presumption of the sovereign independence of Iran and to form the basis for new and additional legal obligations on Iran.

I conclude, therefore, that the IAEA's claim that its decisions regarding Iran have been made legally binding by virtue of Security Council resolutions and that therefore Iran is under safeguards obligations additional to those contained in IAEA-specific legal sources, and that furthermore the IAEA has additional legal authorities to those contained in IAEA-specific legal sources is simply incorrect and derives from a misinterpretation of the Security Council's relevant resolutions.

15. *See* GOV/2012/50, para. 2.

If the IAEA's claim were to be deemed correct, it would mean that since 2010—i.e., for the five years leading up to the adoption of the JCPOA in July 2015—Iran was in essentially the same legal position that Iraq was in following the first Gulf War in 1991, when the Security Council adopted Resolution 687 giving IAEA inspectors *carte blanche* authority to investigate the whole of Iraq's territory looking for evidence of a nuclear weapons program and requiring Iraq's complete cooperation with the IAEA in its investigations. As much as some of Iran's detractors would like this to have been the case, it was not, and it defies logic that it should have been.

Thus, this assessment and dismissal of the IAEA's claim regarding additional obligations and authority created on the basis of U.N. Security Council resolutions leaves unchanged my conclusions in the previous chapters concerning Iran's compliance with its safeguards obligations and the authority of the IAEA to investigate and assess that compliance.

II. THE SECURITY COUNCIL'S DEMAND THAT IRAN SUSPEND ITS URANIUM ENRICHMENT PROGRAM

In its resolutions on Iran's nuclear program, the U.N. Security Council did unquestionably impose legal obligations on Iran, and on all U.N. member states, in a number of non-safeguards-related matters. These include mostly trade-related restrictions, including export controls and financial sanctions. As I noted above, one of the most notable non-safeguards-related restrictive obligations that the Security Council imposed on Iran, specifically in Resolutions 1696 and 1737, is the obligation to suspend its uranium enrichment activities.

Before proceeding to consider the substance of this command by the Security Council, I do want to stress once again that this command to cease uranium enrichment has absolutely nothing to do with the NPT, or with the IAEA Statute, or with Iran's safeguards agreement with the IAEA. The U.N. Security Council derives its authority exclusively from the U.N. Charter. The basis for its acting as it did in Resolutions 1696 and 1737, under Chapter VII of the U.N. Charter, is its authority specifically given in Article 39 of the Charter to:

> determine the existence of any threat to the peace, breach of the peace, or act of aggression and . . . decide what measures shall be taken in accordance with Articles 41 and 42, to maintain or restore international peace and security.

Having acted pursuant to Articles 40 and 41 of the Charter, respectively, in Resolutions 1696 and 1737, the Security Council apparently implicitly exercised its authority in Article 39 to determine that Iran's nuclear program constitutes a "threat to the peace, breach of the peace, or act of aggression." The Council's determinations in Resolutions 1696 and 1737, including the Council's "demand" (in 1696) and "decision" (in 1737) that Iran must suspend its uranium enrichment program, stem directly and exclusively from the Security Council's exercise of this authority and from the Council's apparent determination that Iran's suspension of its uranium enrichment program is a "measure . . . to restore international peace and security."[16]

I think it is important to stress this line of authority, to make it clear that the Security Council in these resolutions was acting completely independently of any legal authority or obligation originating in either the NPT or any IAEA-specific legal sources. The Security Council was not enforcing any obligation of Iran's found in these nuclear-specific sources. Quite the contrary, as I will now attempt to explain.

Since Resolutions 1696 and 1737 were adopted in 2006, Iran has not complied with this decision of the Security Council for it to suspend its uranium enrichment program. In fact, Iran increased the capacity of its uranium enrichment program from around 350 operating centrifuges in 2006 to over 9,000 operating centrifuges as of May 2015 on the

16. This applies specifically to Resolution 1737, which was adopted under Article 41 of the Charter. Resolution 1696 was adopted under Article 40 of the Charter, and thus comprises "provisional measures."

eve of the adoption of the JCPOA.[17] On a *prima facie* basis, it can therefore be concluded that, at the time of the JCPOA's adoption, Iran was in violation of the Security Council's decision and the legal obligation that it produced, for Iran to cease its uranium enrichment program.

Iran laid out the basis for its decision not to comply with these resolutions of the Security Council in a communication to the IAEA on December 12, 2011. As it there explained:

> Requiring suspension of peaceful nuclear activities . . . will be in contradiction "*to establish conditions under which justice and respect . . . can be maintained . . .*" and "*principles of justice.*" In fact, there is not any report by the Agency on the diversion of nuclear material and activities or any determination of "*threat to the peace, breach of the peace, or act of aggression*" . . . due to Iran's nuclear activities, except some vague, baseless and unverified allegations in the so called "alleged studies" which can not substantiate as a means to undermine the "*inalienable right*" of a Member State under Article 4 of the NPT . . . More generally, requiring suspension of peaceful nuclear activities will contradict to the "right to development," right to natural resources" and "right to self-determination." Such rights are among the fundamental rights of nations and their breach entails international responsibility for those who have violated them.[18]

The Iranian representative is here referencing specifically Article IV of the NPT, which provides in paragraph 1:

> Nothing in this Treaty shall be interpreted as affecting the inalienable right of all the Parties to the Treaty to develop research, production and use of nuclear energy for peaceful purposes without discrimination and in conformity with Articles I and II of this Treaty.

17. Alexander Glaser et al., *Agreeing on Limits for Iran's Centrifuge: A Two Stage Strategy*, ARMS CONTROL TODAY, July/Aug. 2014.

18. INFCIRC/833. Quote from paragraphs F(25)(b)(iii) and F(25)(f).

The argument that Iran is making in its communication is that the decisions of the Security Council which command Iran to suspend its uranium enrichment program were invalid, and therefore need not have been complied with, because they were in contradiction of Iran's right to peaceful nuclear energy provided for in NPT Article IV, as well as of a number of other delineated "fundamental rights of nations." Is there anything to this argument?

Along with Marco Roscini, I recently co-organized a special issue of the *Cambridge Journal of International and Comparative Law* devoted to the very topic of the rights of states in international law. Our interest in this question in fact began in our discussions over the years about the meaning and implications of the right to peaceful nuclear energy identified in NPT Article IV(1). We observed that, in addition to NPT Article IV(1), there are a number of provisions in other positive international legal sources that identify or assert the existence of fundamental rights of states in international law. These include notably the right of self-defense in the U.N. Charter, Article 51, but also include the right to self-determination, the right to economic-non-coercion, the right of permanent sovereignty over natural resources, the right to nonintervention, and a number of others.

We noticed that, notwithstanding the fact that these references to rights of states exist in treaties and in resolutions of the U.N. General Assembly, there has been very little judicial or scholarly engagement with the concept of rights of states in international law. What is their legal character? What is their origin? What are their juridical implications, particularly when they come into conflict with international legal obligations, either of the right-holder or of some other international actor? We therefore organized the special issue of the journal and invited an excellent group of international legal scholars to investigate this topic with us. The results of that project are now in print in the journal.[19]

This is an extremely complex and involved topic, and one that implicates international legal history, theory, and doctrine. I would

19. CAMBRIDGE J. INT'L COMP. L., Volume 4(3) (2016).

invite those interested in a more comprehensive discussion of these aspects of the issue to read the various contributors' papers in the journal, where they are thoroughly discussed.

My own individual contribution to the special issue was a paper, not surprisingly focusing on the right to peaceful nuclear energy in NPT Article IV.[20] I will provide a summary of my analysis and conclusions here, but again in order to avoid redundancy I would refer readers to the full paper for a more fulsome analysis.

I argued there that, where a fundamental right of states has been asserted through positive legal sources, and where that right has been supported by state practice and *opinio juris* such that it is accepted by states as a principle of customary international law, it should be understood to comprise an independent rule of international law with juridical implications equal to any international legal obligation. Thus, when the framers of the U.N. Charter in 1945 provided in Article 51 that states have an "inherent right" to self-defense, they were both recognizing and creating this right as an autonomous rule of international law, which was then universalized through its acceptance as a rule of customary international law.

Similarly, when the 190 states parties to the 1968 Nuclear Nonproliferation Treaty agreed in Article IV(1) that states have an "inalienable right" to peaceful nuclear energy, they were both recognizing and creating this right as an autonomous rule of international law and intended for this rule to have a legal meaning and implication at least on par with any obligation created through treaty or customary law. As with the right of self-defense, the right to peaceful nuclear energy became accepted in parallel customary law and was thus universalized as a right of all states.

Furthermore, I argued, once established, a right of states in international law creates an obligation of respect for that right in other states, and by extension in international organizations. This means that other states and international organizations are under an

20. *Fundamental Rights of States in International Law, and the Right to Peaceful Nuclear Energy*, 4 (3) CAMBRIDGE J. INT'L COMP. L. (2016).

international legal obligation not to act in serious prejudice of fundamental states' rights. The precise contours of this obligation will be dictated by the contours of the legal right that has been established. In the context of the right to peaceful nuclear energy, since uranium enrichment is an essential element of a full indigenous nuclear fuel cycle, I concluded that the right to maintain a uranium enrichment program is a lesser-included right within the right to peaceful nuclear energy.

Thus, since the right to peaceful nuclear energy, as a fundamental right of states, creates in third parties an obligation of respect for the right and for the right-holder's exercise of it—i.e., an obligation not to act in serious prejudice of that right, or unduly restrict the right-holder's exercise of the right—it follows that there is at least a negative obligation in third parties not to unduly restrict, through arbitrary or unreasonable means, the access of states to normal, lawful markets in civilian nuclear energy materials and technologies, including those related to uranium enrichment, through export controls or other means. This conclusion is of particular relevance to the Nuclear Suppliers Group (NSG), as this fundamental right of states to peaceful nuclear energy could be asserted by developing states to create a positive legal obligation for all states, including adherents to the NSG's guidelines, which would prohibit arbitrary or unreasonable restrictions on the supply of nuclear materials and technologies for peaceful nuclear programs.

Specifically with regard to cases in which the fundamental right to peaceful nuclear energy comes into direct conflict with international legal obligations, either held by the right-holder itself or by some other actor, I focused in my contribution on the case of Iran and its refusal to comply with Security Council resolutions commanding it to suspend its uranium enrichment program, on the grounds that these resolutions are made invalid due to their contradiction with Iran's right to peaceful nuclear energy.

I argued that this case essentially presents a conflict of rules question. Iran has in essence claimed that it has a fundamental legal right to peaceful nuclear energy, which, for the reasons I explained above, includes the right to uranium enrichment. Iran has therefore argued that the Security Council's command that Iran cease uranium enrichment was unlawful and *ultra vires* the Security Council's authority.[21] In contrast, the Security Council's view is that its decisions are legally binding on Iran, due to Iran's status as a party to the U.N. Charter, which so provides in Article 25. Thus, in the Security Council's view, its command that Iran cease uranium enrichment was lawful and was controlling over any conflicting right or obligation. Supporters of the Security Council's view on the matter have also cited to Article 103 of the Charter to justify its position.[22]

As an initial analytical step in determining the merit of these contrasting arguments, I first considered the U.N. Charter Article 103 argument. I noted that Article 103 is often misused and misunderstood.[23] Article 103 provides:

> In the event of a conflict between the obligations of the Members of the United Nations under the present Charter and their obligations under any other international agreement, their obligations under the present Charter shall prevail.

By the plain meaning of its terms, Article 103 applies only to circumstances in which a state's obligations under the U.N. Charter come into conflict with its obligations under some other treaty. It is a simple conflict of treaty obligations provision that should be read narrowly. The issue under immediate consideration, by contrast, is a circumstance in which a state's (i.e., Iran's) obligations under the U.N. Charter have arguably come into conflict with the same state's legal right, not obligation; and furthermore, a right that has been established independently in customary international law. Therefore,

21. Communication from Iran to the IAEA, INFCIRC/837 (Mar. 30, 2012).

22. *See* Ryan Goodman, *Iran's Purported "Right" to Enrich Uranium, and Alleged Bias at the New York Times*, Just Security, Nov. 19, 2013.

23. *See* Ryan Goodman, *Expert Opinion on Iran's "Right" to Enrich Uranium in the Face of Security Council Resolutions*, Just Security, Nov. 20, 2013.

U.N. Charter Article 103, according to the plain meaning of its terms, as well as by reference to its *travaux preparatoires*, is simply not applicable to the present matter.[24]

At essence, then, what we are left with is a conflict between, on the one hand, a legal right of a state, which, as I have argued, creates an obligation of respect in third parties that is based in customary international law and is therefore binding both upon states as well as upon the Security Council as an organ of an international organization; and on the other hand, a hierarchically equal *jus dispositivum* obligation binding upon the right-holding state (i.e., U.N. Charter Article 25).[25]

In the context of an international organization, such as the U.N. Security Council, exercising its authority under a treaty, I argued that the obligation created by the fundamental right of states to peaceful nuclear energy should be understood to create a corollary obligation in the international organization to respect this right and specifically not to be arbitrary, unreasonable, or disproportionate in the exercise of its treaty powers relative to this right.

This is a very similar conclusion to that which has been argued in the context of the obligations of the U.N. Security Council relative to international human rights law in the exercise of its treaty powers. There is a solid basis in scholarly literature for the proposition that, notwithstanding the Security Council is not itself a party to international human rights treaties, it is nevertheless bound by customary international law–based obligations of respect for human rights when it exercises its treaty-based powers, including its powers under

24. *See* Andreas Paulus, *Article 103*, in Simma et al. eds, THE CHARTER OF THE UNITED NATIONS: A COMMENTARY, Vol. 2, at 2132–2133 (2012) ("The wording of Art. 103 suggests that it only applies to treaties and other agreements, not to customary international law. The *travaux preparatoires* support this view. The drafters refused to adopt a formula that explicitly included customary international law and other legal sources.").

25. A. Reinisch, *Developing Human Rights and Humanitarian Law Accountability of the Security Council for the Imposition of Economic Sanctions*, 95 AM. J. INT'L L. 851 (2001).

Chapter VII of the Charter.[26] I am essentially making the same argument, only in the context of fundamental rights of states that have created similar customary international law–based corollary obligations in third-party holders of international legal personality.

Such an understanding of obligations upon the Security Council and other international organizations, created by fundamental rights of states, I argued, would be potentially transformative in the authority dynamic as between such international organizations and, particularly, developing states. It would provide a justiciable standard against which to measure such international organizations' actions for lawfulness in areas in which states have asserted, and have evidenced through state practice and *opinio juris* their acceptance of, the existence of fundamental rights of states, including in areas in which such international organizations do not otherwise have legal obligations limiting their conduct with respect to these subject areas. It would give states a basis on which to potentially challenge actions taken by the Security Council as being in violation of its obligation of respect for specific rights of states, just as it can be challenged as having acted in violation of specific rules of international human rights law.

So how would this work in the specific context of Iran's asserted fundamental right to peaceful nuclear energy, inclusive of a right to uranium enrichment, versus the Security Council's command through legally binding resolution that Iran cease uranium enrichment? If taken as I have constructed it above, the Security Council should be understood to be subject to a customary international law–based obligation to respect Iran's established right, by not acting in a manner that is arbitrary, unreasonable, or disproportionate in the exercise of its treaty powers relative to the right. The legal standard having been established, the question would then become one of application of law to facts, ideally conducted by an international judicial

26. *See, e.g., id.*; C. Michaelsen, *Human Rights as Limits for the Security Council: A Matter of Substantive Law or Defining the Application of Proportionality?*, 19 J. CONFLICT & SECURITY L., 451–469 (2014).

body of lawful jurisdiction, though in the likely absence of this, by the analyst.

What, then, of Iran's U.N. Charter Article 25 obligation to comply with the decisions of the Security Council? It is important to recall that Article 25 in fact provides that member states are obligated to "accept and carry out the decisions of the Security Council in accordance with the present Charter." This provision has been interpreted by some scholars, myself included, to require member state compliance only with decisions of the Security Council, which are themselves in compliance with the provisions and principles of the U.N. Charter.[27] This interpretation is strengthened by a view of Article 25 in its context within the U.N. Charter, and in particular by the text of Article 24, which immediately precedes it. Article 24 provides:

> In discharging these duties the Security Council shall act in accordance with the Purposes and Principles of the United Nations.

In Article I of the U.N. Charter, one of these purposes is identified as follows:

> To maintain international peace and security, and to that end: to take effective collective measures for the prevention and removal of threats to the peace, and for the suppression of acts of aggression or other breaches of the peace, and to bring about by peaceful means, and *in conformity with the principles of justice and international law*, adjustment or settlement of international disputes or situations which might lead to a breach of the peace.[28]

Thus, the obligation on U.N. member states to "accept and carry out the decisions of the Security Council" is intrinsically linked to the

27. *See* Daniel Joyner, *Non-proliferation Law and the United Nations System: Resolution 1540 and the Limits of the Power of the Security Council*, 20 Leiden J. Int'l L. (2007); Anne Peters, *Article 25*, in Simma et al. eds, The Charter of the United Nations: A Commentary, Vol. 1, at 807–819 (2012).

28. Emphasis added.

Security Council itself acting in accordance with the purposes and principles of the United Nations, one of the foremost of which is to act in accordance with international law. Furthermore, there is, as previously noted, an ascendant understanding both by scholars and by international judicial bodies that the Security Council's powers are limited not only by the provisions of the U.N. Charter itself but also by customary international law.[29]

There are several different procedurally-related arguments as to exactly how it should be understood to occur, but on the basis of the foregoing I argued that there is an essential ascendant understanding that states parties to the U.N. Charter, and to Article 25 thereof, are at legal liberty not to comply with decisions of the Security Council that are themselves in disharmony with the Security Council's legal obligations under customary international law.[30] I am on record elsewhere as being in agreement with this understanding.[31] According to this understanding, if it were to be determined that the Security Council through its decisions violated its obligation to respect Iran's fundamental right to peaceful nuclear energy, Iran would be at legal liberty not to comply with the Security Council's command that it cease uranium enrichment.

I will choose at this point in the analysis not to proceed further to an actual application of the facts of the Iran case to this legal test. I do so because, while I stand by the legal analysis I have given concerning the right of states to peaceful nuclear energy, I also recognize that this analysis is based upon a number of theoretically and doctrinally underdeveloped understandings that do not currently enjoy broad support among international legal scholars. For this reason I do not think it particularly constructive to proceed to an analytical

29. *See, e.g.*, Anne Peters, *Article 25*, in Simma et al. eds, THE CHARTER OF THE UNITED NATIONS: A COMMENTARY, Vol. 1, at 819 (2012); ANTONIOS TZANAKOPOULOS, DISOBEYING THE SECURITY COUNCIL (2011).

30. *See* ANTONIOS TZANAKOPOULOS, DISOBEYING THE SECURITY COUNCIL (2011).

31. Daniel Joyner, *Non-proliferation Law and the United Nations System: Resolution 1540 and the Limits of the Power of the Security Council*, 20 LEIDEN J. INT'L L. (2007).

conclusion as to whether the Security Council's command that Iran suspend its uranium enrichment program is indeed invalid, as Iran has argued.

What I do hope to have demonstrated through this partial analysis and discussion, however, is that the concept of fundamental rights of states, inclusive of the right to peaceful nuclear energy, deserves to be taken more seriously as a doctrinal legal argument than it has been to this point both by diplomats and international legal scholars. In my opinion, the concept of fundamental rights of states, which has itself been pervasive in international legal thinking for centuries, lies at the heart of the very modern struggle for the soul of the international legal system. Over the past two decades, the rise to prominence in role of international organizations as fora not only for coordination of state action but also for lawmaking, monitoring, and verification of state conduct, and in some cases adjudication of legal disputes, has made the international legal system a much different, more complex place than it once was for states, which were once the only and independent actors within it.[32]

This modern structure of the international legal system, in which the legal obligations of states are often made, monitored, adjudicated, and enforced through international organizations, has taken on post-Westphalian aspects of constitutionalism and maturity as a legal system that have changed significantly the position of states. Indeed, a number of scholars have recently recognized international organizations as agents in which a decay in the traditional paradigm of state consent in international lawmaking has taken place.[33]

As the international legal system matures, grows increasingly complex, dense, and fragmented, and moves toward a more complete

32. *See, e.g.*, DAN SAROOSHI, INTERNATIONAL ORGANISATIONS AND THEIR EXERCISE OF SOVEREIGN POWERS (2005).

33. *See* Nico Krisch, *The Decay of Consent: International Law in an Age of Global Public Goods*, 108 AM. J. INT'L L. 1 (2014); Laurence R. Helfer, *Nonconsensual International Lawmaking*, U. ILL. L. REV. 71 (2008); Andrew T. Guzman, *Against Consent*, 52 VA. J. INT'L L. 747 (2012); JOEL P. TRACHTMAN, THE FUTURE OF INTERNATIONAL LAW: GLOBAL GOVERNMENT (2013).

legal system, it would appear to be manifestly sensible and necessary for states, and particularly developing and less powerful states, not only to have clearly developed understandings of their obligations within that legal system but also to have clearly developed understandings of their rights within that system, which can potentially be used as a shield against excessive encroachment upon their sovereign independence by other actors.

The U.N. Security Council in particular is one of the most legally influential of these international organizations (or, in its specific case, one organ of an international organizations). The Council's understanding of its role and powers, and the question of the legal limits of those powers under the Charter, is a subject that has been widely debated by international legal scholars in recent years.[34] In writing on this subject, I have previously argued that the Security Council's understanding of its authority under the Charter has changed significantly since the end of the Cold War, to encompass not only its more traditional executive role in enforcing existing international law but also an ascending legislative and adjudicatory role that has greatly expanded both the scope and substance of its decisions, and has brought its actions into conflict with fundamental principles of international law.[35]

In light of the increased scope of action and self-understanding of authority of the U.N. Security Council in particular, all U.N. member states would appear to have a strong self-interest in developing and clarifying the concept of the fundamental rights of states in international law—rights which can be asserted against and which must be respected by other actors, including the Security Council. This is especially true for developing states, which are particularly susceptible

34. *See, e.g.*, ANTONIOS TZANAKOPOULOS, DISOBEYING THE SECURITY COUNCIL (2011); ERIKA DE WET, THE CHAPTER VII POWERS OF THE UNITED NATIONS SECURITY COUNCIL (2004); DAVID SCHWEIGMAN, THE AUTHORITY OF THE SECURITY COUNCIL UNDER CHAPTER VII OF THE UN CHARTER (2001).

35. *See* Daniel H. Joyner, *The Security Council as a Legal Hegemon*, 43 GEO. J. INT'L L. 225 (2012).

to economic and financial sanctions imposed by the Security Council, as well as unilaterally by powerful states.

This susceptibility has been significantly amplified in recent decades due to the increased internationalization of markets and interdependence of national economies, a phenomenon often referred to as globalization. Globalization has made developing states more vulnerable than ever before to both unilateral and collective sanctions imposed by, and often coordinated between, powerful states, the most powerful of which sit as permanent members on the Security Council. For developing states, therefore, there would seem to be a particular modern imperative to balance the scales of this phenomenon through the development and clarification of fundamental legal rights, which in turn create in other states and international organizations an obligation to respect these rights.[36]

I am of course aware of the considerations which run counter to this push for a reinvigoration of the concept of states' rights. These include the concern that if the Security Council were to be deemed unable to act in any manner that might be construed to contradict some element of a fundamental rights of states, perhaps widely construed, it could lead to the almost complete paralysis of the Council and its inability to effectively perform its role given to it under the U.N. Charter. I think, therefore, that this is an area in which more work needs to be done in understanding the proper balance between states' rights on the one hand, and international organizations' necessary discretion to act on the other.

Returning to the immediate focus of this section, i.e., the Security Council's command that Iran suspend its uranium enrichment program and Iran's argument that this command was invalid, I would at present conclude the following: The Security Council's decision that Iran must suspend its uranium enrichment program never made any sense. Uranium enrichment is an inherently dual use process—meaning that it has perfectly valid civilian uses along with potential

36. *See* GA Res. 66/186 (2011) on unilateral economic measures as a means of political and economic coercion against developing countries.

military uses. NPT Non-Nuclear Weapon States all over the world have uranium enrichment programs, many if not most of which are far more advanced and of greater capacity than Iran's—certainly as it stood in 2006. Add to this the fact that the NPT does explicitly provide in Article IV(1) for an inalienable right for all states to have a peaceful nuclear program and the decision of the Security Council to command Iran to cease a program which no evidence suggested was being used for anything other than civilian purposes, seems to imply an ill-considered and politically motivated decision by the Council to stop Iran from obtaining capacities that many other states possess and maintain without criticism.[37]

From a legal perspective, it is a highly fraught endeavor to attempt to show that the Security Council has overstepped its broadly and vaguely worded Article 39 discretion to determine threats to peace and to adopt measures to restore peace. But this particular decision of the Council seems to push the outer limits of that discretion. Add to this the analysis I have provided concerning the legal implications of the peaceful use of nuclear energy as a fundamental right of states, and I think it is fair to conclude that the legal validity of this command of the Security Council is doubtful.

III. CONCLUSION

I have concluded in this chapter that the IAEA's claim that its decisions regarding Iran during the period of confrontation from August 2002 to July 2015 were made legally binding by virtue of Security Council resolutions and that therefore Iran was under safeguards obligations additional to those contained in IAEA-specific legal sources, and that furthermore the IAEA has additional legal authorities to those contained in IAEA-specific legal sources is incorrect and

37. *See* my book INTERPRETING THE NUCLEAR NONPROLIFERATION TREATY (2011) for a more comprehensive interpretation of the scope and meaning of the Article IV(1) right.

derives from a misinterpretation of the Security Council's relevant resolutions. I have further concluded that, while Iran was at the time of the adoption of the JCPOA in July 2015 in *prima facie* violation of the Security Council's command that it suspend its uranium enrichment program, the legal validity of this command of the Security Council, expressed in Resolutions 1696 and 1737, is doubtful.

PART II

ACCORD

Chapter 7

The Joint Comprehensive Plan of Action and Developments since July 2015

Let us now revisit the summary of the legal arguments of the two sides to the Iran nuclear dispute, which I laid out in Chapter 2. In light of the legal analysis and conclusions I have provided in the foregoing chapters, we can now observe that both sides were partially correct in their legal arguments made during the period of confrontation between August 2002 and July 2015.

As the West and the International Atomic Energy Agency (IAEA) had asserted, Iran was indeed in violation of its safeguards treaty obligations in 2003, when it was found to be so by the IAEA. This placed a legal burden on Iran to remedy that violation, which it did by 2008 through cooperation with the IAEA. Furthermore, while not formally a violation of a legal obligation, Iran had also failed to live up to its political commitments with regard to its 2009 declaration concerning the Fordow facility, as the IAEA had maintained. Finally, Iran's failure to suspend its uranium enrichment program had been in *prima facie* noncompliance with the U.N. Security Council's command that it do so—although this last observation must come with the caveat that the legal validity of the command itself was dubious.

For its part, Iran had been correct in arguing that it had not at any time violated any provision of the Nuclear Nonproliferation Treaty (NPT). It had furthermore not violated its safeguards treaty obligations subsequent to 2003, with regard either to undeclared nuclear material on its territory or to the declaration of new facilities. Therefore it was indeed, as it had argued, in full compliance with its safeguards obligations after 2008 and continuing up through the adoption of the Joint Comprehensive Plan of Action (JCPOA) in July 2015. And it was additionally correct that the IAEA's determinations to the contrary were based upon incorrect understandings both of IAEA safeguards law and of the implications of U.N. Security Council resolutions.

This, then, was the legal situation on the eve of the adoption of the JCPOA. Politically, the diplomatic efforts purposed in finding a political settlement to the at times dangerously tense standoff between Iran and its detractors had proceeded in fits and starts since 2003 with little real progress having being made until the diplomatic breakthrough of the Joint Plan of Action (JPOA) on November 24, 2013. As I explained at the close of Chapter 1, the JPOA was an explicitly interim agreement setting the stage for continuing negotiations, potentially leading to a final and comprehensive diplomatic resolution. Over the next twenty months, negotiators from Iran, the P5+1, and the European Union attempted to reach such a comprehensive settlement. Several extensions of tentative deadlines were agreed, and marathon negotiating sessions were held, ending with a seventeen-day final session at the Palais Coburg in Vienna.

On July 14, 2015, the agreement of the JCPOA was announced through a joint statement by E.U. High Representative Federica Mogherini and Iranian Foreign Minister Javad Zarif. When it was finally made public, the length and detail of the agreement stunned many. There had been a hope that the parties would be able to agree on a comprehensive diplomatic package of commitments, but few believed it realistic that such a diverse group of negotiating parties, with such a history of antipathetic relations among them, could produce an agreement of such scope and depth of detail, even including a dispute settlement procedure for the agreement's implementation. The agreed documents consist of 159 total pages of text, including 18 pages of the JCPOA itself, with a further 141 pages divided among 5 annexes. On July 20, 2015, the U.N. Security Council adopted

Resolution 2231, in which it unanimously endorsed the JCPOA and brought into force the measures relating to the Security Council that were agreed in the JCPOA.

I. KEY COMMITMENTS IN THE JCPOA

The key commitments in the JCPOA can be described as follows. Iran commits in the JCPOA to limit its uranium enrichment activities and to decrease its existing stockpile of low-enriched uranium (LEU). Specifically, Iran agrees to reduce its existing holdings of LEU by 98 percent, from 10,000 kg to 300 kg, and to maintain this level of LEU holdings for fifteen years. It further agrees that this remaining stockpile will be enriched to no more than 3.67 percent purity of the U235 isotope. Iran's excess LEU stockpile is to be sold to a foreign buyer in return for natural uranium delivered to Iran. This foreign buyer, though not stipulated in the JCPOA, is almost certain to be Russia. All remaining uranium oxide in Iran enriched to between 5 percent and 20 percent will be fabricated into fuel for the Tehran Research Reactor.

Iran further commits for ten years to place over two-thirds of its operating centrifuges in storage, reducing the number of centrifuges operating in the country from around 19,000 down to a total of 6,104 centrifuges, divided between the Natanz and Fordow facilities. However, the 1044 centrifuges at Fordow will only be used for continuing nuclear research purposes, and not for uranium enrichment.

Specifically with regard to its heavy-water facility at Arak, Iran commits to redesign and rebuild the facility in a manner in which it will no longer be capable of producing weapons-grade plutonium. All spent fuel produced by the Arak reactor will be shipped out of Iran for the lifetime of the reactor, and for fifteen years Iran commits not to develop spent fuel reprocessing capabilities. All of these commitments regarding the front end of Iran's nuclear fuel cycle were sought by the European Union and the P5+1 in order to reduce Iran's potential "breakout time," or the estimated time necessary for Iran to produce enough nuclear material for a weapon, should it choose to do so.

With regard to safeguards on its nuclear program, Iran commits in the JCPOA to provisionally apply the IAEA Additional Protocol, with a view to seeking its formal ratification. Iran also agrees to fully implement the modified Code 3.1 standard in its subsidiary arrangements relative to its comprehensive safeguards agreement. In addition to these commitments, Iran also agrees in the JCPOA to yet further provisions for enhanced access by the IAEA to sites within Iran. These enhanced access provisions are found in Annex I, Section Q. Paragraph 75 of Section Q provides that "if the IAEA has concerns regarding undeclared nuclear materials or activities, or activities inconsistent with the JCPOA, at locations that have not been declared under the comprehensive safeguards agreement of Additional Protocol," the IAEA may request access to such undeclared locations. And if the IAEA and Iran are unable to reach an access agreement or other explanatory solution satisfactory to the IAEA, the agency can submit its access request to a Joint Commission, made up of representatives from each of the JCPOA parties, including Iran. Iran then commits in Section Q to implement the Joint Commission's majority decision on the matter. These enhanced access provisions are to remain in place for fifteen years. The JCPOA's enhanced access provisions can be viewed as a supplement to Iran's obligations under its comprehensive safeguards agreement (CSA) and Additional Protocol.

Independently, yet in coordinated parallel with the JCPOA, on July 14, 2015, Iran and the IAEA signed a "Roadmap Agreement" for the "clarification of past and present outstanding issues regarding Iran's nuclear programme." This Roadmap Agreement set out an agreed process through which Iran and the IAEA would address the agency's long-standing possible military dimensions (PMD) concerns. It provides that by December 15, 2015, the Director General should submit to the Board of Governors a "final assessment on the resolution of all past and present outstanding issues, as set out in the annex of the 2011 Director General's report (GOV/2011/65)." This final assessment report on the PMD issue, called for by the

Roadmap Agreement, was in fact delivered to the Board of Governors on December 2, 2015, as IAEA document GOV/2015/68 and was accepted by the Board in a resolution dated December 15, 2015. The concluding summary of the Director General's report stated:

> The Agency assesses that a range of activities relevant to the development of a nuclear explosive device were conducted in Iran prior to the end of 2003 as a coordinated effort, and some activities took place after 2003. The Agency also assesses that these activities did not advance beyond feasibility and scientific studies, and the acquisition of certain relevant technical competences and capabilities. The Agency has no credible indications of activities in Iran relevant to the development of a nuclear explosive device after 2009.
>
> The Agency has found no credible indications of the diversion of nuclear material in connection with the possible military dimensions to Iran's nuclear programme.

Finally, in Annex I, Section T of the JCPOA, Iran commits to what might be described as principles supplementing its obligations under Article II of the NPT. As I discussed at length in Chapter 3, the NPT's prohibition on horizontal proliferation of nuclear weapons to Non-Nuclear Weapon States (NNWS) parties, is limited to proscribing the manufacture or other acquisition of a nuclear explosive device. The commitments of Annex I, Section T of the JCPOA go further than this and provide that Iran will not engage in a delineated list of activities short of the manufacture or other acquisition of a nuclear weapon, yet which nevertheless "could contribute to the development of a nuclear explosive device." These activities include, *inter alia*, developing or using computer models to simulate nuclear explosions, developing or using multipoint explosive detonation systems suitable for a nuclear explosive device, developing or using explosive diagnostic systems, and developing or using explosively driven neutron sources. All of these are precursor capacities necessary for developing a functioning nuclear warhead.

While the above described commitments undertaken by Iran in the JCPOA are significant and represent serious compromise on the part of the Iranian government relative to positions they had taken in previous attempts at diplomatic settlement, it should nevertheless be noted that most of these commitments are not of permanent duration. In fact, in its recitation of the preamble and general provisions, the JCPOA makes it clear that the ultimate position of the European Union and the P5+1 toward Iran's indigenous nuclear program, including the uranium enrichment element of that program, will be one of acceptance and normalization. As paragraph iv of the general provisions states:

> Successful implementation of this JCPOA will enable Iran to fully enjoy its right to nuclear energy for peaceful purposes under the relevant articles of the Nuclear Non-proliferation Treaty (NPT) in line with its obligations therein, and the Iranian nuclear program will be treated in the same manner as that of any other non-nuclear-weapon state party to the NPT.

Along with the lifting of economic sanctions, this recognition of Iran's right to maintain a peaceful nuclear energy program, inclusive of an indigenous uranium enrichment capacity, was a primary negotiating objective for Iran.

In return for all of Iran's commitments concerning its nuclear program under the JCPOA, the European Union and P5+1 parties commit themselves, through a carefully delineated schedule of reciprocal concessions, to the comprehensive lifting of all economic sanctions on Iran related to its nuclear program. These include both the sanctions imposed multilaterally by the U.N. Security Council since 2006 and the unilateral sanctions imposed unilaterally by the United States and the European Union since that time. As noted previously, in its Resolution 2231, adopted on July 20, 2015, the Security Council endorsed the JCPOA and agreed to the commitments made therein relative to its past resolutions.

Annex V of the JCPOA provides that initial sanctions relief, in the form of the termination or ceasing of application of the unilateral nuclear sanctions measures imposed by the European Union and the United States and the termination of all U.N. Security Council nuclear sanctions, is to occur on "Implementation Day," which is stipulated to occur upon the verification by the IAEA of Iran's initial completion of its essential commitments. This verification by the IAEA, heralding the arrival of Implementation Day, occurred on January 16, 2016. On that date, U.S. and E.U. officials confirmed the application of their initial sanctions commitments and announced their implementation.

Annex V stipulates that the U.N. Security Council's nuclear sanctions imposed since 2006 are to be terminated as of Implementation Day, subject to "re-imposition in the event of significant non-performance by Iran of JCPOA commitments . . ." This clause is elaborated upon in the Dispute Resolution Mechanism section of the JCPOA in paragraphs 36–37, as well as in operative paragraphs 11–13 of Security Council Resolution 2231, which describe what has been referred to as the "snapback" process of the JCPOA. The procedure outlined in these paragraphs is quite complex, but the essential gist is that any one of the JCPOA's parties can complain that any other party is not complying with its JCPOA commitments. If this occurs, and if no accommodation can be reached to resolve the impasse, including through the facility of the Joint Commission, the complaining party can notify the Security Council of the alleged noncompliance. Paragraph 37 of the JCPOA describes what would happen next in such a scenario:

> Upon receipt of the notification from the complaining participant, as described above, including a description of the good-faith efforts the participant made to exhaust the dispute resolution process specified in this JCPOA, the UN Security Council, in accordance with its procedures, shall vote on a resolution to continue the sanctions lifting. If the resolution described above has not been adopted within 30 days of the notification, then the provisions of the old UN Security Council resolutions would be re-imposed, unless the UN Security Council decides otherwise.

Assuming, however, that the snapback procedure is never triggered, the JCPOA's Implementation Plan in Annex V provides for the final termination of the unilateral nuclear sanctions of the United States and the European Union on "Transition Day," which is set to occur on October 18, 2023; and for the final termination of the U.N. Security Council's nuclear sanctions on "UNSCR Termination Day," which is set to occur on October 18, 2025.

II. GENERAL OBSERVATIONS

Before commencing a more detailed analysis of the JCPOA's legal implications, a couple of preliminary general observations need to be made. The first is that the JCPOA is not a treaty, i.e., it is not a legally binding agreement among states. It is, rather, an agreement among states constituting political commitments only. The text of the agreement is quite explicit and unequivocal on this point when on page 6, following the preamble and statement of general provisions, it leads its recitation of the commitments of each party with the statement: "Iran and the E3/EU+3 will take the following voluntary measures within the timeframe as detailed in this JCPOA and its Annexes." This statement manifests the clear intent of the parties to the agreement that it be understood as legally nonbinding. Additional evidence supporting this conclusion can be found in the fact that the JCPOA was not signed by representatives of the agreeing parties. It was simply announced jointly by the representatives of the European Union and Iran. Nor are there any provisions in the JCPOA for the agreement to be ratified or to come into force.

The reasons why the parties chose a legally nonbinding format for the JCPOA are clear. The subjects addressed in the JCPOA are extremely politically sensitive. For this reason there was an understandable interest, particularly on the part of the United States and Iran, in avoiding the requirement of securing the formal support of their respective domestic legislative bodies for the agreement, which would have been necessary had the agreement been framed as a legally binding treaty. Furthermore, the ambitious scope and level of detail achieved in the JCPOA's text and the agreement's creative approaches to problem solving on what are sure to be a dynamic set of issues raised over the course of the JCPOA's implementation—for example, in the creation of the Joint Commission and the sanctions snapback procedure—would have almost certainly been impossible had the agreement been framed as a treaty. States are typically, and predictably, far more conservative and restrictive in their negotiations of treaty text than they are in negotiations of agreements that are politically binding only. There is an underlying psychology present in the negotiation of a legally nonbinding agreement—however weighty the issues concerned are and however serious the parties are in their intent to abide by their commitments—that takes into abiding account the at least formally available option of noncompliance with the agreement without legal consequence, should necessity so dictate at some future point. This formal possibility, even if the parties have no intention of ever availing themselves of it, allows them to agree to text that is more detailed in its terms and creative in its approach. All of these reasons underlying the choice of form for the JCPOA are in harmony with and predictable according to a well-established scholarly literature on hard and soft forms of international agreement.[1]

Again, however, it must be emphasized that one should not imply from the legally nonbinding form of the JCPOA any necessary deficiency in either the seriousness of the parties with regard to the

1. *See* Charles Lipson, *Why Are Some International Agreements Informal?*, 45 INT'L ORGANIZATION 495, 507 (1991); Robert Keohane et al., *The Concept of Legalization*, 54 INT'L ORGANIZATION 401 (2000); Kenneth Abbot & Duncan Snidal, *Hard and Soft Law in International Governance*, 54 INT'L ORGANIZATION 429 and 440 (2000). *See generally* Arthur Stein, *Coordination and Collaboration: Regimes in an Anarchic World*, in NEOREALISM AND NEOLIBERALISM: THE CONTEMPORARY DEBATE (David A. Baldwin ed., 1993); Joseph Grieco, *Understanding the Problem of Institutional Cooperation*, in NEOREALISM AND NEOLIBERALISM: THE CONTEMPORARY DEBATE (David A. Baldwin ed., 1993); LISA L. MARTIN, COERCIVE COOPERATION: EXPLAINING MULTILATERAL ECONOMIC SANCTIONS (1993).

agreement or in the sincerity of the parties' intention to abide by their commitments undertaken therein. The aforementioned scholarly literature on hard versus soft (i.e., legally binding versus legally nonbinding) international agreements finds no clear correlation between the bindingness of an agreement on the one hand and the compliance of parties with that agreement on the other.[2] The question of when and why states comply with their international commitments is immensely complex and may include, but is certainly not limited to, the influence of this one independent variable. As Charles Lipson has explained:

> High costs of self-enforcement and the dangers of opportunism are important obstacles to extralegal agreements. Indeed, the costs may be prohibitive if they leave unsolved such basic problems as moral hazard and time inconsistency. The same obstacles are inherent features of interstate bargaining and must be resolved if agreements are to be concluded and carried out. Resolving them depends on the parties' preference orderings, the transparency of their preferences and choices (asymmetrical information), and the private institutional mechanisms set up to secure their bargains. It has little to do, however, with whether an international agreement is considered "legally binding" or not.[3]

A second preliminary general observation about the JCPOA is that the JCPOA did not, in and of itself, change anything about the legal situation existing at the time it was agreed. Again, the JCPOA itself is a legally nonbinding agreement. However, the JCPOA does include commitments undertaken by its parties, which, when implemented by them, will in some cases have legal implications. The first of those legal implications, which I will consider in more detail below, occurred on Implementation Day: January 16, 2016. On that

2. *See* Martha Finnemore, *Norms, Culture and World Politics: Insights from Sociology's Institutionalism*, 50 Int'l Organization 325 (1996); Robert Keohane et al., *The Concept of Legalization*, 54 Int'l Organization 401 (2000).

3. Charles Lipson, *Why Are Some International Agreements Informal?*, 45 Int'l Organization 495, 507 (1991).

day, Iran's provisional application of the IAEA Additional Protocol, and its acceptance of the modified Code 3.1 version of its comprehensive safeguards agreement subsidiary arrangements, came into effect. Also on that day, economic sanctions and other restrictions contained in U.N. Security Council resolutions and in the domestic law of the United States and the European Union terminated or ceased application. Thus to be clear, between July 14, 2015, and January 16, 2016, the JCPOA had no legal effects or implications for its parties.

It could be said that the Roadmap Agreement, concluded between Iran and the IAEA on July 14, 2015, in connection with but formally independent from the JCPOA, produced something of a legal effect in the sense that it led to the submission by the IAEA Director General to the Board of Governors of a final assessment of the PMD issue on December 2, 2015, and the acceptance of this report by the Board in a resolution dated December 15, 2015. In that resolution, the Board of Governors agreed that the PMD issue would no longer be on the Board's agenda, effectively ending the IAEA's active consideration of the PMD issue.[4]

III. MORE ON SAFEGUARDS, PMD, MISSILES, AND SANCTIONS

Having made these initial observations, I will proceed to consider in more detail a few elements of the JCPOA, the IAEA Roadmap Agreement, and Security Council Resolution 2231 that have particular legal or normative implications.

A. Safeguards

As of Implementation Day—January 16, 2016—Iran has agreed to accept modified Code 3.1 within its comprehensive safeguards

4. GOV/2015/72.

agreement subsidiary arrangements. I covered Code 3.1 at length in Chapter 4. Again, modified Code 3.1 stipulates that preliminary design information on new nuclear facilities must be reported to the IAEA "[a]s soon as the decision to construct or to authorize construction has been taken, whichever is earlier." Significantly more importantly, as of Implementation Day Iran has also agreed to provisionally apply its Additional Protocol agreement with the IAEA. It will be recalled that Iran signed an Additional Protocol agreement with the IAEA in 2003, though it never ratified the treaty, and thus Iran's Additional Protocol agreement never formally came into force. However, Iran did voluntarily implement the provisions of the Additional Protocol from 2003 until 2006.

In the JCPOA, Iran agrees to provisionally apply its Additional Protocol agreement, effective on Implementation Day, "pending its ratification by the Majlis (Parliament)." Later in Annex V, as part of the commitments scheduled for "Transition Day," which will occur on October 18, 2023, Iran commits to "[s]eek, consistent with the Constitutional roles of the President and Parliament, ratification of the Additional Protocol." So the JCPOA envisions a period of approximately eight years of Iran's provisional application of the Additional Protocol, at which time Iran will seek its formal ratification.

The fact that Iran commits in the JCPOA only to provisionally apply the Additional Protocol has been criticized by some in the West as a weak commitment, because it means that Iran will not be legally bound to apply the Additional Protocol and could at any time cease its provisional application of the treaty. It is important to understand what the provisional application of treaties entails in order to evaluate this criticism. Article 25 of the Vienna Convention on the Law of Treaties addresses the subject of provisional application of treaties but gives little detail about related process or about the meaning and legal implications of provisional application. The jurisprudence of international tribunals and the work of scholars have provided substantial fleshing out of the principle of provisional application, and the subject is currently on the agenda of the International Law

Commission, with Special Rapporteur Juan Manuel Gómez-Robledo having produced three reports as of this writing.[5]

Article 17 of the INFCIRC/540 Additional Protocol template provides that a safeguarded state "may, at any date before this Protocol enters into force, declare that it will apply this Protocol provisionally." Thus, the treaty comes into provisional application at the time of the state's unilateral declaration to that effect. It is correct that, once in provisional application, the safeguarded state may at any time, through unilateral declaration, terminate the provisional application of the treaty. This termination has the same legal consequences as the termination of a treaty in force, including the cessation of all treaty obligations going forward for the state. So to this extent, the critique of the JCPOA's commitment for Iran only to provisionally apply the Additional Protocol is correct—Iran can indeed unilaterally terminate the provisional application of the Additional Protocol at any time through unilateral declaration and by so doing withdraw from any obligation under the treaty going forward.

However, it is not correct to equate this ability to unilaterally legally terminate the provisional application of the Additional Protocol with a lack of legal effect of the Additional Protocol during the time of its provisional application. For the duration of the provisional application of the Additional Protocol, Iran will be legally bound by all of the provisions of the Additional Protocol and subject to the same regime of state responsibility and treaty law implication in the case of a breach of any provision thereof as it would be were the Additional Protocol actually in force during that time. Thus, during the period of provisional application, the terms of the Additional Protocol will, along with the terms of Iran's comprehensive safeguards agreement, together constitute Iran's safeguards obligations under international

5. *See, e.g.*, ANNELIESE QUAST MERTSCH, PROVISIONALLY APPLIED TREATIES: THEIR BINDING FORCE AND LEGAL NATURE (2012); Denise Mathy, *Article 25*, in THE VIENNA CONVENTIONS ON THE LAW OF TREATIES: A COMMENTARY, Vol. I (Olivier Corten & Pierre Klein eds., 2011); Ulrich Klaus, *The Yukos Case under the Energy Charter Treaty and the Provisional Application of International Treaties*, in POLICY PAPERS ON TRANSNATIONAL ECONOMIC LAW, NO. 11 (Halle, Martin-Luther-University 2005).

law. And the IAEA will have the legal authority to investigate and to assess Iran's actions with regard to its nuclear program, according to the terms of both the CSA and the Additional Protocol.

It may be queried why Iran negotiated for a commitment in the JCPOA only to provisionally apply the Additional Protocol, with a view to seeking its ratification after Transition Day. The answer is likely to be found in Iran's desire to maintain some leverage itself during the phased implementation schedule articulated in Annex V. It will be recalled that the economic sanctions imposed on Iran by the Security Council are to be initially terminated on Implementation Day, but that subsequent to that point they may be reimposed through the snap-back procedure discussed previously, up until UNSCR Termination Day, which is scheduled to occur roughly ten years later. This conditionality attached to the permanent lifting of sanctions was no doubt sought by Western states parties in order to incentivize continued compliance by Iran with its commitments throughout the full term of the JCPOA's schedule. One may speculate that Iran desired some reciprocal leverage to incentivize Western states to keep the full measure of their commitments under the JCPOA, in the form of a similarly central commitment the implementation of which would be at least partially within Iran's discretion.

As discussed in Chapter 4, the Additional Protocol supplements a safeguarded state's comprehensive safeguards agreement by requiring the state to produce a more expansive declaration regarding nuclear-fuel-cycle activity being carried out within its territory and by providing for the IAEA to have "complementary access" to that which it has under the CSA. Specifically, the Additional Protocol gives the IAEA the right of access "on a selective basis in order to assure the absence of undeclared nuclear material" to "any place" on the site of a declared facility, and not only to agreed strategic points, as under the CSA. It further provides for IAEA access to all sites on which information has been provided by the state regarding research and development activities on nuclear-fuel-cycle-related technologies, in order "to resolve a question relating to the correctness and completeness of the information provided." It also provides for IAEA access to "any location specified by the Agency" in order to carry out "location-specific environmental monitoring." This provision enables IAEA inspectors to nominate undeclared locations at which they would like to take soil, water, and air samples in order to detect the presence of nuclear materials and thus potentially produce evidence of undeclared nuclear activities. These access supplements to the CSA significantly increase the IAEA's ability to verify not only the correctness but also the completeness of state declarations and allow for increased confidence in the determinations of the IAEA that no undeclared nuclear-related activity is being carried out on a safeguarded state's territory.

With the Additional Protocol in effect, whether through provisional application or through formal entry into force, there should be considerably less controversy regarding the content of Iran's safeguards obligations and regarding the scope of the IAEA's authority to investigate and to assess Iran's compliance with its safeguards agreements than there was during the period of confrontation. The Additional Protocol is in most respects quite clear on these subjects. However, the provisions regarding access to undeclared sites in Article 5(b) and (c) of the Additional Protocol, and the activities that are permitted to the IAEA to be carried out at or near such sites, contain terms that have the potential for controversy between the IAEA and a safeguarded state, particularly in cases where the IAEA has requested access to sensitive sites, such as military facilities. This potential for disagreement over discrete terms of access in Article 5 of the Additional Protocol appears to be the motivation behind the negotiated inclusion in the JCPOA of provisions addressing access in Annex I, Section Q. As described previously, this section provides in paragraph 75 that "if the IAEA has concerns regarding undeclared nuclear materials or activities, or activities inconsistent with the JCPOA, at locations that have not been declared under the comprehensive safeguards agreement of Additional Protocol," the IAEA may request access to such locations. If the IAEA and Iran are unable to reach an access agreement or other explanatory solution satisfactory to the IAEA, the Agency may then submit its access request to the

Joint Commission, and Iran is committed to implementing the Joint Commission's majority decision on the matter.

At first glance, the access provisions in Annex I, Section Q of the JCPOA do appear to give the IAEA a significant card to play in the event that concerns arise regarding activities within Iran that could be characterized as included in the quite broadly worded category of "activities inconsistent with the JCPOA" at undeclared locations. In the past, the IAEA and Iran have disagreed over specific IAEA requests to visit sensitive locations within Iran, and in particular military facilities such as Parchin. Here again, however, the fact of the legally nonbinding nature of the JCPOA, inclusive of this set of enhanced access commitments, should, it would be hoped, incentivize the parties to the agreement, and related actors including the IAEA, to be calculating and reasonable in their approach to disputes over access. The parties should be aware that excessively aggressive or unreasonable demands made by any side—such as unreasonable requests by the IAEA to visit Iranian military facilities—could result in the collapse of the entire JCPOA framework.

Paragraph 15 of the JCPOA provides that the enhanced access provisions of Annex 1, Section Q will be in effect for fifteen years from Implementation Day. It does perhaps bear mentioning by way of clarification that throughout this period and beyond, Iran's safeguards legal obligations will consist exclusively of the terms of its CSA and, as applicable (i.e., so long as it is either provisionally applied or has been brought into force), its Additional Protocol with the IAEA. The access provisions of Annex I, Section Q of the JCPOA are political commitments only and during the term of their duration are not within the authority of the IAEA or any other body to investigate or assess as a subject of safeguards obligation compliance.

B. PMD

As mentioned previously, the Roadmap Agreement concluded between Iran and the IAEA in connection with the JCPOA led to the submission by the IAEA Director General to the Board of Governors of a final assessment of the PMD issue in December 2015 and the acceptance of this report by the Board. The sixteen pages of the Director General's report are quite technical in its review of the IAEA's findings of fact concerning the various PMD allegations made by the IAEA, most notably in its November 2011 report. However, the conclusion section sums up the IAEA's final assessment of the PMD issue:

> The Agency assesses that a range of activities relevant to the development of a nuclear explosive device were conducted in Iran prior to the end of 2003 as a coordinated effort, and some activities took place after 2003. The Agency also assesses that these activities did not advance beyond feasibility and scientific studies, and the acquisition of certain relevant technical competences and capabilities. The Agency has no credible indications of activities in Iran relevant to the development of a nuclear explosive device after 2009.
>
> The Agency has found no credible indications of the diversion of nuclear material in connection with the possible military dimensions to Iran's nuclear programme.

Some excellent technical and political analyses of the IAEA's final PMD report have been offered.[6] I will limit my comments to a brief consideration of the report's legal implications for Iran and its institutional implications for the IAEA.

It will be recalled that at the end of Chapter 3, I said that I was personally persuaded by the view of Robert Kelley regarding the subject of past nuclear weaponization work conducted by Iran. This is the view that while Iran likely did conduct research and development activities on technologies and capabilities necessary for building a knowledge of how to construct a nuclear warhead following its war with Iraq in the 1980s, Iran likely never constructed a complete nuclear explosive device, or any of its primary components, and likely

6. *See, e.g.*, Robert Kelley, *IAEA: Most PMD Claims Groundless*, LobeLog, Dec. 10, 2015; Peter Jenkins, *Iran's Nuclear Aberration*, LobeLog, Dec. 7, 2015.

never conducted any of these activities using nuclear material. It also likely stopped any active nuclear weapon research and development programs by 2003.

The IAEA's final PMD report is significant in essentially confirming this view of Iran's past nuclear weaponization efforts. This is at least normatively important in constituting the IAEA's own determination of the facts of Iran's nuclear weaponization research activities, at a level that does not constitute a violation of NPT Article II's prohibition on the manufacture or other acquisition of a nuclear explosive device. And it is legally important in constituting the IAEA's determination that no diversion of nuclear material to military uses occurred in the process of these research activities. Again, under Articles 1 and 2 of Iran's comprehensive safeguards agreement, the exclusive purpose of IAEA safeguards on Iran's nuclear facilities is to verify that no nuclear material is diverted from peaceful to military uses. The PMD report's conclusions thus represent the IAEA's formal determination that nothing in Iran's past nuclear weaponization research activities constituted noncompliance with Iran's safeguards agreement with the IAEA.

The IAEA's final report on the PMD issue also has, in my view, important institutional implications for the IAEA itself. The report, and its acceptance by the Board of Governors, brings to an end the ill-conceived misadventure of the IAEA into the area of nuclear weaponization investigation and assessment. It will be recalled that at the end of Chapter 5 I argued that the combined systemic phenomena of the gap between expectations and capacity for the IAEA and the deep politicization of the IAEA's governing bodies, added to the pro-Western views of the current IAEA Director General, have created a political environment in the IAEA that produced an overstepping of the bounds of the IAEA's legal authority in its investigations and assessment of the PMD issue in the Iran case. Again, the IAEA has neither the legal authority nor the institutional capacity to act as a general nuclear weapons supervision regime or international bureau of investigation for rooting out and dismantling secret nuclear weapons programs. In its ill-conceived efforts to act as one in prosecuting its PMD agenda in the Iran case, it used third-party intelligence information provided by states that it had no capacity to independently verify and refused to share these sources of intelligence with the state that was the subject of the investigation. This tactic, which cannot but remind one of a criminal prosecution on the basis of secret evidence unavailable to the defendant or the jury, produced increased distrust among states in the reliability of IAEA determinations and in the independence and objectivity of the agency generally. As the Russian representative to the IAEA, Grigory Berdennikov, explained:

> The risk here is obvious. False allegations generated by interested parties in order to exercise political pressure on a State unfortunately remain part of current international landscape. They are quite common in many areas, including nonproliferation and one should admit could be very important sometimes involving issues of war and peace. Moreover, the intelligence services of some States may be tempted to use the IAEA as a tool to verify the information they receive via their operative channels. In other words—they may wish to turn the IAEA Department of Safeguards into their branch.
>
> We do not want this to happen. We stress that the right to use all available safeguards relevant information should not be perceived as a blank check that Member States have given to the Secretariat in the area of information handling. The Secretariat remains a technical body of an international organization, which should work with data submitted via official channels or received during performing its statutory functions . . . We think that if the Secretariat decides to use any information, except for data obtained through its own inspection activity, it should duly disclose its origin and be ready to defend its credibility in an open discussion at the Board of Governors. Every State should have the right to publicly defend itself against false allegations and accusations generated by interested third parties or by the media.[7]

7. Daniel H. Joyner, *Statement by Russian Representative to the IAEA Grigory Berdinnekov*, ARMS CONTROL LAW, Oct. 21, 2014.

The IAEA's decision to embark on its PMD investigation in Iran was doomed to ignominy from the beginning as there were no legal authorities on which to base it and no legal criteria or standards which the agency could apply to determine compliance or noncompliance by Iran. In fact, the JCPOA and the Roadmap Agreement should be seen as constituting an extraordinarily fortunate escape for the IAEA from the metaphorical hole that it had dug for itself by commencing an investigation that had no clear basis for resolution. In the end, as part of the *sui generis* political settlement represented by the JCPOA, and under pressure from the P5+1 to conclude its PMD investigation, the IAEA agreed to produce a limited fact-finding report that contained no explicit compliance determination, and very few facts that were not already in the public domain, on the basis of a minimal level of face-saving cooperation by Iran. And again, the basic findings of the report found no facts to indicate noncompliance by Iran with any actual legal standard, i.e., whether in the NPT or in Iran's comprehensive safeguards agreement.

It can only be hoped that the negligible benefit and huge costs associated with the IAEA's Iran PMD investigation will stand as a cautionary tale for the agency going forward and that in future cases the IAEA will resist the temptation to swim out of its depth, in the interest of preserving the agency's credibility.

C. Missiles

In its Resolution 1929, adopted on June 9, 2010, the Security Council imposed a conventional arms embargo on Iran. It further addressed Iran's ballistic missile program thus:

> [The Security Council] decides that Iran shall not undertake any activity related to ballistic missiles capable of delivering nuclear weapons, including launches using ballistic missile technology, and that States shall take all necessary measures to prevent the transfer of technology or technical assistance to Iran related to such activities.

Iran's diplomats argued consistently that the Security Council's arms embargo and proscriptions on Iran's ballistic missile programs were unwarranted, and when negotiations began on the JCPOA they argued vigorously that they would not include their missile program on the agenda for negotiation along with their nuclear program. There is therefore nothing in the text of the JCPOA itself on the subject of Iran's conventional weapons and missile programs. However, in Security Council Resolution 2231, the Council did make some changes to its treatment of these issues.

Annex B of Resolution 2231 provides for the temporary continuation of the international conventional arms embargo on Iran, inclusive of an exception for transfers approved by the Security Council. However, it further provides that the embargo will cease on the date five years from Adoption Day under the JCPOA. This date will be October 18, 2020.

With regard to Iran's ballistic missile activities, Security Council Resolution 1929's circumscription of course terminated, along with the Security Council's other previous resolutions, on Implementation Day, January 16, 2016. In its place, Security Council Resolution 2231 in Annex B provides the following text:

> Iran is called upon not to undertake any activity related to ballistic missiles designed to be capable of delivering nuclear weapons, including launches using such ballistic missile technology, until the date eight years after the JCPOA Adoption Day or until the date on which the IAEA submits a report confirming the Broader Conclusion, whichever is earlier.

The substitution of the leading phrase "calls upon" in this text in Resolution 2231 has legal significance, as I explained in Chapter 6. The change to this invitational yet legally nonbinding phrase in Resolution 2231 means that, as of January 16, 2016, Iran is no longer under a legal prohibition regarding its ballistic missile activity from the Security Council. The remaining hortatory expression in Resolution 2231 by its terms expires on October 18, 2023.

The removal of the Security Council's legal prohibition on ballistic missile activity by Iran and its disentanglement from the nuclear issue can be seen as a significant victory for Iran in the JCPOA process.

As a general matter, on the ballistic missile issue as well as on the issue of the Security Council's command in multiple previous resolutions that Iran suspend its uranium enrichment program, Resolution 2231 can be viewed as an instance of the Security Council's having to walk back from its prior injunctions with which Iran had refused to comply, and in fact with which Iran consistently did not comply. In the end, the Security Council itself can be rightly seen as one of the parties to the JCPOA whose compromise with regard to its previous demands was required in order for the JCPOA to be agreed. While this was certainly a pragmatic approach for the Council to take, it does beg the question of what implications this walking back by the Council might have for future cases in which it takes strong, injunctive stances against states or other actors. Might the Iran case make such injunctions appear less as immutable commands and more as negotiating positions? Might this perhaps be a positive evolution in both states', and the Security Council's own, understanding of the Council's role and authority?

D. Sanctions

As noted previously, the JCPOA's Implementation Plan in Annex V provides for the initial termination or ceasing of application of both the U.N. Security Council's economic sanctions on Iran and the unilateral nuclear sanctions imposed by the United States and the European Union on Iran, on Implementation Day, January 16, 2016. It further provides for the final termination of the U.S. and E.U. unilateral sanctions on "Transition Day," which is set to occur on October 18, 2023, and for the final termination of the U.N. Security Council's nuclear sanctions on "UNSCR Termination Day," which is set to occur on October 18, 2025.

Among these actors, by far the least predictable with regard to the likelihood of its compliance with its commitments undertaken in the JCPOA is the United States. The question of how the United States plans to abide by its commitments—including the precise legal machinations of presidential waivers and U.S. statutory law—and indeed *whether* it will abide by its commitments, is complex and uncertain. It would be foolish to predict both how and whether the United States will bring its domestic law into compliance with its commitments in the JCPOA. Among the variables in this equation is the U.S. presidential election in November 2016, as well as frequent calls by members of the U.S. Congress for increased non-nuclear-related economic sanctions on Iran to compensate for any relief granted through the lifting of nuclear-related sanctions.

Even if the United States effectively lifts its secondary economic sanctions targeting non-U.S. entities, U.S. legal and natural persons are likely to remain prohibited from engaging in most financial transactions in Iran and with Iranian persons. U.S. businesses, therefore, are likely to miss out on any investment and trade opportunities created for, among others, European businesses through multilateral and unilateral sanctions relief.

Paul Pillar has persuasively made the case that U.S. noncompliance with its commitments regarding sanctions relief under the JCPOA is the single most likely cause of the derailment of the entire diplomatic accord. As he has explained:

> The scenario that presents the greatest danger of the nuclear agreement unraveling is thus one in which new sanctions legislation and other Iran-punishing moves by the U.S. Congress cross a line that leads most Iranians to get fed up and to say to heck with it. The incentives that led them to accept the restrictions on their cherished nuclear program would become too indiscernible to make the bargain seem worthwhile any more. And that would bring the deal-killing result that hardliners on our own side have wanted all along.[8]

8. *What Would Be Most Likely to Unravel the Iran Nuclear Agreement*, THE NATIONAL INTEREST, Feb. 4, 2016.

IV. CONCLUSION

My own view is that the JCPOA, and its associated diplomatic and legal developments, constitute a major triumph for diplomacy and for the peaceful resolution of international disputes. Its negotiators are to be commended for their work in crafting an agreement which demanded compromise on all sides, but which also gave each of the parties the core set of political victories needed to enable them to sell the agreement to their domestic constituencies and give the accord a chance for success. Time will tell, but the JCPOA regime may in retrospect be credited with avoiding war. As such it represents the best possible model of successful diplomacy.

At its essence, the JCPOA sets out an approximately ten-year time frame during which all of the key commitments of its parties are to be implemented. At the end of that ten-year period, if all goes according to plan, all nuclear-related economic sanctions on Iran will have been formally lifted, and Iran will be at liberty to maintain a mature, full front-end nuclear fuel cycle that is recognized as legitimate and that is subject to the same safeguards obligations as the nuclear programs of other advanced civilian nuclear energy states, such as Japan and Germany. A few relatively insignificant limitations on Iran's nuclear program will remain for another five years after that point, with even fewer and less significant ones carrying on for yet another fifteen years. But practically, after ten years of implementation, the JCPOA should produce a new status quo in which Iran has become reintegrated with most elements of the world's financial systems and is on a normalizing path with countries in Europe and Asia.

All of this, of course, depends on the successful implementation of the JCPOA. It cannot be overemphasized that the JCPOA is a legally nonbinding diplomatic accord between its parties. The agreement and commitments it represents could of course fall apart at any time, and for any one of myriad reasons. If this happens, relations between Iran and the West are likely to return to the status of active confrontation over Iran's nuclear program. The next ten years of the implementation of the JCPOA will no doubt be riddled with allegations of noncompliance by all sides, as antithetical elements within domestic political systems attempt to derail the accord. Indeed, these have already begun. The success or failure of the JCPOA, and of the realization of the positive end state it envisions, will depend solely upon the political will of all sides.

I have now come to the end of this manuscript. I have attempted within it to provide an analysis of many of the most important legal questions that have arisen over the course of the past fourteen or so years during both the confrontation and, much more recently, accord phases of the Iran nuclear case. As I said in the Introduction, my hope is that all of this analysis will provide an instructional case study of the application of the relevant sources of international nuclear law, which will in turn inform both the ongoing diplomacy surrounding the Iran nuclear dispute itself, as well as similar future cases.

I would like to close by offering a few words on the IAEA. In this manuscript, I have at times been critical of the way in which the IAEA has handled the Iran case. I would not wish for readers to take from this criticism the impression that I think the IAEA is not overall an excellent and integral international organization, or that its work is unimportant. On the contrary, I think that the IAEA has played an invaluable role in the international nuclear normative regime in the past and that it was fully worthy of its Nobel Prize in 2005. My criticism is meant in the vein of an *amicus curiae*—one whose advice has been unsolicited, but nevertheless is offered in order to assist the agency in fulfilling its important role in international law and international relations. The essence of my critique has been to remind the agency of the importance of staying within its clear legal authorities, which have been carefully negotiated and agreed to by its states parties. I have argued that the IAEA's continued credibility as an independent technical supervisory body of states' nuclear programs depends, at least in part, on its observance of these limitations. And, somewhat gratifyingly, I have some grounds for optimism that the points of critique I have raised, which have also and much more influentially been raised by states in the IAEA General Conference, have begun to find some traction in the Board of Governors and in the Secretariat. As Mark Hibbs has recently observed:

> While for Western states the Iran crisis was about Iran's non-compliance with its obligations, Iran, joined by developing and non-aligned countries, brought forth a narrative which framed the crisis as being instead about the IAEA's objectivity, competence, and authority, and about states' "nuclear rights". . . [The] themes Iran raised in its defence increasingly resonated among some member states in discussion in the board and the IAEA General Conference about the agency's development of the [state level concept], especially since 2012.
>
> Given this background, during implementation of the JCPOA the IAEA may be challenged to demonstrate that it is implementing safeguards in Iran according to the letter of its legal authority and obligations, and that it will not be unduly swayed by powerful member states that have concluded an informal political arrangement with Iran.[9]

9. *Iran and the Evolution of Safeguards*, Carnegie Endowment for International Peace, Dec. 16, 2015.

INDEX

CPSIA information can be obtained
at www.ICGtesting.com
Printed in the USA
BVHW042026250322
632461BV00006B/28

9 780190 635718